S0-BDM-004

COMPUTER
BOOK SERIES
FROM IDG

Selling Online For Dummies®

Cheat Sheet

Your Selling Site Checklist

- ✔ **Selling online means you're operating in a global marketplace, no matter what the size of your business.** Be prepared for the unexpected.

- ✔ **Get a domain name as close as possible to the name of your business or product.** Your domain name is your store's address in Cyberspace.

- ✔ **Accept payment in as many forms as you possibly can arrange.** The best way to sell a lot is to make it easy to buy.

- ✔ **Make your site a site worth visiting.** All the advertising in the world won't help if your site doesn't give something worthwhile to your customers.

- ✔ **Provide a way for customers to contribute.** Chat, discussion groups, and conferences are highly valued by customers — maybe more so than any editorial content you produce.

- ✔ **Invite customers to come back regularly by updating your online store's content often.** Use surveys, themes, promotions, and contests to generate a sense of fun and to encourage participation.

- ✔ **Provide security to protect your customers' privacy.** Your customers will appreciate it.

- ✔ **Avoid sending bulk e-mail about your site.** Even though at first it may seem like a great form of cheap advertising, sending direct bulk e-mail (often called spam) is a bad idea. Find another way.

- ✔ **Take time to study the laws that affect your business online.** Basically the same laws apply in Cyberspace as in the physical world.

- ✔ **Explore new business possibilities created by digital currency.** Look at the possibilities opening up due to the micropayment technologies.

- ✔ **Check out the competition.** When discovering better ways of selling online, you find no substitute for spending time on the Internet yourself.

Accept These Forms of Payment

Make your store more successful by accepting as many forms of payment as possible. Be sure to include these in your list:

- ✔ **Credit cards:** Take security precautions to protect your customers' credit card information online.

- ✔ **Electronic cash:** Not as newfangled as it sounds, electronic cash means instantaneous transaction settlement using banking networks, which is good for your cash flow.

- ✔ **Electronic checks:** Like electronic cash, settlement is fast, and you don't have to pay a credit card service fee.

- ✔ **Debit cards:** Just like an ATM card, many banking services cards today deduct money directly from a specified checking account.

...For Dummies: #1 Computer Book Series for Beginners

Selling Online For Dummies®

Cheat Sheet

Goals for Your Customer Service Department

Check out these essential ideas for creating an outstanding customer service department:

- **Let the customers give you feedback by e-mail or bulletin board.** They love to contribute.

- **Respond to your customer feedback quickly, especially if they send e-mail.** Customers want to hear from you in a few days — not three months from now.

- **Let the customers give each other tips about your product by setting up a bulletin board area just for that discussion.** Often, customers prove a great source of advertising.

- **Keep your Frequently Asked Questions (FAQ) list up to date.** Doing so eventually saves you time and creates happy customers.

- **Spend time developing one-to-one relationships with your customers in whatever ways you can.** You can hang out on your site's bulletin board or chat rooms, too.

- **Publish a newsletter regularly, perhaps pointing out new product features or giving tips.** You keep in contact with your most precious asset — your customers.

Good Selling Sites

Use this space to record Web sites that show you something of interest for your own site. (If you need help looking for good sites, you can look in the Internet Directory in this book or open the bookmark file included on the CD.)

_____

_____

_____

_____

_____

_____

Copyright © 1998 IDG Books Worldwide, Inc. All rights reserved.
Cheat Sheet $2.95 value. Item 0334-0.
For more information about IDG Books, call 1-800-762-2974.

IDG
BOOKS
WORLDWIDE

...For Dummies: #1 Computer Book Series for Beginners

™

References for the Rest of Us!®

BESTSELLING BOOK SERIES FROM IDG

Are you intimidated and confused by computers? Do you find that traditional manuals are overloaded with technical details you'll never use? Do your friends and family always call you to fix simple problems on their PCs? Then the ...*For Dummies*® computer book series from IDG Books Worldwide is for you.

...*For Dummies* books are written for those frustrated computer users who know they aren't really dumb but find that PC hardware, software, and indeed the unique vocabulary of computing make them feel helpless. ...*For Dummies* books use a lighthearted approach, a down-to-earth style, and even cartoons and humorous icons to diffuse computer novices' fears and build their confidence. Lighthearted but not lightweight, these books are a perfect survival guide for anyone forced to use a computer.

"I like my copy so much I told friends; now they bought copies."

— Irene C., Orwell, Ohio

"Quick, concise, nontechnical, and humorous."

— Jay A., Elburn, Illinois

"Thanks, I needed this book. Now I can sleep at night."

— Robin F., British Columbia, Canada

Already, millions of satisfied readers agree. They have made ...*For Dummies* books the #1 introductory level computer book series and have written asking for more. So, if you're looking for the most fun and easy way to learn about computers, look to ...*For Dummies* books to give you a helping hand.

™

IDG BOOKS WORLDWIDE

4/98

SELLING ONLINE

FOR

DUMMIES®

by Leslie Heeter Lundquist

IDG Books Worldwide, Inc.
An International Data Group Company

Foster City, CA ♦ Chicago, IL ♦ Indianapolis, IN ♦ New York, NY

Selling Online For Dummies®

Published by
IDG Books Worldwide, Inc.
An International Data Group Company
919 E. Hillsdale Blvd.
Suite 400
Foster City, CA 94404
`www.idgbooks.com` (IDG Books Worldwide Web site)
`www.dummies.com` (Dummies Press Web site)

Copyright © 1998 IDG Books Worldwide, Inc. All rights reserved. No part of this book, including interior design, cover design, and icons, may be reproduced or transmitted in any form, by any means (electronic, photocopying, recording, or otherwise) without the prior written permission of the publisher.

Library of Congress Catalog Card No.: 98-70129

ISBN: 0-7645-0334-0

Printed in the United States of America

10 9 8 7 6 5 4 3 2

1E/SX/QV/ZY/IN

Distributed in the United States by IDG Books Worldwide, Inc.

Distributed by Macmillan Canada for Canada; by Transworld Publishers Limited in the United Kingdom; by IDG Norge Books for Norway; by IDG Sweden Books for Sweden; by Woodslane Pty. Ltd. for Australia; by Woodslane Enterprises Ltd. for New Zealand; by Longman Singapore Publishers Ltd. for Singapore, Malaysia, Thailand, and Indonesia; by Simron Pty. Ltd. for South Africa; by Toppan Company Ltd. for Japan; by Distribuidora Cuspide for Argentina; by Livraria Cultura for Brazil; by Ediciencia S.A. for Ecuador; by Addison-Wesley Publishing Company for Korea; by Ediciones ZETA S.C.R. Ltda. for Peru; by WS Computer Publishing Corporation, Inc., for the Philippines; by Unalis Corporation for Taiwan; by Contemporanea de Ediciones for Venezuela; by Computer Book & Magazine Store for Puerto Rico; by Express Computer Distributors for the Caribbean and West Indies. Authorized Sales Agent: Anthony Rudkin Associates for the Middle East and North Africa.

For general information on IDG Books Worldwide's books in the U.S., please call our Consumer Customer Service department at 800-762-2974. For reseller information, including discounts and premium sales, please call our Reseller Customer Service department at 800-434-3422.

For information on where to purchase IDG Books Worldwide's books outside the U.S., please contact our International Sales department at 650-655-3200 or fax 650-655-3295.

For information on foreign language translations, please contact our Foreign & Subsidiary Rights department at 650-655-3021 or fax 650-655-3281.

For sales inquiries and special prices for bulk quantities, please contact our Sales department at 650-655-3200 or write to the address above.

For information on using IDG Books Worldwide's books in the classroom or for ordering examination copies, please contact our Educational Sales department at 800-434-2086 or fax 817-251-8174.

For press review copies, author interviews, or other publicity information, please contact our Public Relations department at 650-655-3000 or fax 650-655-3299.

For authorization to photocopy items for corporate, personal, or educational use, please contact Copyright Clearance Center, 222 Rosewood Drive, Danvers, MA 01923, or fax 978-750-4470.

LIMIT OF LIABILITY/DISCLAIMER OF WARRANTY: AUTHOR AND PUBLISHER HAVE USED THEIR BEST EFFORTS IN PREPARING THIS BOOK. IDG BOOKS WORLDWIDE, INC., AND AUTHOR MAKE NO REPRESENTATIONS OR WARRANTIES WITH RESPECT TO THE ACCURACY OR COMPLETENESS OF THE CONTENTS OF THIS BOOK AND SPECIFICALLY DISCLAIM ANY IMPLIED WARRANTIES OF MERCHANTABILITY OR FITNESS FOR A PARTICULAR PURPOSE. THERE ARE NO WARRANTIES WHICH EXTEND BEYOND THE DESCRIPTIONS CONTAINED IN THIS PARAGRAPH. NO WARRANTY MAY BE CREATED OR EXTENDED BY SALES REPRESENTATIVES OR WRITTEN SALES MATERIALS. THE ACCURACY AND COMPLETENESS OF THE INFORMATION PROVIDED HEREIN AND THE OPINIONS STATED HEREIN ARE NOT GUARANTEED OR WARRANTED TO PRODUCE ANY PARTICULAR RESULTS, AND THE ADVICE AND STRATEGIES CONTAINED HEREIN MAY NOT BE SUITABLE FOR EVERY INDIVIDUAL. NEITHER IDG BOOKS WORLDWIDE, INC., NOR AUTHOR SHALL BE LIABLE FOR ANY LOSS OF PROFIT OR ANY OTHER COMMERCIAL DAMAGES, INCLUDING BUT NOT LIMITED TO SPECIAL, INCIDENTAL, CONSEQUENTIAL, OR OTHER DAMAGES.

Trademarks: All brand names and product names used in this book are trade names, service marks, trademarks, or registered trademarks of their respective owners. IDG Books Worldwide is not associated with any product or vendor mentioned in this book.

is a trademark under exclusive license to IDG Books Worldwide, Inc., from International Data Group, Inc.

About the Author

Leslie Lundquist has forged a career out of researching and reporting on cutting-edge technology. She has already collaborated on two books, both published by John Wiley and Sons, dealing with Internet commerce: *Digital Money: The New Era of Internet Commerce,* with Dan Lynch (Chairman of CyberCash, Inc.), and *Creating the Virtual Store,* with Magdalena Yesil (former Vice President of CyberCash, Inc.).

Leslie has worked for computing industry leaders such as Xerox, Apple, and IBM, and she now owns her own writing and Internet consulting business. She holds a degree in philosophy from Stanford University.

ABOUT IDG BOOKS WORLDWIDE

Welcome to the world of IDG Books Worldwide.

IDG Books Worldwide, Inc., is a subsidiary of International Data Group, the world's largest publisher of computer-related information and the leading global provider of information services on information technology. IDG was founded more than 25 years ago and now employs more than 8,500 people worldwide. IDG publishes more than 275 computer publications in over 75 countries (see listing below). More than 60 million people read one or more IDG publications each month.

Launched in 1990, IDG Books Worldwide is today the #1 publisher of best-selling computer books in the United States. We are proud to have received eight awards from the Computer Press Association in recognition of editorial excellence and three from *Computer Currents'* First Annual Readers' Choice Awards. Our best-selling *...For Dummies®* series has more than 30 million copies in print with translations in 30 languages. IDG Books Worldwide, through a joint venture with IDG's Hi-Tech Beijing, became the first U.S. publisher to publish a computer book in the People's Republic of China. In record time, IDG Books Worldwide has become the first choice for millions of readers around the world who want to learn how to better manage their businesses.

Our mission is simple: Every one of our books is designed to bring extra value and skill-building instructions to the reader. Our books are written by experts who understand and care about our readers. The knowledge base of our editorial staff comes from years of experience in publishing, education, and journalism — experience we use to produce books for the '90s. In short, we care about books, so we attract the best people. We devote special attention to details such as audience, interior design, use of icons, and illustrations. And because we use an efficient process of authoring, editing, and desktop publishing our books electronically, we can spend more time ensuring superior content and spend less time on the technicalities of making books.

You can count on our commitment to deliver high-quality books at competitive prices on topics you want to read about. At IDG Books Worldwide, we continue in the IDG tradition of delivering quality for more than 25 years. You'll find no better book on a subject than one from IDG Books Worldwide.

John Kilcullen
CEO
IDG Books Worldwide, Inc.

Steven Berkowitz
President and Publisher
IDG Books Worldwide, Inc.

*Eighth Annual
Computer Press
Awards ▷1992*

*Ninth Annual
Computer Press
Awards ▷1993*

*Tenth Annual
Computer Press
Awards ▷1994*

*Eleventh Annual
Computer Press
Awards ▷1995*

IDG Books Worldwide, Inc., is a subsidiary of International Data Group, the world's largest publisher of computer-related information and the leading global provider of information services on information technology. International Data Group publishes over 275 computer publications in over 75 countries. Sixty million people read one or more International Data Group publications each month. International Data Group's publications include: **ARGENTINA:** Buyer's Guide, Computerworld Argentina, PC World Argentina; **AUSTRALIA:** Australian Macworld, Australian PC World, Australian Reseller News, Computerworld, IT Casebook, Network World, Publish, Webmaster; **AUSTRIA:** Computerwelt Osterreich, Networks Austria, PC Tip Austria; **BANGLADESH:** PC World Bangladesh; **BELARUS:** PC World Belarus; **BELGIUM:** Data News; **BRAZIL:** Annuario de Informatica, Computerworld, Connections, Macworld, PC Player, PC World, Publish, Reseller News, Supergamepower; **BULGARIA:** Computerworld Bulgaria, Network World Bulgaria, PC & MacWorld Bulgaria; **CANADA:** CIO Canada, Client/Server World, ComputerWorld Canada, InfoWorld Canada, NetworkWorld Canada, WebWorld; **CHILE:** Computerworld Chile, PC World Chile; **COLOMBIA:** Computerworld Colombia, PC World Colombia; **COSTA RICA:** PC World Centro America; **THE CZECH AND SLOVAK REPUBLICS:** Computerworld Czechoslovakia, Macworld Czech Republic, PC World Czechoslovakia; **DENMARK:** Communications World Danmark, Computerworld Danmark, Macworld Danmark, PC World Danmark, Techworld Denmark; **DOMINICAN REPUBLIC:** PC World Republica Dominicana; **ECUADOR:** PC World Ecuador; **EGYPT:** Computerworld Middle East, PC World Middle East; **EL SALVADOR:** PC World Centro America; **FINLAND:** MikroPC, Tietoverkko, Tietoviikko; **FRANCE:** Distributique, Hebdo, Info PC, Le Monde Informatique, Macworld, Reseaux & Telecoms, WebMaster France; **GERMANY:** Computer Partner, Computerwoche, Computerwoche Extra, Computerwoche FOCUS, Global Online, Macwelt, PC Welt; **GREECE:** Amiga Computing, GamePro Greece, Multimedia World; **GUATEMALA:** PC World Centro America; **HONDURAS:** PC World Centro America; **HONG KONG:** Computerworld Hong Kong, PC World Hong Kong, Publish in Asia; **HUNGARY:** ABCD CD-ROM, Computerworld Szamitastechnika, Internetto online Magazine, PC World Hungary, PC-X Magazin Hungary; **ICELAND:** Tolvuheimur PC World Island; **INDIA:** Information Communications World, Information Systems Computerworld, PC World India, Publish in Asia; **INDONESIA:** InfoKomputer PC World, Komputek Computerworld, Publish in Asia; **IRELAND:** ComputerScope, PC Live!; **ISRAEL:** Macworld Israel, People & Computers/Computerworld; **ITALY:** Computerworld Italia, Macworld Italia, Networking Italia, PC World Italia; **JAPAN:** DTP World, Macworld Japan, Nikkei Personal Computing, OS/2 World Japan, SunWorld Japan, Windows NT World, Windows World Japan; **KENYA:** PC World East African; **KOREA:** Hi-Tech Information, Macworld Korea, PC World Korea; **MACEDONIA:** PC World Macedonia; **MALAYSIA:** Computerworld Malaysia, PC World Malaysia, Publish in Asia; **MALTA:** PC World Malta; **MEXICO:** Computerworld Mexico, PC World Mexico; **MYANMAR:** PC World Myanmar; **NETHERLANDS:** Computer! Totaal, LAN Internetworking Magazine, LAN World Buyers Guide, Macworld Netherlands, Net, WebWereld; **NEW ZEALAND:** Absolute Beginners Guide and Plain & Simple Series, Computer Buyer, Computer Industry Directory, Computerworld New Zealand, MTB, Network World, PC World New Zealand, Publish in Asia; **NICARAGUA:** PC World Centro America; **NORWAY:** Computerworld Norge, CW Rapport, Datamagasinet, Financial Rapport, Kursguide Norge, Macworld Norge, Multimediaworld Norge, PC World Ekspress Norge, PC World Nettverk, PC World Norge, PC World ProduktGuide Norge; **PAKISTAN:** Computerworld Pakistan; **PANAMA:** PC World Panama; **PEOPLE'S REPUBLIC OF CHINA:** China Computer Users, China Computerworld, China InfoWorld, China Telecom World Weekly, Computer & Communication, Electronic Design China, Electronics Today, Electronics Weekly, Game Software, PC World China, Popular Computer Week, Software Weekly, Software World, Telecom World; **PERU:** Computerworld Peru, PC World Profesional Peru, PC World SoHo Peru; **PHILIPPINES:** Click!, Computerworld Philippines, PC World Philippines, Publish in Asia; **POLAND:** Computerworld Poland, Computerworld Special Report Poland, Cyber, Macworld Poland, Networld Poland, PC World Komputer; **PORTUGAL:** Cerebro/PC World, Computerworld/Correio Informático, Dealer World Portugal, Mac*In/PC*In Portugal, Multimedia World; **PUERTO RICO:** PC World Puerto Rico; **ROMANIA:** Computerworld Romania, PC World Romania, Telecom Romania; **RUSSIA:** Computerworld Russia, Mir PK, Publish, Seti; **SINGAPORE:** Computerworld Singapore, PC World Singapore, Publish in Asia; **SLOVENIA:** Monitor; **SOUTH AFRICA:** Computing SA, Network World SA, Software World SA; **SPAIN:** Communicaciones World España, Computerworld España, Dealer World España, Macworld España, PC World España; **SRI LANKA:** Infolink PC World; **SWEDEN:** CAP&Design, Computer Sweden, Corporate Computing Sweden, Internetworld Sweden, it.branschen, Macworld Sweden, MaxiData Sweden, MikroDatorn, Nätverk & Kommunikation, PC World Sweden, PCaktiv, Windows World Sweden; **SWITZERLAND:** Computerworld Schweiz, Macworld Schweiz, PCtip; **TAIWAN:** Computerworld Taiwan, Macworld Taiwan, NEW ViSiON/Publish, PC World Taiwan, Windows World Taiwan; **THAILAND:** Publish in Asia, Thai Computerworld; **TURKEY:** Computerworld Turkiye, Macworld Turkiye, Network World Turkiye, PC World Turkiye; **UKRAINE:** Computerworld Kiev, Multimedia World Ukraine, PC World Ukraine; **UNITED KINGDOM:** Acorn User UK, Amiga Action UK, Amiga Computing UK, Apple Talk UK, Computing, Macworld, Parents and Computers UK, PC Advisor, PC Home, PSX Pro, The WEB; **UNITED STATES:** Cable in the Classroom, CIO Magazine, Computerworld, DOS World, Federal Computer Week, GamePro Magazine, InfoWorld, I-Way, Macworld, Network World, PC Games, PC World, Publish, Video Event, THE WEB Magazine, and WebMaster; online webzines: JavaWorld, NetscapeWorld, and SunWorld Online; **URUGUAY:** InfoWorld Uruguay; **VENEZUELA:** Computerworld Venezuela, PC World Venezuela; and **VIETNAM:** PC World Vietnam.   3/24/97

Author's Acknowledgments

For technical help, terrific encouragement, and CGI for a wonderful sample, I thank Eric Weaver.

For useful NT sysadmin information and funny Web server/automobile comparisons, thanks go to Don Hackler.

Thanks also to the technical staff at Tripod, Inc., including Jonathan Butler, Hank Zill, Brian Rogers, Chris Warren, Nate Kurz, Bobsquatch, Dewitt Clinton, Oliver Maertz, Derek Scanlon, Derek Bruneau, Jeff Van der Clute, and Don Zereski. And to the other helpful folks at Tripod, including Ethan Zuckerman, Kara Berklich, and Janet Daly.

For general support, helpful ideas and a pattern for living, I thank Dan Lynch at CyberCash.

In addition, I thank my agent, Carole McClendon, who started the ball rolling; Ellen Camm at IDG Books Worldwide, Inc., who worked so diligently with me at the beginning; Mary Goodwin, my editor who helped it all come through clearly for you; and Joyce Pepple and Heather Dismore, without whom the CD wouldn't have happened.

I also thank Christopher Lundquist, who patiently endured my 12-to-16-hour workdays on this book and pitched in with drawings for Herb's Herb Shack; Starbuck's coffee, which kept me writing into the wee hours many nights; and Mom and Dad.

Publisher's Acknowledgments

We're proud of this book; please register your comments through our IDG Books Worldwide Online Registration Form located at: http://my2cents.dummies.com.

Some of the people who helped bring this book to market include the following:

Acquisitions, Development, and Editorial

Project Editor: Mary Goodwin

Acquisitions Editor: Ellen Camm

Media Development Manager: Joyce Pepple

Permissions Editor: Heather H. Dismore

Copy Editors: Diane Giangrossi, Joe Jansen

Technical Editor: Joe Lowery

Editorial Manager: Elaine Brush

Editorial Assistant: Paul Kuzmic

Production

Project Coordinator: Regina Snyder

Layout and Graphics: Lou Boudreau, Linda M. Boyer, J. Tyler Connor, Angela F. Hunckler, Brent Savage, Janet Seib, Deirdre Smith, Michael A. Sullivan

Proofreaders: Christine Berman, Kelli Botta, Michelle Croninger, Arielle Carole Mennelle, Rebecca Senninger, Nancy Price, Janet M. Withers

Indexer: Ty Koontz

Special Help

Joell Smith, Media Development Assistant

General and Administrative

IDG Books Worldwide, Inc.: John Kilcullen, CEO; Steven Berkowitz, President and Publisher

IDG Books Technology Publishing: Brenda McLaughlin, Senior Vice President and Group Publisher

Dummies Technology Press and Dummies Editorial: Diane Graves Steele, Vice President and Associate Publisher; Mary Bednarek, Director of Acquisitions and Product Development; Kristin A. Cocks, Editorial Director

Dummies Trade Press: Kathleen A. Welton, Vice President and Publisher; Kevin Thornton, Acquisitions Manager

IDG Books Production for Dummies Press: Beth Jenkins Roberts, Production Director; Cindy L. Phipps, Manager of Project Coordination, Production Proofreading, and Indexing; Kathie S. Schutte, Supervisor of Page Layout; Shelley Lea, Supervisor of Graphics and Design; Debbie J. Gates, Production Systems Specialist; Robert Springer, Supervisor of Proofreading; Debbie Stailey, Special Projects Coordinator; Tony Augsburger, Supervisor of Reprints and Bluelines; Leslie Popplewell, Media Archive Coordinator

Dummies Packaging and Book Design: Patti Crane, Packaging Specialist; Kavish + Kavish, Cover Design

◆

The publisher would like to give special thanks to Patrick J. McGovern, without whom this book would not have been possible.

◆

Contents at a Glance

Cartoons at a Glance

By Rich Tennant

page 55

page 125

page 261

page 191

page 5

page 233

page D-1

page 279

Fax: 978-546-7747 • E-mail: the5wave@tiac.net

Table of Contents

Part VI: Looking at Legal Necessities 261

Chapter 17: It's the Law 263

Chapter 18: Wading through the Gray Areas 273

Part VII: The Part of Tens 279

Chapter 19: The Ten Commandments of Online Selling 281

Introduction

So you want to start selling online? Smart move. This book is just for you. *Selling Online For Dummies* tells you everything I would have wanted to know when I was getting started. It gives an overview of the issues involved, as well as a lot of important details to help you set up a store that works well for your business needs. This book gives you enough information to help you deal with any eventuality in a knowledgeable way.

Selling Online For Dummies assumes that you want to do as much of the work as possible, but it also points out lots of opportunities you have to hire people to do things for you.

Who You Are and What You Already Know

If you're reading this book, you probably already know a little about the Internet, enough to know that you should be taking advantage of the opportunities it offers for your business. In addition to that, you probably know how to use a Web Browser such as Netscape Navigator or Microsoft Internet Explorer. Maybe you even know a little bit about HTML, which is the language in which documents on the Web are created, but that won't matter much for the purposes of this book. You can pick up what you need from *Selling Online For Dummies* even if you know no HTML.

You may also have some knowledge or experience with marketing online and the special challenges it poses. (If you want to brush up on marketing on the Internet, pick up a copy of *Marketing Online For Dummies,* by Bud Smith and Frank Catalano, published by IDG Books Worldwide, Inc.) *Selling Online For Dummies* can help you put your online marketing ideas to work so that they can earn you some money.

If you want to work with the UNIX operating system, and if you have an old computer sitting around somewhere, this book gives you enough information that you can set up an online store with very little cash outlay. (You can get essentially all the software you need to run an online store using UNIX free on the Web.) If you have a bigger budget, this book covers plenty of hardware, software, and service options for you.

How to Read This Book

You don't need to read this book from cover to cover. Skip around and read the parts that strike your fancy. Then you can go back and fill in the details as you need to.

However, if it's a quiet evening and you have nothing better to do than sit by the fire and read this book from start to finish, I invite you to do just that. You get an interesting and complete picture of what it takes to put together a winning Web site for selling online. And if you happen to have an Internet connection available on your laptop by that fireplace, you can visit some of the sites mentioned in the book, download some software, or read more about topics that interest you most.

Better still, if you have a CD-ROM drive, you can plug in the CD-ROM that comes with the book, copy the HTML template from the CD, open the template, and start creating your site's content right away. (You also may want to take a look at or borrow from the small sample site included on the CD, Herb's Herb Shack.)

What's in This Book

You find the information in this book divided into seven parts.

Part I: Building a Site That Sells

Part I gets you started thinking about your business in new ways, and it helps you draw up a blueprint for your online store. You get a chance to read about the essential elements of a successful online store, and to start thinking about your domain name and your Internet Service Provider, too.

I also tell you what taking your business online may cost you, and how it can help some different types of businesses increase revenues, reduce costs, or both.

Part II: Laying a Strong Online Foundation

Part II talks about selecting the right hardware and software for your site. I give you some tips on configuring sites of various sizes and some advice about managing and maintaining your site.

Part III: Creating Selling Content

Part III emphasizes the content you need to sell your goods and services online. It shows you some ways to create professional-quality content consistently, which brings your customers back time and time again.

Part IV: Keeping Your Web Site Strong

Part IV helps you add power to your store. It looks at ways to get the word out by advertising your store online and offline. It helps you build a great business by offering information about how to use customer databases and some tips for providing excellent customer service in the Internet environment.

Part V: Accepting Payment Online

Part V guides you through the still somewhat-murky waters of electronic cash and credit card purchases. I also tell you what you need to know about providing security for your customers so that they feel comfortable buying from your site.

Part VI: Looking at Legal Necessities

The Internet is an entirely new arena for legal questions about copyrights, jurisdiction, and so on, filled with opportunity and controversy. Part VI charts the legal course for your online store, steering you away from the perils of unknown local and international law, and informing you about legal precedents being established in the courts.

Part VII: The Part of Tens

Part VII includes the Ten Commandments of selling online and ten common mistakes you can avoid. I also suggests at least ten ways you can bring more traffic to your site.

Also floating around in the book is the *Selling Online For Dummies* Internet Directory. To make the Internet Directory easy for you to find, I put it on yellow paper — you can find the Directory quickly when you need to find out about a site in a hurry.

Icons Used in This Book

You find icons sprinkled throughout the text of this book to help you quickly find information that's key to your platform and your site, along with special items of interest.

Points out important information you won't want to forget as you construct your commercial site.

Gives tips on how to do things better, faster, or cheaper. Items marked by this icon tend to come from real experiences of operating online stores.

Marks possible pitfalls. If you can avoid the potential problems mentioned in a warning icon, you may save yourself a few major headaches.

Points out technical details that you really don't need to know — just glide on by if you don't care about such things.

Highlights information of special interest to Macintosh users.

Indicates information of special interest to Windows NT/95 users.

Shows you information of special interest to users of the UNIX operating system.

Indicates that you can find an item on the CD-ROM that comes with this book.

Part I
Building a Site That Sells

The 5th Wave   By Rich Tennant

"Just how accurately should my Web site reflect my place of business?"

In this part . . .

I talk about basic issues surrounding your online store. In addition to pointing out the goals for your selling site, I discuss the fundamental elements of your store. And if that weren't enough for one part, I also throw in a great description of options you should consider when deciding how you want to connect your store to the Internet.

Chapter 1

From Physical Store to Virtual Store: Establishing Your Online Selling Vision

● ●

● ●

Many people think of Web sites that sell online as merely "online catalogues." That comparison works only so far. You need to offer more on your Web site than just an on-screen copy of your product catalogue. Why? Paper-based catalogues still have one advantage over online commerce sites: The potential customer doesn't have to do anything particularly unfamiliar or specialized to look at a paper catalogue anytime or anyplace. A shopper in a physical store doesn't need to turn on a computer and type a bunch of mumbo-jumbo before he or she sees information on a product.

Your job is to make sure that your customers can find your online store, and that it's appealing and easy for them to buy things there. Making sure that your site rewards your customers' efforts to find your online store takes some work. The biggest myth in online selling is that the world will beat a path to your door just because you hang out an online shingle. Would you expect that to happen on a street or in a mall?

Contrary to what you may have heard about orders rolling in as soon as you open your doors, selling online actually requires the same amount of work, and in many ways the same kinds of work, as selling offline — maybe more. But with this book by your side, you can minimize the work involved by organizing an effective battle plan based on the type of business you're in, and by avoiding common mistakes. This chapter shows you the advantages of online selling and gives you an overview of how to make it work for you.

Is Selling Online Right for Your Business?

The advantages of selling online are manifold, and the disadvantages are few (now that the trend toward doing business on the Web has caught hold). You really don't have reason to stay away from that crazy thing called the Internet any longer. Online selling is here to stay, it's moved into the mainstream, and many of your competitors may have already adapted to the new business climate that these opportunities are creating.

Just in case I haven't convinced you yet, here's a minimum list of benefits that can result from selling online:

- ✔ Your market reach isn't limited by geography, so you can reach a global market while keeping costs low.

- ✔ You can easily accept orders 24-hours a day.

- ✔ If you design your site well, customers can educate themselves about your products and services, so you can spend less on sales and marketing.

- ✔ You can build a loyal customer base by using the Web to create closer interaction and better customer service.

Okay, great. Selling online sounds like a great idea — but you should be aware of some disadvantages to going online, disadvantages that may convince you to focus your resources offline:

- ✔ The cost of purchasing server equipment and software can be high.

- ✔ The time required to set up and maintain a site can be substantial.

- ✔ Technology changes quickly on the Web, and you need to update your store frequently (in addition to normal maintenance and operation) to keep pace.

Hopefully, by pointing out possible pitfalls and opportunities, this book can help you cut the disadvantages of selling online and maximize the benefits — which means maximizing your profits. If you design and build a site that's within your ability to maintain, you can reasonably expect your online business to be profitable.

A few words of encouragement

A small company called Entertainment Merchandise, Inc., which sells movie-related memorabilia from a mall-based kiosk, made $36,000 in 1994. Tiring of the slow pace of sales and fearful of the threat of big players like The Disney Store, Entertainment Merchandise moved online. Part of that move was also the decision to accept credit cards, in what had previously been a cash-only business. For 1997, Entertainment Merchandise expects to exceed $1 million in sales across 18 electronic storefronts. They're gearing up to accept debit cards and e-cash, as well as online credit card payments.

Four Things Your Online Store Must Do

Regardless of what products or services you sell online, your store must fulfill four basic functions in order to be successful and turn a profit.

Displaying your products and services

Design your store so that it displays your products and services to their best advantage. Be sure to let your customers know about the benefits and advantages of your products over others that are similar.

By the way, more technology is not necessarily better, even online. What I mean is, you don't have to go all out and create a virtual reality to display your products effectively. Let the display fit the merchandise. For example, if you were designing a physical store to sell high-technology widgets, you may not want to display them in a Victorian rose garden setting, unless you intended to jar your customers' sensibilities "for effect." The online environment can be jarring enough; let the experience be as predictable as possible inside your online store.

Processing inquiries and orders from your customers

Your online store is built upon information. Remember, when customers can't see or touch your products, your excellent descriptions are called upon (literally clicked upon) to fill in the gaps. You need to provide lots of ways the customers can find the information they need, and ways to get in touch with you if they don't find what they're looking for.

Navigational elements on each page enhance your customers' ability to get information quickly and also make them feel comfortable in your environment because they feel more sense of control. The more comfortable they feel, the more likely they will make a purchase.

When customers get ready to order, it won't do to keep them waiting. The point of ordering is the most critical point in the sales process. You need fool-proof, failproof ordering scripts so that no orders "slip away" due to customer frustration. You also need a server that's as fast as you can afford — the ordering process is where it pays off (see Chapter 4 for more information on servers).

Processing payments

If all goes well, you need to equip your store to handle payments. Experience suggests that the more types of payment you can accept, the better — credit cards, electronic cash, checks, physical cash, perhaps even different currencies (see Part V for more information on payment options). And the more methods by which you can accept all those payments, the better, including online (over the Internet), by phone, by e-mail, by fax, and even in person, should that situation arise.

For your security-conscious shoppers, you face the challenge of providing security for all these forms of payment. (And everyone should probably be a security-conscious shopper on the Internet, even if they aren't yet.) Accepting payment directly over the Internet is the most risky; however, using encryption, your secure server can create protected connections with your customers' browsers while they transfer sensitive information such as credit card data (or shoe size, if that's a sensitive topic, too).

After you collect the payments from your customers, you need an account with a merchant bank who can settle all the transactions for you. (I usually think of this process as happening behind the scenes, in the "back room" of your online store, because the customers don't see it.) If you don't have a merchant bank and your business is too small or too new to qualify for an account, hosting services such as First Virtual can handle settlement for you. (For more information about First Virtual and other payment transaction services, please see Chapter 16.)

Delivering your products and services

If you sell an information product — a product made out of data bits — delivery is relatively easy, and quite inexpensive. You save on all sorts of manufacturing, packaging, and shipping costs.

If you sell regular retail products — "hard goods" — delivering your product after an online purchase is about the same physical process as delivery is for stores in the physical world.

Using the Ferengi Approach to Making Money

The Ferengi are a race of creatures on *Star Trek* who are motivated solely by profit. The Ferengi offer one important lesson in this universe: When it comes to setting up your online store, it's gotta pay for itself (at least). Some businesses have ventured into selling online looking for big easy profits, but with unrealistic expectations. Some, even big corporations, have spent a bundle and shown little or no profit so far, although they gain in "coolness" and mindshare on the Web.

In many ways, the online selling craze may remind you of the Gold Rush in 1849 when thousands of people went to California to get rich, but not many actually did get rich by panning gold. Somehow people have gotten an idea that as soon as they put up a Web site, the money will come pouring in. The bad news is, that hasn't happened to very many people. The good news is, if you set realistic expectations for your online success, you're likely to be quite happy with the results you do get from a little hard work.

Over time, selling online can actually pay for itself in the following two ways:

- ✔ By increasing profits through increased sales (of course)
- ✔ By lowering the expenses associated with sales you're already making (which may be less obvious)

The type of business you're in can influence the way your online site is likely to help you most. I categorize businesses into three types to help you see where you fit in:

- ✔ **Retail businesses:** They earn money by selling products, including software.
- ✔ **Service businesses:** They earn money by selling one or more services, such as consulting.
- ✔ **Media businesses:** They earn money by selling subscriptions and advertisements.

Your type of business affects what part of your business is improved most by being online, whether it's better customer service, increased sales, or more efficient product delivery.

Retail business

If your business is retail-oriented, you can increase your sales by adding a new "storefront" that reaches a wide audience on a 24-hour basis. If your business also has high expenses for sales literature and customer support, setting up an online presence can help you lower your costs, in addition to any additional sales you may close online.

How's that on reducing costs, you ask? For example, car dealerships are finding that their customers who use the Web come in knowing a lot more about their cars because they visit a site online for basic facts and comparison shopping. The salespeople find their time is used more effectively, which saves money.

For a retail business, remember that half of the equation is your online presence and half is your fulfillment department — even if people buy your product on the Web, you need to ship it to them in the real world. You may want to think of selling online as the showroom for your physical business, or an additional showroom if you already have physical stores.

Make sure that your online store's budget includes a fulfillment budget. If your online store is your only showroom, don't spend every penny in your savings account on the site right away, because packaging materials and shipping costs can add up.

One special case: Retail software business

A retail software business, or any business whose product is strictly "bits," is a hybrid between a retail business and a media business. The software sales model looks like retail, because the product is purchased a single time, not a recurring purchase like a subscription. Like other retail businesses, a software business can benefit from having a 24-hour storefront online in terms of increased revenue.

However, the delivery model for an online software business looks like a media business because the entire product can be delivered over the Internet. Unlike a media business, developing your software product certainly should be your biggest expense for this type of business, not working on your site. (In a media business, the site IS your business.)

An online store makes a lot of sense for these types of businesses, because online delivery can save you a lot on manufacturing and shipping costs. (Just think, no floppies or CDs to press, no manuals to send to the printer, no product boxes, no cover design, no shipping boxes, no shrink-wrap, no postage meter.) Your software or information retailing business is a prime candidate for making money both ways: by generating revenue and by cutting fulfillment costs online.

Service business

Your service may be at least partially deliverable over the Internet. For example, dating services can get people together online, but eventually they want to meet in person.

Service businesses notice a difference in the area of reduced costs. A great example of a service company using an online store to reduce costs while providing better customer service is FedEx. Customers love tracking their own shipments, and that ability of customers to help themselves to the information eventually reduces the ratio of customer service representatives needed for a given number of customers. (Of course it was a gargantuan task to integrate a Web site with the existing legacy of FedEx databases, but that's another story.) Customers with FedEx accounts can even ship their packages and pay online.

My own business, writing, seems to be a good partly-online business, because I can deliver text and graphics electronically to the publisher over the Internet. (I've never met the editor of this book in person, for example.) However, I haven't generated new business strictly from my online presence thus far, so for me it's a cost-savings thing. Unlike producing a software product or writing a Web-based magazine for subscribers, my writing revenue comes strictly on a contract-by-contract basis; the Internet is just a convenient delivery vehicle. That's why I tend to think of writing as a service business that can reduce costs by delivery online.

Online service businesses will become more diverse and interesting as technology continues to develop. I recently heard about a plastic surgeon who offers a consultation over the Internet — if you have a color video camera connected to the Internet and pointed at your face (or other parts!). He can even take a still frame, delete your features, and paste in others to show you what your new face looks like. All this is done online for about $100 per 15-minute consultation. Think of the possibilities.

Media business

For an online media business, the site is the business. Selling online for a media business means selling subscriptions or selling ad banners on the site.

Media businesses are the darlings of the Web. They're the ones who can utilize all the graphical, multimedia, video and audio, 3-D and virtual reality capabilities that make the Web so exciting.

Media businesses probably show more of what the future will be like than any other entity at this point. But media businesses are hard; people are accustomed to getting things for free on the Web, so it's a challenge to find subscription services they're willing to pay for. Print publications such as *The Wall Street Journal* are having some success with adding interactive editions to their publication. Some Web-based publishers that started out small, such as Tripod, are having success at offering inexpensive subscriptions with services that attract many subscribers (half a million, last time I checked with them, and growing strong). Tripod's secret seems to be a tight focus on a narrow demographic (18- to 34-year-old GenX-ers). America Online (AOL) is a media business as well as a service provider.

For a media business, it may be a good goal to eventually see half the revenue come from subscriptions and half from advertisements. Expect the advertising revenue to start small and build as you build your subscriber base. You need to check your site statistics to convince big name advertisers to buy ads on your site. Meanwhile, you need to work on selling subscriptions like crazy to get your site going. Advertise online and offline, everywhere you can think of. (See Chapter 12 for more about checking site stats and selling ads.)

Actually, all these kinds of businesses can increase their revenue by selling advertisements on their site, as long as the site generates enough traffic to interest advertisers.

Here's the Main Idea of This Book

If you really get this one sentence I'm about to write, you may not need to read the rest of this book, no matter what your business sells — that is unless you want more of the details. Ready, set, here it is:

Make it easy to buy, and you will sell a lot.

And that's really the gist of it.

Make it easy to pay

One aspect of making it easy to buy online is making it easy for customers to pay. For a great example of this, take a look at CDnow, a site that sells CDs at www.cdnow.com. They got one thing really right: They accept almost every imaginable form of payment, secure and unsecure, that a buyer may want to send. That includes

✔ Credit card orders over secure and unsecured server links

✔ Credit card orders over secure and unsecured e-mail

✔ Credit card orders by an 800 number and fax number

✔ Money orders or personal checks by mail

✔ Electronic cash

Online store owners should eventually consider accepting foreign currencies as well, because they are likely to be limited by accepting payment in only their own country's legal tender. For example, people in Japan who don't have easy access to U.S. dollars may not purchase from your site unless you can accept payment in yen. Currency exchange information is available online, so this option isn't as far-fetched as it may seem. For now, however, international buyers are often limited to credit card purchases.

For more discussion of payment methods, please see Part V. But basically, plan on accepting as many forms of payment as you can, which will increase the chances of maximizing your sales from the start.

Make it easy to find prices

A few of your ideas need to change in small but important ways to adapt to this new business environment. For example, scrap the technique of saving the price sheet for last in your sales presentation. Most Web shoppers won't put up with having to click several times before they know the price of an item. They're comparison shopping, and they're in a hurry. If you want their business, put your price list up front. Better yet, integrate your prices throughout your online showroom. Include prices on cleanly-designed pages with descriptions and artwork that show off your product in an appealing, attractive way.

Give full-featured product descriptions

You may have heard of the old idea of conserving brochure space by limiting your product descriptions to 25 words or less. Not needed on the Web, where essentially you have as much space as you need.

If you think people will call or send e-mail for more information, think again. What the Web promises is immediacy, and immediacy of information is part of that promise. Write full-featured product descriptions rather than short, stingy ones.

Create an environment of trust

For successful selling online, it's extremely important to create an atmosphere of trust for your customers. When you think about it, all business is based on trust. Remember the days when people didn't want to order merchandise from direct mail catalogues because they were afraid the company wouldn't accept returns? The development of the Internet is at a similar point as a business medium.

Just as in a physical store (as catalogue merchants know), you can create trust online by adopting customer-centered, service-oriented policies, such as liberal return policies. For example, there's a certain urban myth I heard concerning a fellow who once returned all his clothes to Lands' End because he needed some money — does their guarantee really say that they take back anything you ever bought from them?

Essential Elements of a Successful Online Store

In creating your online store, just as in a physical store, your goal is to *draw in* your visitors ("Just browsing, thanks"), so that they become paying customers. Hopefully, they become repeat customers, too! Toward accomplishing that goal, successful online stores of all types — retail, services, and media — seem to share a few important qualities.

Trust, without which no transaction ever takes place

It's a little more tricky establishing trust in an online store than in a physical store. To establish trust, you must establish clear policies for what you can do in case of defective merchandise, returns, and similar situations — and you must convey the policies clearly to your customers. Ideally, your policies cater to the customers' needs and interests.

When you're an online store instead of a physical store, even your physical persistence as a store can be questioned by your customers. You don't want to leave questions like this in your customer's minds: "Well, Joe's Boxing Supplies was there yesterday, but with the way things change on the Web, I wonder if they'll still be there next time I need new gloves?" It may take some time and hard work to build your reputation in an online store, just as it would in a physical store. If your customers permit it, communicate with them frequently by e-mail so they know you're still kicking. A short, friendly newsletter does an excellent job of reminding them of your presence. (And a newsletter might be a good way to tell them about sales and special promotions, too.)

Direct-mail catalogue merchants faced many of these same hurdles a few years ago, and they managed to overcome the trust hurdle in many cases by offering frequent catalogue mailings, generous return policies, and a 24-hour ordering presence.

A clear statement of the benefits of your products and services

The benefits and advantages of your products and services should appear on your site prioritized and, if appropriate, compared honestly to competitive products and services. (If they don't compare favorably, well, get some new products!)

When I think about clear statements of benefits and advantages of products, by the way, the Lands' End catalogue comes to mind. I love reading about the fine quality of their cotton, or how their towels are five inches longer than the nearest competitor. These are the types of statements you can use just as effectively in your online store. (If you haven't seen a Lands' End catalogue, try their Web site at www.landsend.com.)

Support for the customer's decision to buy

Support for buying online is called *information*. Make available as much information as possible about your business, your products, and services, including detailed product specifications, price sheets, and so on — in easy-to-find locations, not tucked away somewhere in back.

Again, going back to the catalogue comparison, one of the biggest fears people have in ordering clothing from a catalogue is that the item will not fit. Catalogue merchants support the customer's buying decision by providing size and measurement charts right there in the catalogues (as well as specific information about their return procedures and policies, just in case). You might need to think about what types of supporting information your products and services could use. (Hint: Especially if you sell services, a few testimonials from previous clients is always a good place to start.)

A pleasant and convenient shopping experience

In an online store, pleasant and convenient means the following things, practically speaking:

✔ **Not too many clicks to get to the ordering page:** If you make your customer click too many times to get to the ordering page, find the product they want, and so forth, it's increasingly possible with each click that she may become impatient and leave your store. If you're running advertisements on your site, it's increasingly possible that your customer will click on an ad banner and vanish that-a-way. (Of course, there's a balancing act here between wanting a nice set of pages on which you can earn revenue by selling ad banners, and not letting your customers vanish in a sea of "salable page views.")

✔ **Easy navigation that gives customers a good sense of control over their shopping experience:** In an environment without physical clues telling you where you are, it's easy to get lost. That's the basis of the traditional problem of Web sites — getting lost in Cyberspace. Giving customers a sense of where they are within your site at all times is important. It's equally important to let them get anyplace else they may want to go as quickly as possible (that is, in as few clicks as possible).

One method that's becoming popular as an aid to site navigation is the left-hand column containing, more or less, a table of contents for the site, whose entries are clickable links. By combining left-hand column navigation links with header and footer navbars on every page, you give your customer control of the navigation process pretty much all the time. This is a good thing. Don't fall into the trap of thinking someone would never want to go *here* from *there*.

✔ **Straightforward and even simplistic page design and site design (wherever possible):** Simple design is a must. After all, your customers may never have seen your site before. Your graphic designer's beautiful creation — a new page layout or image-mapped navigation bar — may be completely nonintuitive to a new visitor. It's a tough problem, balancing the need to keep your site fresh with the need to keep it elegantly simple.

✔ **Good server response, no long waits or timeouts, especially when ordering:** Having a connection to the Internet that's more than adequate to serve several customers at once is important. You want to measure the number of visitors to your site and plan accordingly. Third-party auditing services such as Nielsen I/PRO (www.nielsenmedia.com) can provide statistics about how many people are visiting your site and what they are looking at. After you have some information about your site's traffic, you can adjust your Internet connectivity through your Internet Service Provider (ISP) if needed — as long as you have an ISP that can give you enough bandwidth, that is.

✔ **Lots of opportunities for customers to give you feedback about their experience at your site:** A good way to provide lots of opportunities for feedback is to put an e-mail address or a link that reaches your customer service department at the bottom of every page. It's easy to do if you create a standard footer to use on every page of your site; then use a template containing that footer to create every HTML page. (On the CD that accompanies this book, there's a site template that you can use to get started.)

✔ **Attention to customers' needs for privacy and security:** The Internet is open to all who come. In this era of computerization and networks, it's so easy to get information about people that maybe our better judgment tells us we shouldn't have. People will give you sensitive financial information and who knows what else. The right things to do are protect their privacy by asking permission before distributing information about your customers, and to protect your site from information break-ins with judicious use of password protections, firewalls, and other security measures such as encryption, when called for.

Those are the basics. Get those right first. If you want to go beyond the basics, if you want to create an online store that brings people back and encourages them to stay longer, try creating chat rooms and bulletin boards through which they can talk with each other about your products and services. People love to talk and they love to feel they contribute something of value to you or to other customers. (For more information about creating chat rooms and other forms of interactivity in your online store, please see Chapter 11.)

A consistent corporate message, understandable by real people

You want to create an online store with products and services that are helpful, and you want to reach real people who want what you sell, right? It's easy to say but sometimes difficult to accomplish.

It's important to communicate the same corporate message repeatedly so that your customers feel comforted and reassured. If you repeat a statement several times in pretty much the same words, but not like a broken record, they feel like you really mean it — and you do, don't you? Repetition builds trust, and agreement with your message creates customer loyalty. The easiest messages to communicate over and over, ideally, are *simple messages.* When you create the selling content for your site, spend time boiling down your thoughts to their simplest terms. It is time well spent. You don't want your customers (or your staff, for that matter) to spend time thinking about your company's products, goals, intentions — do it for them.

Articulating your corporate vision is especially important if you have a staff of several people, all creating pages for your site and explaining the corporate policies in their own words. But it can be true even if you do it all yourself, because your understanding (not to mention your mood) changes from day to day.

A corporate style guide helps you convey your message consistently and clearly. You want to apply your corporate style guide to all the text you write for your online store. (For more information about style guides and how to use them, please see Chapter 10.)

Knowing Where to Start

The process of setting up an online store isn't always simple right now, though it's likely to get simpler as more off-the-shelf solutions become available over the next year or two.

You face several "in-house or outsource?" decision points as you create the framework for your online store. I've created a checklist designed to help you address those points with as much clarity as possible. Also, the chapters are structured so that they offer you information pertinent to each decision as it comes. For example, you must decide whether to have your entire (basic) site hosted by an ISP-type service provider; then you may face a hosting versus do-it-yourself decision again when it's time to set up your storefront. You also face a similar decision when you decide how to process transactions — get your own software or hire a transaction service. Clear as mud? See if the following checklist helps:

Decision 1: Operating and connecting your site

In-house: If you have space and other resources available, you can choose to operate and maintain your own server machines and pay only for a connection (such as a dedicated phone line) to the Internet. You probably need to hire a full-time Webmaster to maintain your machines.

Outsource: Otherwise, you can choose to upload the HTML pages and other materials for your site onto a server machine that's operated by an Internet Service Provider. All you have to do in that scenario is regularly create and upload the updates to your site. (You can also choose to co-locate your own machine with a service provider, but that's a slightly more complicated option that's discussed in Chapter 3.)

At this point it's a good idea to decide who's actually going to develop your site — including Web pages, database materials, ordering forms, and such. It could be an in-house job (you do it), or you could look into hiring a Web page development and design firm to do it for you. I give you some design resources in the Internet Directory section of this book.

Decision 2: Selling and storefront choices

In-house: In many cases your "storefront" is your entire site, but a few businesses divide their site into an informational portion and an online store portion. In fact, many businesses that already have Web sites (that don't offer commerce) can think of selling online as adding some capabilities and a few new Web pages to their existing site. You can purchase storefront software that's compatible with your choice of hardware and operating system platform, and then install and run it yourself (see Chapter 7 for more about storefront software). Because electronic storefront software runs on top of your Web server software, if you already run your Web site, it's just a little more to do.

Outsource: Even if you operate and maintain your own machines (an information site, without commerce capabilities), you can hire a service to host a storefront and electronic commerce-capable portion of your site. Well-known businesses like *Rolling Stone* magazine have done exactly this. To set up this option, you just create a link from your existing site into the hosted portion.

Decision 3: Choosing commerce capabilities

In-house: Even some electronic storefront products don't contain capabilities for conducting electronic commerce right on your site. Many of the products available off the shelf today require that you use a commerce transaction service, such as CyberCash (see Chapter 16). If your electronic commerce needs go beyond what your storefront product offers, you can look into hiring a programmer to develop customized transaction capabilities for your store. In Chapter 7, you find some storefront options that include the ability to complete your selling transactions right at your site.

Outsource: Actually, the majority of online stores today seem to be outsourcing their electronic transaction processing to companies like CyberCash. The services generally are reliable and fast, especially if your store's needs are straightforward—such as if you use online credit card transactions only, no digital cash. Chapters 15 and 16 give details about the ins and outs of electronic commerce for your store.

This section sums up the major decisions you have to make, except for all those other choices that are perhaps a little more familiar these days, such as what kind of hardware do I need, what's the best operating system, and so forth. Chapters 4 and 5 in this book help you along with those decisions.

Throw money at the problem: Of course, many services offer an entire package for you, from Internet connection to electronic commerce. They host your entire site, including settling transactions into your merchant account. For a fee, many can even develop the HTML and databases for you. This may be the way to go if you don't already have an existing site that you operate in-house, and especially if you don't have the resources available to operate your own site. That makes all of these decisions simpler, yes?

A Room with a View: Creating the Right Impression

Your Web site is a reflection of your whole business image, so you really need to work at making your image a good one. Your site may be the only thing that many of your customers see to make a sales impression.

No matter what your budget, you want your site to have three basic qualities, probably in this order of importance:

- Responsiveness (as in quick downloads)
- Clear, simple organization that makes information easy to find
- Visual attractiveness

These elements of a site make your business appear capable, trustworthy, and competent. Most first-time builders of online stores fail in one of these areas. For example, you can easily use too many graphics or animations in an attempt to make your store look exciting and dynamic. It's easy to bury information that customers want to see right away (such as prices) under a glowing description of your company's Christmas party. It's easy to make files that take so long to show up in a Web browser that your customers click away in despair. (Luckily, this book can help you avoid at least a few of these pitfalls, so you make a more professional impression on each new customer that comes your way.)

You have to make that impression with the resources (time and money) that you have available, which can be challenging. One proprietor of a well-known online store once said to me, "It's possible to do the Internet inexpensively, but it often looks it. Your personality always shows through." What kind of personality do you want to show your customers? (See the "Fictional Site Profiles" section later in this chapter to look at some options and some ballpark figures about prices you can expect to pay for three sample sites.)

As with dressing for success, build the best site you can afford. Yes, it's great to have a site up there and open for business, but don't sacrifice quality if you can help it.

Just before you go on to the following budget section, stop by Virtual Vineyards (www.virtualvin.com) for a breath of fresh air. Take a taste of an online retail food and wine site that's gone full-out to create an experience of quality for its customers. I never cease to be amazed by the feeling I get of having stepped into a posh boutique, even though I never leave my chair. It's not just how the site looks, it's not just that it has that snappy "at-your-service" response time of a good butler — it's how the site *feels*. Maybe it's the personal wine recommendations from the sommelier, maybe it's the "Selection of the Week" page, maybe it's the deeper pages with background on wineries and families who make the wines that Virtual Vineyards sells. I guess it's just everything all added together. It works for me, what do *you* think? And you can find lots of other sites out there, just as refreshing as this one.

Budgets to Live By

You definitely need to create a realistic budget for setting up and maintaining your online store. This section helps you marshal your resources. It provides some important monetary questions that help you judge what you can afford to offer your customers. Later in this chapter, you can find examples of a big-budget site, a moderate cost "online discount store" site, and a truly inexpensive option. You can pick and choose and adapt from these samples to fit your needs for selling online.

Here are some questions you should ask yourself when you think about budgeting your site:

 ✔ **Who will design and implement your site?** You have a few choices here: You can (and probably should) hire a full-time Web designer if your site changes often. If you need a lot of work to get going, then just a little regular updating after that, you may consider hiring a design firm to get you started. Also, your ISP or hosting service may offer Web page design and construction services for an additional fee. The Internet Directory section of this book contains a list of some well-known design firms that can help you get started, if you don't already know of one.

✔ **How often will your Web site need to be updated?** The more frequently you need to update your site, the more "HTML-and-GIF-generating" staff hours you need to budget. Professional Web pages probably take about three to five staff-hours per page to produce, on the average. You can expect to pay $45 to $65 per hour to hire out this kind of work on a contract basis.

If you have a relatively stable catalogue of products, you can plan your site so that large areas don't need to be updated often. That leaves you more time and budget free to focus on other areas, such as product introductions, advertising, or customer promotions.

✔ **Who will manage and maintain your site?** You may not need a full-time programmer, but a full-time Webmaster (with a few programming skills for Perl and CGI) is an excellent choice. You may think: What for, after those machines are set up, what would that Webmaster do all day? Hah! Computers are like children — it's amazing the ways they can get into difficulty. Computers need babysitters, too. At anywhere from $3,000 to $5,000 per month, on the average, these babysitters are not cheap, but they're worth their weight in gold if you run your own site.

Fictional Site Profiles

Just for fun, and to help you start putting together some ideas, I present some fictitious profiles of different-sized Web sites. I point out their different needs and what kind of hardware and connectivity they may find cost-effective. (Beware, these folks don't always do the right thing. I point out where they sometimes go wrong, so you can avoid making these mistakes.)

By the way — I include Herb's Herb Shack on the CD that comes with this book as a sample site. The sample includes an HTML template and a CGI program to help you with simple database searching. Of course, to experinece the full functionality of CGI program, you need to install it to your hard drive. (For more information on CGI, read *Creating Web Pages For Dummies*, by Bud Smith and Arthur Bebak, published by IDG Books Worldwide, Inc.)

Jim's Coffee House

Jim used to work for Apple Computer, so he has a couple of Macs sitting around. Now he runs a coffee house in Houston, Texas, but he can't get away from the old desire to be a nerd sometimes. He decided to set up a small Web site for his coffee house and let people order bulk coffees that he'll package and ship out during the slow times of the day. Because he's a one-man operation, he doesn't want to worry about running a Web site all week. He just wants to keep the Web site open during business hours.

Jim decides to install another phone line and buy WebSTAR for his Macintosh Quadra 840AV (it has 32MB of memory and a TelePort Gold II modem). He gets an account at his local ISP with unlimited access, so he can stay connected from 7 a.m. when his store opens until 7 p.m. when it closes.

Even though he used to work for Apple and knows what can happen on a network, he doesn't care much about security and can't afford fancy hardware, so he doesn't get a firewall (see Chapter 3 for more information on firewalls). He knows a little HTML, so he puts together some pages himself and hires a guy to write some CGI scripts in Perl for ordering the coffee.

The effectiveness of this site is pretty low. I recommend that Jim use a hosting service. For not much more than he's paying anyway for his ISP, he gains the advantages of full-time accessibility and a firewall. Also, the performance of his site would improve tremendously over the 28.8 Kbps dial-up line he's using. He will leverage his investment in the Perl scripts by uploading them to the hosting service. He can use the same HTML pages.

I also recommend keeping the new phone line and setting up that Mac Quadra in his coffee shop with a Web browser, allowing people to surf the Web while drinking their coffee. He'll probably sell more coffee in the shop. Perhaps he could charge a nominal fee for using the computer, and then he can pay for that phone line out of the proceeds. He can have the best of both worlds.

Because Jim already owns a business, he probably has a merchant account and doesn't need a service such as First Virtual that can handle merchant banking transactions on Jim's behalf (see Chapter 16 for more information on merchant banks). Instead, Jim could look for a hosting ISP that offers secure electronic commerce services if he's really serious about selling his coffee online.

Herb's Herb Shack

Herb lives in southern Vermont on a small farm where he raises herbs and organic produce. His wife, Eleanor, makes small sachets and other items using the herbs that Herb grows. Herb's brother Bill got them interested in the possibilities of reaching a wider market with their products by opening an online store.

By keeping their small-to-medium-sized Web site operating full-time (which you can find on the CD that comes with this book), Herb figures they can increase the revenues of their small, family-owned business by about 20 percent. If they make more revenue, they can afford to hire a neighbor to help with the sewing and stuffing of the sachet packets and other items.

Also, it will be especially helpful to Herb if he doesn't have to pay so much to the distributor who handles his products. Herb figures he can charge the customers less and still keep more of the profits when he can distribute the products himself.

They set up their online store, Herb's Herb Shack, in the basement of their old farmhouse. After a good family meeting, Herb took $1,500 they were saving to buy his daughter a used car upon graduation from high school and used it to buy a server machine, a Sun SPARC 1 Plus. The store opened using a regular 28.8 phone line, dedicated to the server connection, so it cost about $300 per month. His daughter uses Adobe PageMill at her school, so she created some Web pages advertising Herb's products.

Herb placed ads for the site in *Vegetarian Times* and other appropriate publications, and he put up notices on community bulletin boards in (physical) stores nearby, such as Wild Oats market in Williamstown, Massachusetts (because it's a college town and he figured it was likely to have lots of Internet users among the students). He also put an ad in the student newspaper at Williams College. And just for fun, he placed an ad in *Wired* magazine, too.

Herb is worried because his business is growing fast, and his rural community doesn't have the infrastructure to support high-bandwidth network services such as T1. Also, Herb doesn't have the cash reserve to invest in new equipment, but he really needs a bigger machine.

As the store grows, Herb decides that leasing a hosted machine is his best option for growth. It means less money up front for him, and he gets the benefits of a hosting service and better bandwidth. Heck, the hosting service even runs site statistics for him. And the whole package only costs $2,000 per month. (See Chapter 3 for more options on connecting to the Internet.)

Herb finds an acceptable ISP (that will lease him a server machine running Solaris, because his site was designed to run on a SPARC server), offering T1 and better, located in Troy, New York. It's about 45 minutes away by car, but he doesn't have to go there much, because the service runs everything.

Pretty soon stores like Wild Oats are buying ads on Herb's site, and his business begins reaching out to the compatible health and nature-oriented community with community awareness newsletters. And that company with all those young kids in Williamstown — what's it called — Tripod? is buying an ad, too. Turns out lots of those kids like herbs.

Herb has always accepted online payments by credit card. At first, he had no real security system, so he offered people a phone number to call with their orders. But most people just typed in the credit card numbers anyway. Herb likes the idea of protecting people's privacy, so now Herb's Herb Shack accepts electronic cash payments using DigiCash's ecash system, as well as secure credit card transactions (because his ISP runs Netscape's Commerce Server on his leased machine). He's looking into CyberCash's CyberCoin system for handling small purchases, but finds CyberCash's services a little confusing and thinks it would be difficult to configure them for his site without hiring a consultant. (See Part V for more information about security and accepting payment online.)

Now Herb is worried about running out of innovative ways to sell herbs. He's planning to diversify his business into slightly-gourmet, healthy foods and wines. But he knows he needs to find out a lot about regulations for shipping alcoholic beverages. (Herb turns to Chapter 17 of this book to read more about his legal responsibilities.)

Jane's Parent Line

Jane is setting up an online version of the print magazine that she works for — this magazine is focused on 35- to 45-year-old professionals who have children. Because the site is media-intensive, an excellent and fast connection to the Internet is a very high priority for Jane. Jane wants to use online commerce to let subscribers pay their subscription fees, and to offer special promotional items for sale.

Also, a high priority for Jane is to develop engrossing and professionally produced articles and other content for her site. Jane is looking forward to developing a lot of the site's content herself, because she has been the editor of the printed version of this magazine for two years already (and has grown the subscriber base from 10,000 to 40,000 parents). Jane's boss, Dick, has given her a budget of $60,000 to get this medium-to-large online venture up and running, with $10,000 per month for ongoing development and support costs for the first year.

An important feature of the online site, designed to draw in new subscribers and get the current print subscribers to move online, is ParentTalk, a message-based discussion forum on which parents can get advice on their child-rearing questions. ParentTalk is a moderated forum, and the moderator conducts a weekly chat as well, centered around parenting issues for kids in grade school and junior high school.

Jane chooses a Gateway NS9006 as her server machine. It runs Windows NT. Of course she'll need two machines because her market research tells her that her subscriber base will be large enough to require a mirror site, so there goes $26,000 of her budget (plus tax). To link the two machines together, Jane chooses a 10BaseT Ethernet Hub. She also needs a router. She chooses an Ascend Pipeline 130 router, with the optional integrated Secure Access Firewall. (See Chapters 4 and 5 for more information on servers and server software.)

To save money after spending such a bundle on hardware, Jane goes to the Apache HTTP Server Project at www.apache.org, downloads Apache 1.3 (which works with NT), and installs it on her computer. She also turns to Matt's Script Archive (at www.worldwidemart.com/scripts) and downloads CGI scripts written in Perl (Perl for NT) for a bulletin board and chat room. (Whoops, she forgot that she needs to recompile the scripts, so she also downloads Perl.)

Meanwhile, Jane is arranging a T1 line to be installed on her behalf at her selected ISP, because she has chosen co-location as her best option for site management. She wants to be focused on the content of her site, not on the demands of site management. There's a $2,000 installation charge for the T1 line, plus $1,000 per month fee.

What's wrong, Jane? No time to write? I think Jane is trying too hard to do it all herself. Just for one thing, Jane won't have time to build ad revenue because she won't be able to monitor her site traffic. But because her site is large and very frequently updated, hosting may not be a good option for Jane. She needs a Webmaster (at $4,500 per month), whom she can charge with the task of traffic monitoring and CGI management (among other things), while she focuses on the site's content development and on a host of freelance writers whom she manages. Jane needs to develop a site-wide style guide and apply it to the freelancers' pages.

Chapter 2

Drawing Up a Blueprint for Your Online Store

In This Chapter

▶ Looking at the anatomy of your store

▶ Seeing a store through the customers' eyes

An online store resembles a physical store in many ways, even though it doesn't look much like one (and you don't need a broom to clean your online store). As an essential part of planning your selling site, this chapter takes you on a tour of the four major features that build your selling site.

If you're thinking of using an advertising or design agency to help you create your online store, this is the place to start. Sit down with your agency and design a solution for every one of the points listed in this chapter — a solution that fits your particular business and your goals. (Please see Chapter 1 for more information on setting your online-selling goals.)

Designing the Parts of Your Store

In any store, physical or virtual, you need to show your products, let the customers pick them up, and then handle the details of the purchase. Of course, in an online store, all the elements that accomplish these tasks are actually software.

This section introduces you to the elements of your store, which you'll be creating and getting to know well:

- ✔ The storefront
- ✔ The shopping cart
- ✔ The cash register
- ✔ The back room

Figure 2-1 illustrates the parts of your online store, conceptually speaking. (After all, it's always a good idea to draw up real blueprints, isn't it?)

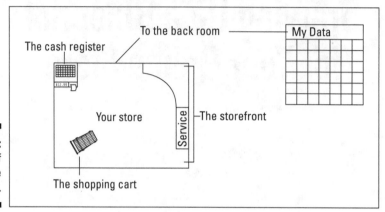

Figure 2-1:
The parts of
an online
store.

Keep in mind that your store is connected to the Internet, but I'm not showing the connection in Figure 2-1, just your store itself. (Chapter 3 has more details about how to connect your store to the Internet, including information about how to use firewalls to protect your valuable information.)

The very front doorstep of your store is your *home page.* It's the page your customers see as they arrive at your online store. Make your home page as welcoming as possible — simple, quick, and functional — like a good doormat. If you like, you could include any of the following features on your home page:

- A directory of your site
- Contact information for your company
- Information on current specials
- All of the above

The storefront

The storefront, like the aisles of a physical store, welcomes your customers, makes them as comfortable as possible, and introduces them to your products. Within the storefront, you display your products (or services), which means that the customers can get information about them and order them.

The storefront content

The storefront contains almost everything commonly referred to as the *content* of your online store, which could include any or all of the following items:

- ✔ HTML pages
- ✔ Images
- ✔ Interactive forms, such as order forms
- ✔ Whatever else you need to describe your products and services, such as pictures or lists of questions and answers

(For more information about developing content for your storefront as professionally as possible, look in Part III. Chapter 6 of *Marketing Online For Dummies,* by Bud Smith, published by IDG Books Worldwide, also offers tips on creating effective content.)

Setting up a storefront is something like setting up a window display for a physical store. You want the display to be as neat and attractive as possible. For example, to add visual interest, you may display icons or thumbnail-sized pictures of your products along with their descriptions.

When setting up your storefront, try to refrain from writing product descriptions of the type you may be accustomed to — meaning 25 words or less. Actually, customers on the Web like to get as much information as possible, so "long copy" sells your products best. After all, the customer has gone to all the trouble of sitting down at the computer, starting up the browser, and typing in your URL, why not give the customer a nice reward — all the information he or she could want.

Media site content

If your business is media-centered, instead of using the physical metaphor of the storefront as the aisles or display cases of your store, you should think of your published articles and other editorial content as your storefront — like the pages of a magazine. You may tend to think of your "magazine pages" as your product, but they are only part of the product — you may say they enable the product. Your subscriptions and your advertising space are actually your salable products.

Subscriptions are the result of successful editorial content. How? Editorial content creates an attractive "display case" that makes customers want to return to your site frequently, as subscribers. You're even luckier if your media site handles time-sensitive information such as sports scores or stock quotes; the customers return again and again. All online stores should think of themselves as being in the media business and should develop their content with commensurate care.

The storefront framework

Your *electronic storefront software* displays your products, and it contains a framework of other software designed to help you with the nuts and bolts of operating your store online (operating your store means processing orders, inquiries, payments, returns, and so on). This entire software framework generally is called electronic storefront software.

Sometimes your electronic storefront software includes a shopping cart for your customers, sometimes it doesn't. Online malls usually provide their members with electronic storefront software, and often with "back room" utilities, such as order tracking and processing, as well. You can find quite a few off-the-shelf storefront products (and shopping carts, too). I discuss these products at length in Chapter 6.

The shopping cart

The *shopping cart* is just what it sounds like, though a virtual shopping cart is a little more sophisticated than the ones that roll on wheels. A shopping cart in your online store keeps track of the items that your customer "picks up" (by clicking on them) until it's time to check out.

Shopping cart software varies widely. Some people look at the entire product display and purchasing system as the shopping cart. Others think of the shopping cart as the software that keeps track of a customer's purchases during a shopping session, before the items are actually purchased. Commercial shopping cart software products exist at both ends of this spectrum, so look carefully when you're selecting a shopping cart and make sure it goes gracefully down the aisles of your store, electronically speaking. Chapter 6 goes into more detail about shopping cart software.

The cash register

You need a cash register in your online store that can accept as many forms of payment as possible, including the following:

- Credit cards
- Cash
- Checks
- Electronic cash

Here's where security comes in. When you're collecting money online, it's a very good idea to use secure network connections. Otherwise, it's too tempting for mischievous or malicious individuals to "walk off" with your customers' credit card information. It would be like leaving a credit card sitting unguarded on your display counter or leaving the drawer of the cash register open. In that situation, it may be difficult even for honest people to resist such a temptation.

If you collect payments over the Internet, several companies provide software or payment services that protect your customers' information, and yours as well. Also, many of the servers discussed in this book offer secure data transfer using Secure Sockets Layer (SSL) or other encryption protocols. So if you run your own server, you can still provide security. If you don't collect payment over the Internet, just using an 800 number or other method, security is not such a big issue for you, though it never hurts to be cautious. Many customers appreciate a secure server even when transferring ordinary data such as their address and phone number online.

For more information about online payment security, see Chapter 15. For more specific information about payment software and services available, please see Chapter 16.

The back room

Many companies recognize the need for good storefront software. However, there's been a slower response to the need for excellent back room software designed specifically for online stores.

Your back room needs to offer the following services:

- ✔ **Recording customer information:** For this information, you need a customer database. You can use your customer database to keep track of what customers have bought previously. That way, you have a good "tickler file" to give you hints about additional or future products they may like. This time-tested technique of letting previous purchases suggest additional purchases is called *cross-selling:* Would you like some fries with your hamburger, sir? Or would you like some paper for that new printer? (Databases for your online store are covered in Chapter 13.)

- ✔ **Tracking your inventory:** With appropriate file protection safeguards in place, your customers can just check into your inventory database to see whether the item they need is in stock. Lots of electronic storefront software lets you create Web pages "on the fly," based on the results of customer searches. Chapter 6 talks about several storefront packages in detail.

✔ **Processing payments with your bank:** If you don't already have one, you'll need a merchant account so that payments from customers can be deposited for you. Chapter 16 talks about how to set up a merchant account.

✔ **Delivering your products and services to your customers:** If your products aren't delivered online, you also need an *ordering and fulfillment system.* All these tasks are part of your online store's back room — facilities for performing these tasks are included in many electronic storefront software packages.

You can integrate different databases in your back room in order to improve customer service. For example, with PeaPod's online grocery shopping service (at www.peapod.com), I can set up a personal shopping list, which is stored for me. If items on my list aren't in stock at this time, the site offers alternates from their list of current inventory. I can schedule my own delivery time, and they never forget my address. Making a service like PeaPod work takes at least three databases: an inventory database, a customer database, and a delivery scheduling database, all working together. (For example, electronic storefront products such as Cat@log let you integrate information from several databases onto a single Web page, if you want to do something similar at your store.)

Tracking your site traffic statistics can also be considered part of your back room, especially if you are running your own server rather than using a hosting service (see Chapter 3 for more information on hosting services). Accurate site traffic statistics are important for increasing your ability to attract advertising revenue (as you see in Chapter 12, which gives a lot more information about collecting site statistics). The more traffic you generate and substantiate, the more likely you'll be to attract high-paying advertisers.

You also need a way to track your expenses and income, and if you use a computer to manage these files (you are, aren't you? Excel is very easy . . . Quicken is helpful), you probably won't want to connect it directly to the Internet. You want to protect data sensitive to your business operation behind a *firewall,* which is a barrier to unauthorized access to your site from the Internet (see Chapter 3 for more information).

Challenges of online delivery

If online delivery of your products is part of your back room, you face a few unique challenges due to the ease of copying digital bits and the openness of the Internet's communications channels:

✔ Look into secure delivery for your products, just to make sure that no one obtains illegal copies along the way.

✔ Bone up on export restrictions, especially if your product contains any sort of encryption techniques for protecting your

data. Encryption is considered a munition by the U.S. Government, and it is highly restricted.

✔ Investigate copy protection for your products because copying digital images and text is so easy.

Some technological solutions are on the way for these potential difficulties. For more information about export restrictions and copy protection, turn to Chapter 17.

A Trip through an Online Store

Not only do online stores have pretty much the same parts as physical stores, they work pretty much the same way, too. When customers come in, they usually go straight to the displays and look at the merchandise (unless they have an inquiry or a return, in which case they go to the customer service desk).

When customers find something they like, they put it in a shopping cart and eventually, perhaps after browsing some more, they head for the cash register. At the register, they pull out a wallet and pay for the items. You accept the payment, and the customer goes along his or her way with a new purchase.

Figure 2-2 is a visual representation of this basic trip through the store, as seen from the customer's viewpoint.

After the customer leaves, you enter the purchase into your records, perhaps updating your inventory list. Or maybe you do the updating at the time of purchase, if you have the right systems in place. You report the transaction to your bank for settlement with the customer's bank. And you get your money. In Figure 2-3, I show you what the whole process looks like to you, the seller.

Figure 2-2:
What the customer sees, conceptually at least.

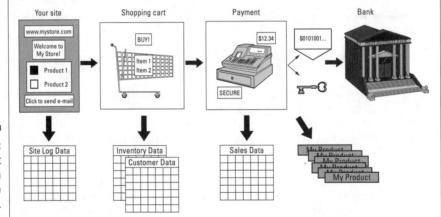

Figure 2-3:
What happens in your online store.

As you can see, a lot goes into setting up and running your business online. For example, at each point in the process, you have an opportunity to record information about a transaction into a database. But don't worry — you can get all kinds of software available to help you, and it's getting better every day. (When you're ready to select the hardware and software that will run your online store, be sure to look at Part II. Also, you find information about using databases in Chapter 13.)

Chapter 3

Connecting to the Internet

• •

• •

*O*ne of the most important decisions you face in setting up your online store is determining the nature of your connection to the Internet. You need to decide whether to go with a hosting service, which means you pay someone to run the site for you, or whether to run the site yourself.

After you decide on a host for your site (either yourself or a service), you need an address on the Internet, which is commonly called a *domain name*. Next thing you need is a pipeline, the biggest you can afford, for shipping your essential product information out to your customers and taking their orders in return. Or for receiving customer feedback and sending your response. Or for letting them chat with each other at your site and trade tips. Or . . . well, you get the idea.

Hire a Host or Host It Yourself?

Choosing whether to hire a hosting service or hosting your own site is like choosing the right lease for a physical store; it can make a big difference in your customer traffic and in your overhead expenses over the long term.

Consider the following points when deciding whether to pass the buck to a professional hosting service, or whether to keep that buck for yourself:

> ✔ **Hiring someone to host your site for you:** If you're just trying out online selling for the first time, or if you're going about it in a small way, you could start by using a hosting service. That way, you haven't committed to buying a lot of expensive computers and software.

Lots of high-traffic, successful sites are run by hosting services. Don't be fooled into thinking you have to do it yourself to be a success!

If you decide to have someone host your site for you, this chapter tells you some specifics to look for in a hosting service, and the rest of the book adds to your ability to tell whether your hosting service is doing a good job.

✔ **Hosting your site yourself:** On the other hand, you can find a lot of freeware to get you started, and jumping in with both feet can really get a project going. It's up to you — you have lots of room for your personal style in how you go about setting up your online store.

If you decide to host your site yourself, this book gives you a good start toward everything you need to know to put together an online store that works for you.

This Way to Your Web Site: Web Hosting Services

Hosting services spring up like mushrooms after a rain. Look in the back of a trade magazine and there they are — scads of ads for Web hosting services.

What you get

What's a hosting service, you say? Basically, for a flat monthly fee, a Web hosting service provides the following services:

✔ Space for your site's content files (typically, at least 20 to 25MB or so, and you can usually buy additional space in increments as you need it)

✔ E-mail accounts for you to send and receive e-mail

✔ Sometimes, domain name registration services (see "Getting a Domain Name" later in this chapter for more information on domain names)

✔ Other ancillary services associated with your online presence:

• Some hosting services perform backups or collect site statistics for you. Site statistics show you who visits your site and what they look at. (For a lot more specific discussion about site statistics, please see Chapter 12.)

- Some provide software, such as Microsoft FrontPage, to let you build your Web pages.

- Many offer consulting help in creating your Web site for you.

A hosting service relieves you of the technical headaches of maintaining your site. You can concentrate on advertising, merchandising, and other aspects of your business.

The worst thing about a hosting service is that you have less control over certain aspects of your site, including the precise update schedule for your content.

It's gonna cost ya . . .

Prices and service packages for Web hosting are all over the map now — this industry is far from standardized yet — so be sure to look around.

Right now I can pick up a trade magazine and see a number of back-of-the-magazine ads that offer basic Web hosting services from $14.95 to $24.95 per month (when I say *basic,* I mean those services described in the preceding section). That could be a good option for a modest site (or even a personal site, just to get your feet wet) if you can handle your electronic commerce and security needs independently. For example, some people still don't want to send credit card information over the Internet, so you could offer a toll-free phone number for purchasers. If your hosting service offers the ability to put up *CGI scripts* (which let your customers fill in forms online), you can usually arrange some kind of commerce directly through your site in any case.

In another price category are hosting services (such as some online malls) that offer full electronic commerce hosting capabilities, along with all the other services offered in basic hosting. For *secure commerce* hosting options, the cost of Web hosting ranges from $34.95 per month (for secure credit card acceptance online) to $150 per month for top-of-the-line hosting service, including:

- ✔ Secure commerce, which means sensitive information is protected using encryption

- ✔ Shopping cart software, which is an essential part of the online shopping process

- ✔ Backups, to make sure your data is always recoverable in case of a disk failure

- Database access, which means you can make database information available on the Web

- Password protection, which keeps unauthorized users out of areas you want to keep private

- A library of other programs you may need, including guestbooks, counters, chat, and more

Usually the hosting service charges a set-up fee, typically equivalent to about a month's service. Some hosting services offer discounts for paying a year's lease up front; some require a year's contract as a minimum. Most likely you have to pay an additional fee to register your domain name, which you can read about in "Getting a Domain Name," later in this chapter.

Asking the right questions

No one likes quizzes, but I assure you that you need to ask any potential hosting service a few questions to make sure that they are right for you. You need to ask the following questions of any hosting service that you're considering (and heck, I throw in a few bits about what to look for, to boot):

- **Exactly what is included in your monthly service fee?** You may see a list of services at the site, but it's always a good idea to contact the site directly to get the most current information and to find out about any special offers they may have coming up in the future.

  Get backup arrangements and support guarantees in writing, because sometimes they're not actually spelled out in a general service contract.

- **Are there any restrictions on my service?** Some hosting services may limit the number of file transfers that you're allotted or the types of content that you can use.

- **What guarantees do you provide about my site's accessibility for my customers?** Some services provide a statistic, such as guaranteed 99.7 percent uptime.

  Ask whether you get compensation if the accessibility guarantees are not met. You don't want your customers having the problem that so many of America Online's customers had at one point — inaccessibility — for whatever reason.

  Sometimes your site works perfectly, but your customers still can't reach the site due to heavy Internet traffic or a nonfunctioning node between your store and their machine. Such is life.

Online malls — hosting services in disguise?

It's a bit confusing. What's the difference between a hosting service and an online shopping mall? Sometimes you can't see much of a difference on the surface. In fact, online malls may offer you hosting services, even online commerce processing, as part of an attractive package that encourages you to join. But it's just as easy to be part of an online mall if you want to run your own server and link to the mall from your site.

Remember, no one can tell the difference in the virtual world. An online mall may be no more than a group of online stores that work together and treat each other preferentially through mutual linking, ad banners, and other perks.

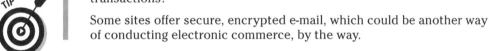

✔ **What site statistics do you provide?** For example, you may inquire about what log file analysis software the service uses, how frequently you get reports, and whether the site can provide a report on just one section of your Web site?

✔ **What type of security do you provide?** Look for security for your site, such as a good firewall, and security for electronic commerce transactions, such as SSL security. Does the host charge extra for secure transactions?

Some sites offer secure, encrypted e-mail, which could be another way of conducting electronic commerce, by the way.

The domain name game

A hosting service can save you time and bureaucratic hassles by helping you apply for your domain name (if you're interested in that help, make sure you ask about that service before signing with a host). But if you decide to transfer to another hosting service, you usually have to pay another fee, even though you already have registered your domain name.

If your chosen hosting service doesn't offer domain registration as part of your package, don't worry. It's pretty easy to do it yourself, or you could use a domain registration service to help you. (For more information about domain registration, please see "Getting a Domain Name" later in this chapter.)

Caveats about Web hosting services

A couple of areas bear closer examination when you search for a hosting service — these issues can end up costing you, either in fewer customer visits or in actual dollars you have to pay out. Specifically, look out for these two top-priority items when selecting a hosting service:

  ✔ **Keeping the pipes clear:** Check to see whether the service provides an adequate "pipe" of Internet connection so that customers find your site easily accessible and responsive at all times.

  ✔ **Hemming you in:** Check whether they limit in some way the amount of data you can transfer over the Web on a monthly basis. That is, whether they limit the number of file downloads you can provide of your site's content into your clients' browsers, either by counting hits, or by counting the megabytes of data sent out from your site.

The size of the pipe

Besides the package of services they provide, hosting services vary a lot in the size of the "pipe" they can offer you to the Web. You want to select a provider that provides the right pipe for you — some offer a trickle, and some offer a floodgate, relatively speaking. (Turn to "How Much Bandwidth Do You Need?" later in this chapter for tips on choosing the right size pipe.)

The bottom line on pipe size: You want your customers to shop 24-hours a day, with as big a pipe as you can afford. Pick a hosting service with lots of capacity, because you share that capacity with other sites hosted by that provider. (Or host your own site and pay for your own connection, right?)

Limited data transfer

Another thing to look at when selecting a hosting service is whether they charge extra when your site exceeds a specified number of *hits* (files accessed by visitors), or if they limit the total amount of data per month that your site transfers over the Web.

You don't want to have to pay extra for people to get information about your products or services, especially when you can find service providers who enforce no such limits. Look for a service with no limits, or with limits at least three times higher than you think your site will receive. That way, you have some room to grow before you have to incur the time and expense of hiring a bigger hosting service.

Hosting Your Own Site

Ah, you've decided to host your own site? Welcome to the wonderful world of the Web. You're about to experience it to the fullest.

Picking Internet Service Providers

An Internet Service Provider (ISP) is a company that provides a connection to the Internet. Looking for an ISP resembles looking for a hosting service, because essentially all hosting services are value-added services for a basic ISP. The major difference between using a hosting service and an ISP is that an ISP does not offer extra services like site statistics, backups, and so forth. That's okay — you can do that stuff yourself.

Look for the least expensive service you can find that offers the biggest pipe with the fewest frills to meet your site's needs. See "How Much Bandwidth Do You Need?" later in this chapter for tips on picking out the right size pipe for your site.

If you run your own server, you won't need space on their server for your Web files. If you set up your own e-mail server, you may not need their e-mail service, either.

You also want to consider the whole package of services offered; some may suit your business needs better than others, for example, by offering domain name registration services or free technical support. Here are the key questions you want to ask any ISP you consider:

- ✔ What types of connections do you offer?

- ✔ What is your access range? Do you offer national, international, or worldwide access?

- ✔ How many Internet POPs (Points of Presence) do you have? (Almost all ISPs have their own backbone, by the way.)

- ✔ What types of switches and routers do you use? How redundant are they at each transfer point?

- ✔ To what NAPS and MAEs are you connected?

- ✔ What firewall system do you use?

- ✔ What additional services do you provide? (For example, site analysis, arranging for telco lines on your behalf, installation, service agreements, domain registration services, hosting services, database hosting services, and of course, electronic transaction services.)

- ✔ What are your hours and charges for tech support? (Most advertise 24-hour tech support — it's just the manner of service that varies. Some provide e-mail-only support during certain hours, while some offer round-the-clock telephone support by real human beings.)

Reliability and then some

ISPs, who stake their reputations on reliability and availability of their servers, strive to keep their machines fully operational and connected to the Internet 99.99 percent of the time. About one minute of outage per week is the acceptable figure for many such services.

One service provider in Palo Alto, California, called IDS (Internet Distribution Services) utilizes a clever way to let a group of interconnected server machines on the Internet help each other stay operational. Each machine runs a process that makes it "wake up" every few minutes and "look around," by using the network to "ping" other machines. If the awakened machine sees all the other machines and sees the Internet, it can go back to sleep. If the machine can't see another machine or can't see the network, it calls in a message to a centralized phone number. On this local network of a dozen computers or so, usually two or three machines are awake at any particular time. If any of the machines is truly nonfunctional, all the awakened machines report it. Thus, several messages reach the centralized phone number and a Webmaster receives a call on a pager. The machines often are able to reconnect or restart themselves, but if not, the Webmaster can restart the machine remotely in most cases. This system lets fewer Webmasters manage a greater number of machines without sacrificing high standards of reliability and connectivity.

Nationwide and international Internet Service Providers

If you need reliable, full-time, high-bandwidth service for a large online store, consider a nationwide ISP, and probably one that serves business customers (not just individuals). Many of the ISPs that provide nationwide service are connected directly to the Internet backbone, some even own part of the backbone. (The Internet was turned over from the NSFNET backbone at the end of April 1995, and transitioned totally into commercial operation.)

One of the most important things to look for in a nationwide Internet Service Provider is how they route their traffic. Those who own their own portion of Internet backbone are likely to offer more reliable service and often faster than providers that rely on others for transporting your data over the Internet.

You can find at least 15 worthwhile providers of business-oriented Internet services that have U.S. or international reach. To shop around for an ISP, just fire up your browser and do some research online. (Going online gives you access to an ISP's most current prices.) You could start your search at `thelist.internet.com`.

ISPs and Internet traffic

In the early days, the only thing an online business had to worry about was the possibility that their ISP would go out of business. You could select a service provider easily, on the basis of features provided and cost. For large businesses, at least, the selection process has become more taxing as the Internet comes to its knees in a tidal wash of packet traffic. Certain ISPs have better ways to work around the flood (at least for now) than others.

Many ISPs have spent billions of dollars to improve the bandwidth and redundancy (and therefore the performance and reliability) of their own portions of the Internet. However, the public backbone itself presently is creating a bottleneck of Herculean proportions. So, the thing to look for in finding an ISP is how they route their traffic around or through the six troublesome intersections that connect the Internet (see the following sidebar "Internet traffic jam"). You're likely to get faster and more reliable transmission from a provider that has a good work-around plan.

You also want to consider whether an ISP has equipment stationed at the major interchange sites. If it does, you know that your data has a more direct route onto the Internet than if your ISP relies on transfers by other hosts at interchange sites. When traffic is very heavy, every little bit helps in getting your files to your customers faster.

Internet traffic jam

Because of the current levels of traffic on the Internet, it's been stated by those in the know that over 60 percent of businesses are unhappy with their ISPs.

Why is the Internet traffic so bad? The public portion of the Internet backbone is overloaded because it depends on only six "intersections," which eventually must transfer literally every one of the trillions of packets on the network. These intersections are of two types:

✔ Network Access Points (NAPs), where public packets flow onto the network

✔ Market Area Exchanges (MAEs), where packets are routed onto the appropriate major subnets for further transmission

Two of these intersections, MAE East in Washington, D.C., and MAE West in San Jose, California are reportedly so busy that they drop up to 40 percent of the packets flowing through them between the hours of 3 p.m. and midnight most days. (Not to worry, all the packets are retransmitted by the sender, but retransmission uses up more bandwidth on an already crowded interchange.)

Co-location

In a co-location arrangement, you rent space in a climate-controlled computer room for your server hardware. You can rent "rack space" for extra equipment such as modem banks.

The co-location host provides power, an Internet pipe, and so on, and they may even reboot your server machine for you in case of a hard crash. You still perform all the site maintenance and operation tasks, such as gathering statistics, backups, and site updates.

If you have server software that allows *remote administration* (site updating and management using a customized tool or through a Web browser window), co-location can be a great option for you. Sometimes co-location gets you a great view, too. I know of a site that has co-located its computers into a huge room with a panoramic view of the Manhattan skyline. Sorry, no sleep-overs allowed.

Especially good reasons to consider co-location include the following:

- ✔ You live in a rural area and want more speed.
- ✔ You expect a lot of site traffic.
- ✔ You want another mirror site in another part of the country to make access quicker or easier for customers in a certain region.

Console servers

In a co-location deal with an ISP, you end up doing a lot of remote site management. It's convenient to log in remotely to individual machines for troubleshooting and backups, but you're not always able to do that when you're co-locating a large site.

If you find yourself in that situation, you may need a *console server*. A console server is a computer into which you can log in using a modem and talk to any machine on your Web farm *as if* you were typing on its own keyboard. The console server usually is physically near the machines it controls, so you normally put it wherever you keep your server machines.

A console server can talk to other "intelligent" network equipment, too, not just servers. The server can talk to your router, for example. It takes some work to set up a console server, but hey, it's better than having to drive somewhere on a dark and stormy night when a machine crashes.

Like a lot of fancy equipment designed for professional networks, console servers are expensive. You can expect to pay at least $10,000 to $15,000 for a console server.

Sometimes a co-location ISP also leases you a server, which could mean a big savings to you on up-front costs for your site if you don't have to buy one. The following site on the Web gives you pointers to some ways to lease servers: union.ncsa.uiuc.edu/HyperNews/get/www/leasing.html.

ISDN and coffee, please

If you live in a metropolitan area that offers the service, and if you can afford it, you can go directly to your telephone company for ISDN (Interactive Services Digital Networks, 128 Kbps) service for your online store. The speed of ISDN adequately supports a small site, such as one you may operate with a home business, coffee shop, book store, or similar endeavor, especially if you don't want or need to keep your site available 24-hours per day. Using ISDN offers a good intermediate stopgap before leasing a dedicated line.

If your online store expands, you may want to consider moving beyond ISDN and look into large-scale ISPs such as Exodus Communications (www.exodus.net), which primarily services corporate customers. They offer bigger pipes, such as T1, dedicated lines, and more.

Racing into the future

When you run your own site, how can you provide for new technologies coming along? You need to plan on "redecorating" to accommodate new technology.

A hosting service can usually take care of the redecorating for you.

For example, one new technology that may affect your online store is *cable modems*. Cable modems perform even faster than ISDN. Your site has to keep up — if you start off with an ISDN connection, you have to upgrade as your customers begin to adopt faster communications technology such as the cable modem. Cable modems offer the ability to receive data from the Internet through a cable box at about 10 Mbps, using the cable companies' existing underground fiber optic cable.

(A few techno-weenies love their cable modems already. In a show-of-hands "market survey" at a conference I attended last year, about three-fourths of the attendees said they'd gladly chase the cable truck down the street if they could get their hands on a cable modem. Two attendees had them; they gloated, visibly. I expect to see cable modems becoming more commonplace in about five years.)

Sample ISDN costs for the San Francisco Bay Area

As an example of ISDN costs, in late 1997 I spoke with Pacific Bell, which provides ISDN services in the San Francisco Bay Area:

✔ To convert an existing phone line to ISDN, Pacific Bell charges a $125 conversion charge.

✔ They charge a monthly fee of $29.95 for the two channels needed for full ISDN.

✔ The service has a measured rate, which means that Monday through Friday, 5 a.m. to 5 p.m., you pay 3 cents for the first minute, and 1 cent per minute thereafter, for each channel. Thus it costs 6 cents and 2 cents respectively for two-channel access such as Internet usage. If you stayed connected 24 hours a day, it costs you an additional $288 per month for these hours, added to your bill for measured charges.

✔ Pacific Bell now gives 200 free usage hours for use after 5 p.m. or on Saturdays and Sundays.

✔ Before ordering ISDN, you have to purchase your ISDN terminal adapter equipment and be able to tell Pacific Bell the brand name, because they are all slightly different. (Terminal adapter equipment costs between $200 and $500.)

✔ Only a few ISPs offer ISDN-capable Internet connections. Those services range from about $30 per channel, to about $100 per month. Pacific Bell is among the few ISPs who offer ISDN-capable connections (which makes sense, because then they sell more ISDN service, right?).

✔ It takes about 15 days to convert your line to ISDN.

Because of tremendous demand for ISDN services in the San Francisco Bay Area, Pacific Bell offers a one-stop-shopping deal for ISDN, called HomePack, which is suitable for home office use. The HomePack includes a 3Com brand adapter (ImpactIQ) which normally costs about $200. They waive the installation fee of $50, and they provide software for connecting to the Internet through ISDN. Also, Pacific Bell provides Internet access in the Bay Area, so they throw that in for $50 per month when you buy the HomePack.

Getting a Domain Name

Part of hosting a Web site (whether you decide to let a service host for you or whether you do the whole shebang yourself) is choosing and registering a domain name for your site.

A domain name gives a name to your own little corner of the Web; it's the thing you may think of as someone's "Web address," which usually has the form www.domain.com for businesses in the United States.

Domain names have to be registered with an Internet authority called the InterNIC. It costs $50 per year to maintain your domain name, with two years paid up front. (See "Checking and registering a domain name" later in this chapter for more information.)

Creating your domain name

Hold up here. Before you start to think of that new and innovative domain name to increase hits to your site tenfold, you need to be aware of some domain name conventions. Domain names have to follow a certain form, and they have to be unique. Here are the basics of domain naming:

- ✔ A commercial business must have a domain name with the extension of `.com`
- ✔ A network service provider may have an extension of `.net`
- ✔ An educational institution has the extension `.edu`
- ✔ A government organization, for example NASA, has the extension `.gov`
- ✔ A non-profit organization may have an extension of `.org`
- ✔ Countries have identifying extensions as well. For example, the nation of Tonga has the designation `.to`

These days, you see so many entries in the `.com` portion of the Internet's registration, you may find it difficult to get the domain name you want. Plan on thinking of alternative spellings, or including hyphens and underbars in multiword names.

The closer your domain name is to your company's brand name, the easier you make it for customers to recognize your business online. (I assume that you can still get something resembling your brand name.)

Chapter 4 of *Marketing Online For Dummies,* by Bud Smith, published by IDG Books Worldwide, offers great tips on creating a domain name that markets your site to its fullest.

Don't read this — no really!

Only read this if you're in for a bit of Internet trivia and a personal rant. In the old days, the InterNIC was called the NIC. NIC used to stand for Network Information Center. It was a small group of people down a hallway and around the corner from my office at SRI International in Menlo Park, California, and that was all there was of it — it was all that was needed. We were very cozy.

How times have changed! Now some organizations are filing suit against the InterNIC for "monopolistic" control of domain name licensing, and of course, the associated revenue.

Setting up domain name servers

Before you can fill out the InterNIC's form to register your domain name, you need to set up two *name servers* that host your domain name. A name server is a computer on the Internet that translates domain names into IP addresses, which are a bit like street addresses for computers on the Internet. (They look something like this: 207.46.32.10.)

If you're buying server machines, it's fairly straightforward to set up a single machine with an IP address and matching domain name — you edit a file called the *hosts file*. Hosting a domain name just means that the host machine has information on file about how to match up the name and the number, in the hosts file, of course.

This aspect of getting your site going can seem a little scary, but don't worry: Your server software contains tools that help you edit your hosts files, because it's a normal part of site operations. (Chapter 7 has some examples of editing a hosts file on UNIX, and the concepts are similar for any type of Internet server.)

If you already have a domain name and you want to check who's listed as contacts for your domain, you can also check that on the InterNIC's WhoIs service at rs.internic.net/rs-internet.html. Another site (European) that offers domain name researching tools is www.demon.net/external/ntools.html. Just enter your domain name into the box called Generic whoislookup (about the third box down, with stars beside it).

Checking and registering a domain name

After you think of some good ideas for your domain name, your hosting service can check their availability for you. Or you can check for yourself by hitting the Virtual Internet site at www.vi.net (European) or the InterNIC Registration Service at rs.internic.net/rs-internic.html.

Here's how to check a domain name:

1. **Using your Web browser, go to** rs.internic.net/rs-internic.html.

2. **Scroll down to the WhoIs link and click on it.**

   A search screen appears.

3. **In the input box, type in the domain name you'd like to have, and then press Return.**

If your domain name is already taken, you see a record of who the contact names are for that domain and where its home server resides. Sorry, try another one.

If your choice of domain name isn't taken, congratulations! Click on Register Domain Name and fill out the form. Yes, you can even pay online. If you're planning to have a hosting service or ISP register the name for you, tell your service about your new domain name right away.

Domain registration costs $100 up-front, which covers two years' registration. After that, it's $50 per year, and the billing contact you specify will be notified by e-mail and invoiced by regular postal mail. Internet domain registration applies worldwide, by the way.

After you register your domain name, be sure that you're listed at the InterNIC as one of the contacts for your domain (or at least someone at your company). Don't let someone from your hosting service or domain registration service appear in all three slots. Three contact names are required by the InterNIC: administrative, technical, and billing. Pick one (that is, assuming you're not already doing all three of those jobs yourself). Otherwise, how can you know when your fee is due or if there's another sort of problem? By the way, the billing contact name doesn't show up when someone does a domain name search at the InterNIC, so if you want to be a bit incognito, that's your best choice.

Virtual nation-states?

Domain names are a new kind of worldwide entity. They stand quite aside from copyrights and patents, which are based on national authority. Although domain names resemble trademarks or copyrights in certain ways, no one else has the right to use your domain name after you registered it. And domain names have value; they can be bought and sold.

There have been several cases of "little guys" running out and registering potentially popular domain names, such as janetjackson.com, and then offering to sell the names to major companies. In some cases, that tactic has paid off handsomely. The name business.com sold for $150,000.

Recently I came across a company that had a domain name very similar to mine, and it really threw me for a loop. My company's domain name is cre8tive.com, and there's a design firm in Huntsville, Alabama with the domain cre8ive.com. (I get a fair amount of e-mail intended for employees of their company, which is how I found out about it.) Things like this can happen to you on the Internet. You can't do much about it, except to politely forward their e-mail, I guess — and try not to read it first. A strangely personal medium, for one so huge.

There's a service for everything

If you flinch at the possibility of registering your own domain name, you can hire a service to register for you. Your hosting service or Internet Service Provider usually can register a domain name for you, if the name is available.

Be sure to ask your potential domain registration service these questions:

- ✔ **For how long do I own the name after you register it?** This ownership should be at least two years, or indefinitely as long as you pay your fees.

- ✔ **How will I be notified when further fees are due?** For example, I get U.S. mail and e-mail from the InterNIC every year when it's time to pay the annual registration fee for my domain name, `cre8tive.com`.

How Much Bandwidth Do You Need?

Bandwidth refers to the amount of data that can pass through an Internet connection, measured in bits per second (bps). Typically, Internet bandwidth comes in large numbers: megabits per second (Mbps), or at least kilobits per second (Kbps). Well, then when you dial in to surf the Internet, your 28.8 Kbps modem offers about 28,800 bps of bandwidth. It's the data equivalent of a sipping straw. Compare that to a T1 line, which offers about 1.5 Mbps or 1,614,807 bps. That's a good-sized drinking glass. (The old 2400 baud modems were really about 2.4 Kbps modems, in modern lingo. Like sipping through a chopstick.)

You must set up your online store with the right amount of bandwidth so that your customers get a snappy response when they come to your site. If you have too little bandwidth, your server keeps your customer waiting. If you plan to have more than about three customers at a time visiting your site, and if you expect to give them a quick response time, you absolutely need a T1 line.

Actually, just for the sake of accuracy, a 28.8 modem theoretically offers 29,491.2 bps of bandwidth. Computers, which do everything in terms of powers of two because of their binary methods of data storage, use 1024 instead of 1000 as 1 kilo. 1024 is 2 to the 8th power.

As bandwidth of your Internet connection goes up, so does the cost of buying your bandwidth (from whoever is providing service to you). Here's a stepthrough of bandwidths and approximate costs (current as of witing):

✔ **Dial-up service ($20 to $30 per month):** A 28.8 modem connection, the kind that commonly uses Serial Line Internet Protocol (SLIP) or Point to Point Protocol (PPP) is what your customers generally use to reach you. (That's why your server needs to be fast — because the lines your customers are using are likely to be so slow.) This connection is barely adequate for surfing the Web. You can't run your online store using a regular modem connection, even if your provider lets you keep the line busy all the time (which is another story). It's just too slow, especially for selling online — secure transactions require speed intensive.

✔ **ISDN ($300 to $600 per month):** ISDN delivers 56 Kbps to 128 Kbps, which starts at twice the bandwidth you can get from a normal telephone line. That means, roughly speaking, about three or four customers could be visiting your site at a time and getting decent response.

If you have a home business with light selling traffic, a coffee shop or small Internet Cafe, an art gallery, or some other small business, an ISDN line may serve you adequately. ISDN is especially useful if your Internet site is only online part of the time, such as when your physical place of business is open (or when it is closed!). That's because your phone company charges you a small amount *per minute* for ISDN connectivity.

✔ **T1 ($1,000 to $3,000 per month):** Laying aside cable modems for a moment, because they aren't actually commercially viable yet, the next big step up in bandwidth from ISDN is T1. For a site that expects to be in operation 24 hours a day, 7 days a week (24 x 7), T1 is your minimum bandwidth need. A T1 line offers over a million and a half bits per second of bandwidth. Divide that up into customers visiting your site on 28.8 modems, and it looks like, off-the-cuff, you could handle about 56 visitors at a time. Now that's starting to sound like a Web site!

Actually, many offices already have T1 installed, because it's the type of phone line needed for a PBX or multiple phone line system. If you're in an office such as this, you just need another T1 reserved for Internet use, sort of like having an extra regular phone line at home for modem use.

✔ **T3 ($10,000/month or more):** At 45 Mbps, a T3 line is equal to almost 30 T1 lines. With a T3 line, my back-of-the-envelope math indicates that about 1,680 visitors could have access to your site at any given moment at 28.8 modem speeds.

Many online commerce sites end up using two or more T1 lines when they run out of bandwidth, but aren't ready to step up to T3 connectivity.

Figure 3-1 gives you some idea of the difference in the amount of data that can be transferred per second using varying types of Internet connections.

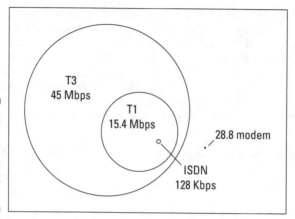

Figure 3-1:
Approximated
relative
pipe sizes
for Internet
connections.

You have other options that fall between the cracks of those given here, such as multiple T1 lines, or fractional T3. The ones listed provide a benchmark.

The more traffic you're expecting, the more bandwidth you need to purchase for your Internet connection. (Sort of like purchasing more potato salad when you're expecting more guests at your picnic.)

Denied — not everyone can get a T1

In some rural areas, T1 access is sometimes unavailable, because it requires actual (underground) cable to be laid and connected into a main trunk. If you live in the country and want T1 speeds, co-location may be a good option for your site. See "Co-location" earlier in this chapter for more information.

Part II
Laying a Strong Online Foundation

The 5th Wave   By Rich Tennant

Meditations, Inc.
BOOKS • SEMINARS • TAPES

"Sales on the Web site are down. I figure the server's chi is blocked, so we're fudgin' around the feng shui in the computer room, and if that doesn't work, Ronnie's got a chant that should do it."

In this part . . .

Nope — you don't need any shovels, mortar, or sand to construct your online store. What you do need are some hardware, software, and tips and hints about putting those two items together and making them run smoothly. I tell you everything you need to know about these "bricks" in your online store in this part.

Chapter 4

The Machine Age: Choosing Your Hardware

The main job of every Web server is to deliver Web pages from the server, across the Internet, to the client's browser. (More or less, that's the colloquial origin of the term *server,* in the sense that it "serves up" pages for viewing by a client, or it "serves" several clients at once.)

You must choose a server that can handle the content of your site and the number of customers you expect. For example, if you offer mostly text at your site, you need less hardware horsepower on your server than if you show animated online movies to help sell your products and services. Similarly, serving more customers means you need more server horsepower.

This chapter helps you understand which server machines give you the most for your money. I also tell you a little about some other hardware you may need, depending on the configuration of your online store.

Looking at the Basic Stuff You Need

Theoretically, you can install your Web server software, your database, your HTML pages, and any other information you need on one server machine, hook it up to the Internet, and start selling your product. It sounds simple when you say it like that, doesn't it? Actually, in practice, you only really need the following to set up a single server machine:

✔ Your server machine, including whatever disk storage, backup devices, printer, monitor, scanner, digital camera, or other peripherals you may choose

✔ Your operating system

✔ Your Web server software (see Chapter 5)

✔ An account at an ISP with the right bandwidth; see Chapter 3 for more information

✔ Equipment for your Internet connection; that is, whatever specific communication equipment you need for your type of connection, such as modem for dial-up, converter box for ISDN, T1, and so on

Many sites start out by using a single machine, and then they grow into local networks as the site gets larger. Larger can mean different things, but generally speaking, a larger site has the following characteristics:

✔ More traffic, especially more customers who want to use the site at the same time

✔ Bigger databases

✔ More HTML pages

✔ More forms and other interactive areas of the site

How will you know if your site is too large for a single machine (or at least for the machine you use)? Things run slowly, really slowly. That's when you need to think about getting a larger machine or setting up a local network of machines. For example, you could have a separate computer running each of the major components of your site — one for the database, one for the transaction software, and so on. If you want to set up a local network of server machines, you probably need the following items:

✔ Your machines, including disk storage (such as RAID), backup devices, printers, monitors, scanners, digital camera, and other peripherals you may choose.

✔ Your operating system.

✔ Your Web server software (see Chapter 5).

✔ An account at an ISP with the right bandwidth (see Chapter 3 for more information).

✔ Your Internet connection along with the specific communication equipment needed: modem for dial-up, converter box for ISDN, T1, and so on.

✔ A router, which is the traffic cop that connects your network to the Internet and "routes" your local packets onto the network in an orderly manner.

✔ A firewall, which protects your site and is now included in many router products.

✔ A hub, which connects all your machines onto the local network.

✔ Individual network connectors for each machine if needed. For example, Ethernet connectors are built into most Macintosh hardware, but they need to be purchased separately for many other machines.

✔ Network cable, such as Ethernet cable.

✔ A few other sundry connectors and adapters, as needed.

✔ Possibly a console server for co-located sites; see Chapter 3 for the details on co-location.

Web sites spread across local networks are sometimes called *Web farms*. You can read more about configuring Web farms later in this chapter.

Comparing Server Platforms

Web server software runs on top of an operating system. These days, you have the following choices when it comes to operating systems:

✔ Windows 95 and Windows NT

✔ UNIX (of various versions)

✔ Mac OS

The server platform you select depends on what you feel most comfortable using, because excellent server software exists for essentially every operating system on the market. (Turn to Chapter 5 for more information on choosing software for your server.)

Although UNIX used to be the platform of choice for serious Web sites, Windows servers are gaining popularity because they are easy to use and familiar to non-UNIX users.

UNIX offers certain advantages as a server platform. Perhaps the biggest natural advantage is that the UNIX operating system has built-in security features. Hackers have been attacking UNIX systems for decades, and as a result, most of the security holes have been exposed and repaired. The same can't be said for Windows NT and other Windows platforms that are becoming popular as servers; they have not yet faced the test of time.

Super nerdie stuff about client/server software

The *client/server* software model for building computer software became prevalent in the 1980s. Project teams found it efficient to use a large-capacity, centralized storage machine as a repository for their data files, while relying on smaller machines on each desktop. The teams connected to the central storage computer and to each other using simple, local area networks. Individual workstations and the software that executed on them were often referred to as *clients*, in reference to the centralized machines that came to be called *servers*.

These early networks were a convenient way to get a group of machines (and, of course, their users) within a single building or a single company talking to one another and sharing information. These networks weren't usually connected to the Internet. Today, the Internet employs a similar client/server software model for the Web server/Web browser software that people use now.

The Macintosh system was not designed for security; however, Macs do resist outside tampering. The biggest security hole for the Macintosh is the ability to sit down physically in front of a Macintosh computer and type commands (such as file access commands) without first entering a password. However, the legendary Macintosh ease of use, when applied to problems of server and site configuration, makes the Macintosh a desirable server platform nonetheless. Also, the Macintosh offers many superior tools for Web site content development, because the Mac remains the industry leader in the specialized areas of desktop publishing and multimedia development.

Choosing Hardware and Figuring Costs

Just for a moment, consider the price of what you need to set up a site in the usual way: a dedicated server machine, server software, a router and/or a firewall, at least one hub, cable, and Internet connectors.

That sort of set-up starts around $2,500 at rock-bottom and easily climbs to the $10,000 price range. Administering such a site is an added expense and time commitment, because with a complicated system like that you are bound to run into security holes and configuration "gotchas."

You need to look yourself in the mirror and ask yourself the following questions about servers and your online store:

  ✔ What kind of server machine(s) do you need?

  ✔ How big should those machines be?

✔ How much bandwidth capacity do you need?

✔ How much storage capacity do you need?

The answers to each of these questions impact your setup costs. You are not alone in answering these tough questions. Everything you need to know about making your server selection is in this section.

I divide the hardware into sections for UNIX, Windows, and Macintosh operating systems. Of course UNIX and Windows NT operating systems both can run on Intel hardware, so sometimes the distinctions are blurred. Just think of the operating system you'd most commonly find on a particular hardware platform, and you won't go far wrong when reading this chapter. (For example: pair Windows NT with Compaq, UNIX with SPARCstation, and Mac OS with Macintosh hardware.)

Web server machines running Windows NT require a lot more hardware horsepower to deliver the same performance (per traffic load) than the same machine running one of the versions of UNIX that's designed for Intel-based PCs. And that bigger machine costs you a lot more money!

In general, UNIX is a good operating system choice for cost-conscious sites, because so much of the software you need to run a UNIX site, including the Web server software itself, is available for free online. You find a superabundance of freeware available for UNIX platforms, for *everything* from file serving to viewing video files. If you don't know UNIX, you can probably find a starving hacker nearby who does (or you can get ambitious and check out *UNIX For Dummies,* 3rd Eition, by John Levine and Margaret Levine Young, published by IDG Books Worldwide, Inc.). Unless someone forces you to use NT servers, try selecting UNIX as the operating system for your online store. The UNIX operating system also scales up well as your store grows.

Servers have more horsepower

A Web server generally is a much more powerful machine than the PC that sits on your desk. It has to be, because it serves hundreds or thousands of customers every day.

Besides having more horses under the hood, Web servers are designed for greater reliability than any desktop PC. (And by PC, I do mean to include all brands of personal computers.)

Accordingly, Web servers usually are a lot more expensive than desktop models.

A smaller site — say, one that's expecting less than 50 customers at once — can often make use of an older, slower, or less powerful machine, such as a Mac IIci or IBM 486 PC. The secret to setting up a cheap site in this way is finding a 24-hour, seven-days-a-week connection to the Internet that you can afford and that gives sufficient bandwidth. However, because ISPs are so competitive nowadays, and they offer complete services for ridiculously low prices, you may find it cheaper just to spring for a hosting service instead of buying software and getting Internet access to set up that old machine in your closet as a Web server. (See Chapter 3 for more information if connecting to the Internet.)

A medium-to-large site may use a Sun SPARCstation running Solaris (or other larger workstation), especially if it wants a full-time, higher-bandwidth connection to the Internet, such as a T1 line.

If your site is large, you may need to link machines together into a Web farm to improve server response time, or you may need a way to make your remote site administration easier if you plan to co-locate (see Chapter 3 for more information on co-locating). You may also need extra storage devices for all your customer databases. Never fear; in the great march of technology, solutions get better and cheaper all the time.

About UNIX sites for cheap

If you aren't required to run NT, and are comfortable with basic UNIX administration, one of the x86 UNIX servers work fine on just about any old leftover machine. A 66 Mhz 486 machine can easily saturate a T1 running Linux or BSDI with an Apache Web server, for example.

For "real" UNIX hardware, Sun and SGI systems start at about $5,000 and may cost $10,000 to get "on-the-air." Rather than spending money on big monitors or fancy video systems, invest in RAM and CPU horsepower and get basic video hardware.

Both SGI and Sun make "industrial strength" hardware that is well-supported by the likely Web server software for these platforms, Apache and Netscape. The choice between one or the other is more likely to be based on external factors, such as who you can get to support it. You need somebody familiar with Solaris or IRIX administration to set up the system initially, and to update the system when patches are released by the vendors. These systems are less of a "do-it-yourself" project than various PC solutions.

UNIX workstations

Among the most popular servers running UNIX on the Web is the Sun workstation. One reason UNIX workstations are so popular is the inherent networking capabilities of the UNIX operating system. Another is the ubiquity of free software available for UNIX operating systems. For example, Apache Web server (see Chapter 5) runs on UNIX. (I'd estimate that about one-third of all sites on the Web are now powered by Apache Web server software.)

Many small-to-medium-sized sites choose SPARCsations as their server hardware, typically the SPARC10 and SPARC20 workstations. These machines start at about $5,000. They are very powerful and fast.

Even better news: Sun Microsystems recently announced a new low-end machine starting at about $3,000, designed to compete with the Intel platforms (such as Compaq and Dell) for the desktop and low-end Web server market.

Larger UNIX sites often move up to models such as the Sun Ultra Enterprise 2 or the Ultra Enterprise 3000. These machines are quite expensive, starting at $10,000 to $15,000 each, and they can often take the place of several smaller machines for a growing site. The machines come equipped to run large databases or to let customers search your site very quickly.

You can get the technical specifications and prices for these machines at the Sun Microsystems site at www.sun.com.

Intel-based PC servers

Dell, Compaq, Hewlett-Packard, IBM, Digital Equipment Corporation, and Gateway 2000 are major manufacturers that provide some of the more commonly used Intel-based server hardware. Many Web sites that use this hardware generally run Windows NT servers; however, some versions of UNIX are available for these Intel machines, notably Solaris. (For more information about operating systems and server software, please see Chapter 5.)

Don't consider this a comprehensive list of server equipment — it's only a group of examples. Shop around for the equipment that best suits your needs and budget.

Intel for small to medium-sized businesses

Small to medium-sized businesses should look at what's commonly called a *workgroup server*. Workgroup servers handle several users at once, perhaps four or five easily, which distinguishes them from desktop computers, which support only a single user. In the workgroup server category, you find the following comparable models, among others:

- Compaq ProLiant 800
- HP NetServer LD Pro
- Dell PowerEdge 2100
- IBM PC Server 325
- Digital Prioris XL

Typically, a workgroup server offers the following features that make it an especially good choice to function as a server for a small to medium-sized selling site:

- A Pentium 166, Pentium 200, or Pentium Pro processor, which means a very fast computer (giving your customers quick response times)
- 256K or 512K of level-two-cache (which is used by the processor to speed things up even more)
- 32MB of RAM, good for running several applications at once
- The capability to accept several gigabytes of hard disk storage
- Allowance of a RAID controller attachment (see "RAID: Reliability in a can" in this chapter for more information on RAID)
- The capability to expand to two-processor configurations, which can allow for easier growth of your store to handle more customers at the same time

Intel for medium to large businesses

Suitable for a faster-growing business (or one that needs to serve quite a few customers at the same time, perhaps 10 to 20) would be another group of products. These machines are slightly more powerful and slightly more expensive:

- Compaq ProLiant 1200 workgroup server
- HP NetServer E45 and LD Pro
- Dell PowerEdge 2200

The preceding servers generally come with more RAM, bigger hard disks, and more opportunity for expansion (say to four processors) than their smaller cousins.

 The bigger the machine you get, the more bandwidth you need in your Internet connection so you can utilize your machine's capacity to the fullest. For information about selecting your connection to the Internet, please see Chapter 3.

 These machines also can run Solaris UNIX as well as Windows NT (if your business want to capitalize on all that free software available on the Web for UNIX systems).

Intel enterprise-class servers

Large online businesses (such as airlines or online financial services) that can endure little or no downtime often go for a class of servers commonly called *enterprise servers.* These server machines are highly fault-tolerant, which means they can recover on their own from many kinds of errors that would make a desktop machine crash. Of course, a fault-tolerant architecture is more expensive to manufacture, so hold on to your hats when you see the prices for these babies.

Here are some good examples of comparable enterprise-class servers:

- ✔ Compaq ProLiant 5500
- ✔ HP NetServer LXe Pro
- ✔ Dell PowerEdge 6100
- ✔ IBM PC Server 704

These machines typically offer the following tasty features:

- ✔ **Supports RAID array storage:** See "RAID: Reliability in a can" in this chapter for more information on RAID array storage.

- ✔ **Offers hot pluggable drive bays:** The disk drives, the most commonly-failing component of a computer component most likely to fail, can be replaced without shutting down the system.

- ✔ **Accepts tasks from one to four processors:** Enterprise servers can distribute the system tasks and speed up the throughput considerably beyond the processor speed (which, in the Compaq ProLiant 5500, is a Pentium Pro 200 Mhz processor, for example).

 This category of machine can run Windows NT Server, Enterprise Edition, which means you can process online commerce transactions on your own machine while running NT, without appreciable loss of performance for other users. The Compaq ProLiant can run Solaris 2.50, 2.51, or 2.6, as well. The IBM PC Server supports Solaris 2.50.

Looking at sample Intel setup prices

As a sample of market prices for Intel-based server hardware, the Gateway NS-7002 workgroup-class server currently sells for about $3,300, and an enterprise-class server NS-9006 sells for about $13,000. Both are RAID-capable. The enterprise-class server comes equipped with two Pentium processors, and the workgroup-class server is expandable to two processors.

You can contact Gateway at 1-888-888-0951 or `www.gateway.com`. They have an excellent Web site on which you can compare sample configurations and pricing.

Macintosh workgroup servers

Apple has several offerings of powerful hardware bundled with all the software you need to set up a Web site. These solutions may be especially attractive for sites that sell graphical or design-related products, or for any small-to-medium-sized site.

Just as an example to whet your appetite, take a look at the features in the Apple Workgroup Server 6150/66:

- PowerPC 601 processor
- Built-in 1.2GB hard drive
- 16MB of RAM

Obviously, this Macintosh option may prove quite inexpensive and appropriate for a small site. The accompanying software package includes WebSTAR, Adobe PageMill, and MacDNS server software for setting up your domain name. The whole thing currently sells for about $999.

Apple's other current server offerings include the larger Workgroup Server 9650/350, 9650/233, and 7350/188. The Workgroup Server 9650/233, for example, compares to any of the Intel machines listed earlier in this chapter, with its

- 233 Mhz PowerPC 604e RISC chip
- 512K level-two cache
- 64MB RAM
- 4GB internal hard drive
- Built-in Ethernet capabilities for 10BaseT or AAUI Ethernet
- Six expansion slots (PCI)

You just can't keep a good Mac down

You can even run an online store using a souped-up Mac IIci, the older Mac that is becoming a favorite machine among Mac fans, if you dare.

Try souping things up with a Dayton accelerator, 17MB RAM and 1GB hard drive. The Mac IIci is definitely "the little Mac that could." I still use mine as a file server and scanning station on my local network.

Although perhaps not suitable for the largest online businesses (some people would give you a healthy debate about that), Macintosh servers can be an especially good solution for the small to medium sized store, especially if you already know the Mac operating system. Macintosh sites have been shown by independent research to be cost-effective Web sites to operate, because the initial server cost is lower and the system maintenance time is less.

Configuring Your Site as It Grows

Picking the right server machine is a good step along the way to getting your online store up and running. But what if you grow to need more than one machine? What if your server (or servers) will be co-located, and far away from you geographically? What if you absolutely, positively can't stand to lose any data on your site? Take heart, configuration options exist for these situations that can make your life a breeze.

In these situations, the equipment you need to resolve your online selling challenges may not come cheap. But it can be fun.

Web farming

If your site grows truly large, you may want to set up a series of linked machines and some duplicates, some specialized on your own local Ethernet network. You then use a router to connect your entire Ethernet to the Internet.

In the lingo of the Webmaster, a group of machines that works together to serve up a Web site often is called a *Web farm*. Figure 4-1 shows a schematic representation of a possible Web farm configuration for what would be a large, very sophisticated Web site.

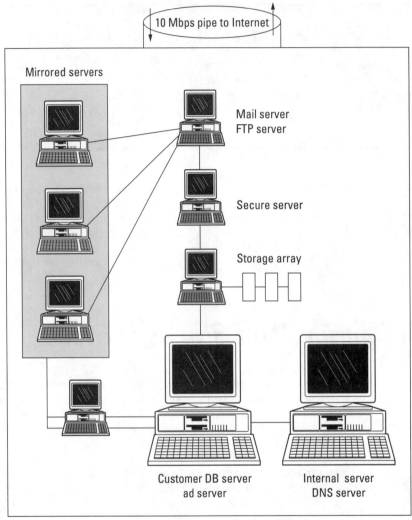

Figure 4-1:
A Web
farm:
Raisin' up
some bits,
'n' waxin'
'em down.

Notice the three machines linked together in Figure 4-1 as *mirrored servers*. Mirrored sites are just what they sound like: exact duplicates. Mirrors are needed on sites that get a lot of traffic, so that the visitors are distributed evenly across several machines that are identical replicas, instead of trying to bottleneck the visitors onto one poor, overworked machine. (See Chapter 7 for more information on mirroring.)

Mirroring is often better than getting a bigger machine, because a computer runs out of capacity for I/O (reading and writing files, such as when you download them to browsers) long before the machine runs out of capacity to compute. Web serving is an I/O-intensive process.

Okay, so maybe the setup in Figure 4-1 is too much — that setup contains a lot of machines, and maybe your business has a smaller budget? A simpler Web farm is shown in Figure 4-2.

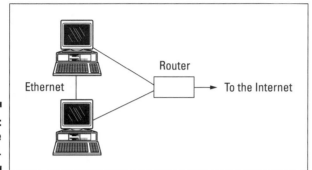

Figure 4-2:
A cozy little
Web farm.

Figure 4-2 shows a local network of two machines connected to the Internet through a router. It's an excellent configuration for a medium-to-large-sized site. On one machine you could run your database and the rest of your site, or you could distribute information across both machines as needed to even out your site traffic.

Don't get burned: Picking out your firewall

A lot goes into setting up your online store — storefront software, maybe special shopping cart software, your site content that advertises your products, your customer databases, and so many other items. But that's not all — you also need a few more pieces of equipment specifically designed to connect your store to the Internet and protect your precious store from malefactors.

Figure 4-3 shows the relationship between your store and the Internet. Notice that something separates your site and the actual Internet, called a *firewall.*

Think of your basic firewall as a sort of alarm system for the Internet. The firewall keeps a lot of otherwise honest people out, but some folks who really want to get in could still find a way.

Firewalls protect the information stored on your site, such as customer names and credit card information. If you care about security (which you should if you run an online store), you need a firewall.

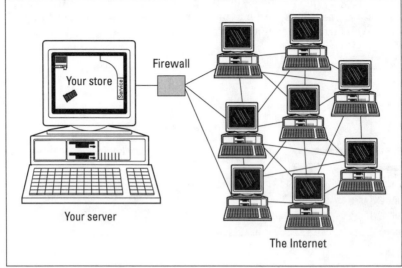

Figure 4-3:
Your store lives on your server, and it talks to the Internet through an ISP and your router/firewall.

A firewall often comes as part of your site's router, which is the hardware box that connects your local network to the Internet. The firewall/router combination is the easiest kind to install. The router and the firewall must be configured specially for your site when you install them. You may need to get professional help to set up your firewall.

One way to find out more about firewalls is by visiting Web sites of firewall vendors, such as Raptor (www.raptor.com) or CheckPoint (www.checkpoint.com). If your needs are more than simple, such as if your site contains a lot of sensitive information, you can always hire a professional to help you find the right firewall product for your store.

If you use a hosting service, the service's firewall protects your store (see Chapter 3 for more information on hosting services). But if you run your own server, you should have a firewall of your own.

CheckPoint, currently the market leader in firewall products, is getting some stiff competition from Microsoft, which introduced Proxy Server 2.0 in October 1997. (A proxy server is a minimal sort of firewall.) Microsoft Proxy Server sells for $995. Also, the next release of Windows NT is expected to have improved proxy-server-based firewall capabilities.

Really nerdy stuff about how firewalls work

A firewall protects your site from unwanted intrusions by restricting the passage of Internet data packets onto your local network. The Webmaster or system administrator establishes certain rules, saying effectively that only packets of this type or from a certain destination can go to this particular machine at your site. Other packets are refused.

For example, all e-mail-bearing packets (called smtp packets) may be restricted to go to a mail server on your local network, where they are scanned for viruses. Certain types of packets may need a password identification before the computer accepts them, too.

Firewalls operate on a simple idea: they make sure that all the packets of data that arrive at your site are "as advertised." A favorite ploy of hackers is to monitor a stream of data packets flowing by on the network (sort of like cars on a freeway), falsify an IP address to create an "evil" packet, and insert that bad packet as a sort of "trojan horse" into that otherwise legitimate stream of data. That's probably exactly what Jeff Goldblum did to the alien mother ship when he uploaded the virus in the movie *Independence Day*, right?

At under $1,000, firewalls-in-routers are low-end firewall products. High-end firewalls sell for as much as $18,000 to $20,000. The average price of a firewall is expected to fall to between $2,000 and $3,000 in 1998. For this price, you could expect to get a firewall or firewall appliance that handles more complex tasks, such as detection of intruders, blocking specific URLs, and virus protection.

RAID – Reliability in a can

RAID (which stands for *redundant array of inexpensive disks*) is a special set of disk drives linked together in ways that make them many times more reliable. RAID provides reliability for your store when you can't afford to be disconnected or lose any data. RAID also makes your disk drives less likely to lose information, even when they fail (which all disk drives eventually seem to do with the workout they get on the Web).

RAID isn't cheap or new, but I want to mention it because RAID creates a completely stable foundation for your online store.

Flavors of RAID

The following four types of RAID are in common use:

✔ **RAID 0** is called *striping*, which means that data is written in small "stripes" across several disks. Because the I/O processor need not wait out the seek time of an individual disk drive, data can be written (and read) much faster.

✔ **RAID 1** is called *mirroring*, which means that disks are created that contain exactly the same data. Mirroring provides data redundancy and therefore reliability: If any single disk fails, the mirror disk still contains the same information. (Notice how the idea of *mirror Web sites* is related to the mirroring of disks in a RAID array?)

✔ **RAID 2** is called *concatenation*, which means that many disks can be treated as one for the purposes of data retrieval.

✔ **RAID 5** is called *parity*, which means that when a file is written, parts of it are spread across several disks. If n disks exist in a RAID array, the data is written onto (n-1) of those disks, and on the nth disk some parity information is stored. If any one disk fails, the information in the file can be recreated from the remaining data plus the parity information.

You may want to look into RAID to save you from losing your order database or your customer database, both of which are priceless assets for your business.

RAID is not a substitute for backups, but it provides safety for your data in case of a bad disk failure.

When you run a RAID array, you have the option to create *hot spares,* which are formatted, but blank, disk drives, all ready to go except for the data. When you have hot spares available, if one of the disks in a RAID array fails, there's usually software installed so that the other disks can immediately create a new duplicate of the one that failed. That reminds me of the Borg from *Star Trek,* somehow.

Also, RAID storage arrays are arranged in groups called plexes that can be mirrored for even greater reliability and redundancy. For example, you may have a situation like the one shown in Figure 4-4, in which plexes are mirrored and hot spares are available as well.

Typically, the individual disks in a RAID array have an unbelievable *mean time to failure,* something like 40,000 hours. They are often variable-density drives, which means that they have more writable sectors at the outer edge than in the center portion. And because the tolerances between the spinning disk and the disk head are so fine, the disks are typically variable-geometry drives, which means that they monitor their own heat expansion and correct themselves accordingly.

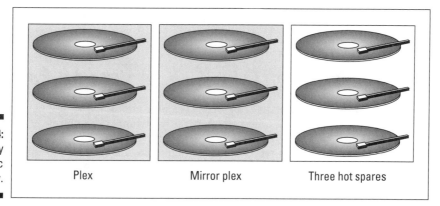

Figure 4-4:
A totally
terrific
RAID array.

Plex   Mirror plex   Three hot spares

Alternative Servers for Your Site

I don't really know what to call these servers. They're just a different idea altogether — a unique package of hardware and software designed to get you up and running fast if your requirements are minimal. How does Alternative Internet Connection Devices (AICDs) sound?

I expect more of these specialized, innovative solutions to appear, so these examples seemed like an excellent way to tell you that all kinds of other hardware is available besides what you traditionally think of as a server machine. (By this I mean, it's not a Dell, Compaq, Mac, or anything like that.)

If your online presence is small, or part of a corporate network (that is, if you provide information or sell your products within a single parent company), you may benefit from these new and relatively inexpensive alternatives to purchasing a server machine and lots of other hardware. They present out-of-the-box solutions that provide the minimal functionality for the minimal price.

AICDs are useful for

✔ Businesses that need a small Web site and don't have the in-house technical experience to manage it

✔ Organizations that need Internet access and don't know the first thing about it

✔ Organizations running on Novell-based networks, which don't easily connect to the Internet

AICDs generally come with step-by-step instructions and wizards for creating Web pages quickly by using templates or configuring a group for Internet connection easily. And AICDs are cheap in comparison to "standard" hardware solutions.

With these ACIDs, you need a lot less money and staff. And they connect to the Internet at speeds ranging from 28.8 to T1.

Twister: Instant Web server in a box

Twister (from Compact Devices) sells for about $1,295 and can literally be up and running in minutes. It's quickly become the quintessential AICD.

The setup wizard lets you create departmental Web sites or other home pages from templates. (But don't use this one to set up your store; it's too small and can't do transactions! Recommend the product to your friends and customers, though. If you want a store in minutes without hiring a hosting service, see Encanto in the next section.)

Twister has a SCSI expansion port so you can add an external hard disk, and it understands the essential Internet protocols (ftp, telnet, RCP, TFTP, Syslog, and Bootp). Twister supports any TCP/IP client, and it can be managed remotely using a browser.

For more information about the Twister, see `www.devices.com`.

Encanto

Some AICDs are not designed for actual electronic commerce, only for information serving; however, at least one company, Encanto, produces a commerce-enabled version that's expected in stores at about the same time as this book. (That's a Silicon Valley scoop, folks.) Keep your eyes and your mind open.

The Encanto "online store in a box" device sells for about $995. Encanto presents a simple electronic commerce solution that "anyone" can set up.

Backed by such visionaries as John Sculley, Encanto hopes to be making the online store accessible to anyone, with an interface that lets you set it up in minutes and a built-in program that automatically sets you up with an Internet Service Provider (ISP), too.

For more information, visit `www.encanto.com`.

Chapter 5

Selecting Server Software

· ·

In This Chapter

▶ Understanding what server software does

▶ Looking at Netscape server products

▶ Considering Microsoft server products

▶ Peeking at server software from O'Reilly, AOL, and Novell

▶ Giving server software from small or overseas companies a chance

▶ Taking a tour of UNIX server software

▶ Discovering Macintosh server software

· ·

*I*n the coming months, server software that supports Web-based electronic commerce is likely to be a fast-growing area of development for Internet tools. Quite a few good tools already exist, but no server product has yet achieved the smooth integration that most Webmasters envision between the core function of a Web server — namely, delivering Web pages to client browsers — and other server utilities designed to facilitate secure electronic commerce. Basically, technology is moving away from a simple model of servers as "deliverers" of software.

This chapter walks you through the amazing variety of server software that you see in the store. I help you make sense of the possible features and match them to your site's needs.

I also compare the features supported by various Windows NT and Windows 95-compatible Web servers, UNIX servers, and Macintosh servers. I offer some advice on which server products may be best suited for a certain type of site. For example, some server software products are better suited to larger sites, some are best for smaller sites. Some server products are designed for a certain operating system, while others are compatible with several.

Your Server Software Wish List

Beyond the basic duty of delivering content to your customers, you should expect your Web server software to also help you out by letting you do the following:

- ✔ **Control, limit, and monitor access to your site by individual users and by groups.** For example, keeping track of visitors from a certain IP address can help you in case of a security breach, or help you know who your customers are.

- ✔ **Create and publish documents on your site.** And I mean doing it easily using semi-automated page-building tools that are fully compatible and integrated with your server (tools such as Adobe PageMill, Microsoft FrontPage, Tripod QuickPage, and so on).

- ✔ **Place and update pages on your site automatically.** This includes the ability to build new indexes of the pages on your site automatically and generate customized Web pages on the fly.

- ✔ **Support one or more powerful database tools.** Databases such as Oracle are already in use by many companies.

- ✔ **Manage your site remotely by using your Web browser.** Remote site management lets you manage your time more efficiently, too.

- ✔ **Conduct secure electronic commerce.** Security is an important feature for creating an environment of trust with your customers.

Software for Windows NT and UNIX

While this section focuses on Windows-compatible servers, several of the servers are also compatible with UNIX operating systems. Almost every server product that runs on Windows will run on UNIX platforms, and vice versa, with only a few exceptions. That's because both Windows and UNIX run well on Intel-based PC hardware.

Netscape server software products

Netscape server software is proving to be nearly as popular as its Netscape Navigator browser. Netscape does an excellent job of providing fully-featured, well-integrated products with outstanding documentation.

For more information about Netscape's products, including the most current prices, check out the Netscape Web site at www.netscape.com.

FastTrack Server 3.01

Netscape's FastTrack Server 3.01, which currently sells for about $295, amounts to a good value for small or medium-sized sites. You can consider FastTrack for any of the following server platforms:

- ✔ Windows NT
- ✔ Many UNIX platforms, including HP/UX, Digital UNIX, AIX, SGI, Sun, BSDI, SCO

FastTrack doesn't scale well as your site grows. But it's relatively easy to upgrade to Netscape's Enterprise Server (covered in the next section) when the need arises.

Here's a list of the features included in FastTrack:

- ✔ HTTP 1.1
- ✔ SSL 3.0
- ✔ Usage logging
- ✔ Remote site management through a browser
- ✔ Netscape Communicator for content creation (but includes little provision for content management)
- ✔ JDK 1.1, support for Java server applets (servlets) and JavaScript
- ✔ LiveWire, which includes a visual site management tool, database access tools, and the JavaScript compiler, which speeds up your site's delivery of JavaScript, HTML, and image files

Enterprise Server 3.0

The Netscape Enterprise Server 3.0 is the cream of the crop for large electronic commerce sites. It's a high-end server designed to help large groups of people create and manage a huge Web site containing large volumes of information. This server is powerful, scalable, and easy to use. It's probably the most commonly-used secure Web server software (Apache is the most common otherwise).

Enterprise Server 3.0 currently sells for about $1,295. (The most comparable Microsoft server product is Microsoft Site Server, Enterprise Edition, which sells for $4,999.)

Enterprise Server 3.0 runs on the following platforms:

- ✔ Windows NT
- ✔ Every version of UNIX except Linux

Netscape packs the following features into Enterprise Server 3.0:

- A graphical site management tool, called Netshare, provides a seamless view of files and directory trees on your server. Netshare also provides document management functionality during content development — for example, work flow rules about orderly access to certain files on your Web server and the tools to enforce them.

- A directory services utility to manage setting up users and groups, which also supports LDAP (Lightweight Directory Access Protocol) so that directory services can be apportioned across several server machines.

- Limiting, logging, and controlling access to your site with password protection and authorization API.

- Direct support for high-end database connectivity with ODBC on NT and UNIX, native to Informix, Oracle, Sybase, IBM DB2. (A valuable Enterprise feature is its ability to connect to more than one kind of database.)

- Support for video and audio streaming with plug-ins.

- The capacity to publish documents to site directly from your Web browser.

- Virtual servers.

- Proxy servers.

- Security via SSL 2.0 and 3.0 and support for Certificate Authority.

- Support for CGI, server-side JavaScript and LiveWire, server-side Java, CORBA tools.

This list of features looks impressive, and it doesn't begin to explain how powerful Netscape's Enterprise server really is. For example, you can use the Enterprise Integration tool to mirror several separate databases so that all your site's updates stay consistent (see Chapter 7 for more information on mirroring). You can give individual site administrators subsets of administrative functionality, such as access to log files only, using the Distributed Administration feature.

Microsoft Web server products

The range of Web product offerings from Microsoft may seem a bit confusing at first. For example, as I was about to write this book, I kept hearing people mention Microsoft Commerce Server and Microsoft Transaction Server. Turns out they're not actually servers, as such, at all. When I looked on the Microsoft Web site (www.microsoft.com), I discovered that Microsoft Transaction Server is actually a development environment (discussed later in this section), and Microsoft Commerce Server is now part of Microsoft Site Server, Enterprise Edition, and it is not sold separately (but Site Server, Enterprise Edition is covered later in this section). Here's hoping that I can get you comfortable with Microsoft's generous selection of product offerings in the Internet area.

Server products change rapidly, so when you're about to make your server software decision, visit the Microsoft Web site to check out the latest pricing and options.

Windows NT Server 4.0

Windows NT Server 4.0 is the basis for any Microsoft-based Web server solution. All other server capabilities are sold as add-ons to NT Server 4.0.

NT Server 4.0 doesn't provide any electronic commerce capabilities, but it provides tools for site management and tracking. It may be good for managing an intranet or small extranet site.

You can get full product for five licenses for $809, and ten licenses for $1,129.

Microsoft offers the following features in Windows NT Server 4.0:

- ✔ Full integration with Windows NT
- ✔ Network management capabilities, including adding user accounts, licensing, and tracking network packet traffic
- ✔ Compatibility with FrontPage, making it easy to create and post new Web pages

If you're looking to use your Windows NT server to manage an Internet site, download Microsoft's Internet Information Server, which is tightly integrated with NT. (In fact, it's so tightly integrated that it's not sold separately.) See the next section for details.

Internet Information Server 4.0

Internet Information Server (IIS) adds to the basic capabilities of Windows NT. The only other product you need is some electronic commerce software to run on top of Internet Information Server's SSL 3.0 security. (For more information about electronic commerce software, please see Chapter 6.)

The Microsoft IIS server is a free download from Microsoft's Web site. However, it is only "free" if you buy the NT Server 4.0 product for several hundred dollars. None of the other NT Web server products require anything more than an NT workstation; they work directly with the NT operating system and don't require NT Server 4.0 as an intermediary layer.

The real story on Internet Information Server 4.0

Some confusion surrounds this product. Several trade magazines recently reviewed Internet Information Server 4.0 in direct comparison to stand-alone freeware or commercial Web server products. However, when I visited Microsoft's Web site, I found that it isn't offered as an independent product at all, only as an integrated part of several other Web server products. In other words, you can't get it unless you buy Windows NT or another of Microsoft's Internet products. Think of Internet Information Server 4.0 as sort of a "plug-in" module that adds a certain set of Internet/Web-server features to other Microsoft networking products.

In any case, this pseudoproduct offers capabilities that, as a part of other products, enhance your Web site in several ways:

- ✔ Audio, video, and streaming ability through NetShow.
- ✔ Search capabilities with the Index Server search engine.
- ✔ Compatibility with Active Server Pages (ASP), which means IIS can generate Web pages on the fly using ActiveX technology. (When you use ActiveX, you can combine HTML, VBScript, JavaScript and ActiveX components on the same page.)
- ✔ Works with FrontPage to generate Web pages easily.
- ✔ Crystal Reports facility for generating reports from site log files on Web traffic, and so forth.
- ✔ Remote administration of the server and NT through a browser.
- ✔ Integration into NT means access to Web documents and management of the files on the server is controlled by NT's core security and directory access system.
- ✔ Full support for SSL 3.0 secure communications over the Internet.
- ✔ Support for transactions.

IIS is not priced separately, and it's not really free, either, in the sense that Apache is a free stand-alone product. It's integrated into several Microsoft Web products, for example, the Windows NT 4.0 server product.

To run Java applets, you have to install Microsoft Internet Explorer, because NT does not include native support for Java.

Microsoft Site Server

Microsoft Site Server, which retails for $1,499, does not offer integrated electronic commerce functionality. It does, however, come through with the following features:

✔ Good utilities for measuring and tracking your Web site

✔ Dynamically generated Web pages

✔ Staging

✔ Mirror servers

✔ Usage analysis tools

✔ Site analysis tools

Microsoft Site Server, Enterprise Edition

Microsoft Site Server, Enterprise Edition is directed at larger sites that specialize in Internet commerce. This is the product that allows Internet commerce; to do commerce with NT, you must buy this software package. It seems very comprehensive in the range of utilities it provides; however, with a price tag of $4,999, it may not be the best choice for the budget-conscious startup.

The former Microsoft Merchant Server is now just a part of this product, and it is now called Microsoft Commerce Server (but Commerce Server is not sold separately).

If you decide to purchase Site Server, you can look forward to the following features:

✔ Order processing and customer tracking tools

✔ Compatibility with Verifone and other digital payment methods

---

Microsoft Web development tools

These tools help you develop and maintain your site's software, especially your customer databases (or other databases). I cover them here just to avoid confusion with Microsoft's actual Web server products.

✔ Microsoft Transaction Server is not a Web server product, but it's easy to confuse them because of its name. Instead, it's a development environment for creating applications that use transactions, such as database access applications that you can use on your Web site.

✔ Visual Interdev is another development environment that helps you create database-related applications to run on your site. It's listed here, again, because it is frequently confused with Microsoft's Web server products.

For more information on these tools, visit the Microsoft Web site at www.microsoft.com.

Other Web server products

Believe it or not, some Web server products are made by companies other than the well-known Microsoft and Netscape. You can find plenty of excellent offerings.

In most cases these products are much less expensive than the Microsoft and Netscape software, which is intended primarily for larger sites, although some of these products function quite adequately for all but the largest online stores. Two of these products are free.

WebSite Professional 2.0

O'Reilly and Associates' WebSite Professional, which currently sells for about $799, may be the best all-around solution for Windows-based, small- to medium-sized sites devoted to electronic commerce. It is easy to use, well-integrated, and complete.

WebSite Professional 2.0 comes with tools that make creating content for your site and making purchases electronically much easier, including the following:

- HomeSite 2.5, a tool for creating Web content and managing content on your site. It makes publishing your documents a point-and-click operation.

- iHTML Professional, a server-side scripting tool that lets you manipulate files on the server dynamically. It also lets you incorporate conditional statements into your site applications, so certain pages are constructed differently (in real time) depending on what values are entered by customers. This tool allows connections to an ODBC-style database using simple commands much like HTML. That makes it possible to develop simple database access scripts without hiring a specialist.

- iHTML Merchant, a tool that lets you build one (or more) storefronts on your server machine, just by using a graphical interface. This tool provides storefront templates that make development easier and faster. iHTML Merchant also lets you set up banner ad rotations, and generate sales reports dynamically. If that isn't enough, all these features can be administered through a Web browser. All in all, iHTML Merchant makes creating a virtual storefront a "doable" task, even for nontechnical users.

- Two additional utilities, WebView and WebIndex, let you view your site to find broken links (and then edit those pages directly), and see what's on your site, respectively. WebIndex creates document indexes for you automatically.

These O'Reilly and Associates Web server products run under the Windows NT operating system. Both of the iHTML products use Microsoft Active Server Pages, which means that you can use scripts to create some of your server pages dynamically. WebSite Professional does not claim to support the HTTP 1.1 standard, although it supports many of the features. WebSite Professional supports CyberCash secure credit card transactions over the Internet using SSL 3.0.

Here are some other outstanding features of WebSite Professional 2.0:

- ✔ Excellent documentation, including tutorials, available in print and online
- ✔ Virtual servers; sharing IP addresses and with individual IP addresses
- ✔ Server-side Java using JDK 1.0 interpreter

If you're relatively inexperienced with Web sites, WebSite Professional, with its ease of use and excellent documentation, may be the server you're looking for. For more information, please see website.ora.com.

AOLserver 2.1

Yes, America Online offers a server product. And not a bad one, at that, especially for small to medium-sized online stores. The price is certainly right — it's free.

AOLserver 2.1 is compatible with the following platforms:

- ✔ Windows NT
- ✔ Several versions of UNIX, including Solaris, SGI, and Linux

AOLserver is comparable in some respects to Stronghold (another excellent SSL-compatible server for UNIX systems only, which costs $995). However, AOLserver is perhaps somewhat easier to use than Stronghold, partly because you can configure it using a graphical interface.

AOLserver allows for secure electronic commerce because it's SSL-compatible. Using AOLserver, you can also publish and delete documents from your server using the Put and Delete commands that comply with the HTTP standard.

Other features of AOLserver 2.1 include the following gems:

- ✔ Support for hosting virtual domains
- ✔ Basic database integration capabilities with some SQL databases
- ✔ Integration with AOLpress, AOL's HTML editor
- ✔ Automatic uploading and publishing of documents created with AOLpress

For more information, you can hook up to the Web at `www.aolserver.com`.

Novell server products

Many companies use Novell NetWare to support their internal corporate networks (often called *intranets*), if not their full Internet operations. If your site is based on NetWare, you may well consider a third-party commerce service, such the service CyberCash provides, to process your electronic transactions securely.

Novell Web Server 3.1 is ideally suited for intranets or small sites that hire out their transaction processing. It's a good choice for organizations that are already running their networks using NetWare Directory Services (NDS). Novell Web Server 3.1 offers these features:

- Authentication for access to (and publication of) documents on the Web
- Supports Java and CGI programs
- Provides SSL for secure electronic transactions
- Interfaces with the Oracle 7 database
- Requires no TCP/IP stack for Internet access from IPX networks if using Microsoft Internet Explorer

Novell Web Server is a good bridge server when traversing between a Novell-based network and the Internet, because it lets each side use the protocols that it already handles.

For more information about Novell server products, visit the Novell Web site at `www.novell.com`.

Server software for Windows only

These server products may be worth a look by small Windows sites. They may be especially useful if you want to set up an online store outside the United States, or if you have a very limited budget.

Alibaba

Alibaba, which retails for $99, is made by Computer Software Manufaktur GmbH. It supports SSL and most standard Web protocols, but it has no direct database hooks. It is available for Windows NT and Windows 95.

At $99, Alibaba may be worthwhile for a small site that's on a tight budget. After all, a page that's up and running on the Web is worth more than one that isn't yet.

For more information, visit the Alibaba Web site at `alibaba.austria.eu.net`.

Commerce Builder

Commerce Builder, by The Internet Factory, is SSL-enabled server software. The product includes support for proxy server, databases, a Usenet news server, and a chat server. Commerce Builder runs on Windows NT and Windows 95, and it sells for about $395.

For more information, fire up your browser and head to `www.ifact.com`.

Server Software for UNIX

These servers, Apache and HTTPd, are unique in that they rely on the UNIX shell commands for configuration and administration, whereas other server products have proprietary (usually graphical) interfaces.

Apache

Apache 1.2 grew out of NCSA's original Web server software, HTTPd, which in UNIX parlance refers to the *HTTP daemon* — or more completely, a HyperText Transfer Protocol daemon. (HTTPd is the name of the file that a UNIX system uses to process http requests.) Apache's name reportedly comes from the phrase "A PAtCHy sErver," because it was developed by a group that produced software fixes, or patches, to the NCSA HTTPd1.3 server's code.

An informal survey of Web sites, conducted in August of 1997 by some Webmasters I know, found that about two-thirds of commercial sites currently operating on the Web use some version of the Apache Web server (which runs on UNIX and NT platforms, and there's speculation about a Mac OS version).

On a recent visit to The Apache Project's Web site, I read a similar claim — that 48 percent of sites currently use some version of Apache. Among the reasons given by Webmasters for using Apache is the ease with which it can be customized to suit an individual site's requirements. Because the Apache source code also is available for free, it is easy to patch in modules that enhance the functionality of Apache.

There be daemons . . .

A *daemon* (pronounced "demon") is a program that takes care of crucial system functions by running in the background, invisibly, while other processes are still running in the "foreground" of a UNIX system.

With just a bit of programming talent behind the scenes, Apache can be a dream come true for a Web site on a budget. It's a grassroots solution that has been tested and adapted for almost any kind of site you can imagine on the Web.

Apache 1.3 is compatible with Windows NT and Windows 95. The Apache Project Web site mentions that Version 1.3 may run slower on UNIX systems than Version 1.2, because of its expanded platform capabilities.

Apache (which you can find on the CD that comes with this book) provides a robust server engine for publishing your content on the Web. Apache supports all the current Internet standards for distributing Web content. Those standards include

- ✓ Complies with HTTP 1.1. standard
- ✓ Extended Server Side Includes (XSSI), directives that enable users to use conditional HTML and other features to create Web pages more easily
- ✓ (In Apache 1.2) a CGI debugging mode
- ✓ (In Apache 1.2) logging capabilities that let you keep track of visitors to your site

You can't administer Apache 1.2 through a browser, because it relies on text-based UNIX shell commands for installation and configuration. However, anyone familiar with the UNIX OS will have no trouble installing and configuring Apache.

Apache on its own does not support secure electronic commerce. For that purpose, sites built with Apache servers often turn to a product called Stronghold, described a bit later in this section.

Apache does require some knowledge about programming to install and configure. For example, although Apache comes equipped with modules for limiting and logging access to your Web site (just as the popular Netscape and Microsoft server products do), these features are not automatically set up when you install the software. The modules must be placed in the correct directories. The configuration files must be edited manually to configure the Apache server for your site's needs; then the HTTPd server file must be compiled. If you find you need to change something in a configuration file, you need to stop and then restart the Apache server, too.

Setup and maintenance of Apache can be time-consuming for someone who's not familiar with UNIX. And the documentation is just as "uh . . . patchy" as its name, consisting primarily of README files, FAQs and RFCs. There's a newsgroup, `comp.infosystems.www.servers.unix`, which provides a bit of technical support. But for a basic freeware server, the price certainly is right!

Features of Apache include the following:

- ✔ Limiting access to your Web site
- ✔ Controlling access to your Web site
- ✔ Logging access to your Web site
- ✔ Text-flow and other publishing functions for your Web site

Apache maintains user and group information in a file that a system administrator can edit, thus it's easy to set up users and groups on an Apache server. Also, Apache utilizes the built-in security of the UNIX system, which lets you restrict IP addresses, as well as access permissions on individual directories and files. However, for maximum security in transferring sensitive financial information online, sites running Apache may want to use a transaction service such as CyberCash, or look into developing customized transaction software (hire a professional).

Although it was originally developed for UNIX platforms, Apache also is available in versions compatible with OS/2, Windows 95, and Windows NT.

For more information, please visit the Apache Project at `www.apache.org`.

Server software for UNIX only

The server products in this section provide secure commerce capabilities for UNIX platforms, for a smaller price than some other server software that's available.

HTPPd

Although HTTPd is the precursor of Apache, it also has survived as server software in its own right. Because Apache was, in fact, based on Version 1.3 of HTTPd, the two products have much in common. However, one of the biggest differences lies in the way you install HTTPd 1.5.2a. When you go to NCSA's Web site, there's a form from which you choose seven directives that will get your Web server up and running. Then you submit your form, and a preconfigured, customized copy of the software is downloaded for installation on your server hardware. This process is easy, hooray! But if you prefer, you can download the individual modules, configure, and compile them in much the same way as you would Apache. Not me.

The form can be found at `hoohoo.ncsa.uiuc.edu/docs/setup/ SingleClick.html`.

HTTPd (which is on the CD that comes with this book) offers these features, among others mentioned in the section on Apache:

✔ Full support for CGI, forms, and image maps

✔ Multiple IP addresses on one server machine (sometimes called *multihoming*)

✔ Server Side Includes (SSI) which lets you create Web pages built on the fly from the output of other commands or files, such as from CGI scripts

✔ Tutorials and good documentation

HTTPd 1.5.2a is free, but if you're not familiar with UNIX, it's probably not your bargain. On the other hand, if you've got time on your hands, there's no time like the present to pick up UNIX, right?

Like Apache, HTTPd doesn't include security for transferring credit card and other sensitive information online. If you choose HTTPd as your store's Web server software, you may want to hire a transaction processing service such as CyberCash.

Stronghold 2.0

Stronghold is a commercially adapted version of Apache that supports secure Internet transactions using Secure Sockets Layer (SSL), Version 3. It's created by C2Net (in California). Stronghold is used by many sites in the U.S. that want to run their own commerce transactions.

The Stronghold 2.1 server supports 168-bit symmetric encryption for transmitting sensitive data, and it comes equipped with the basic tools that let you maintain *digital certificates.* Stronghold sells for about $995. It's a bare-bones server system that suits many sites well. Many sites that use Apache and find they want to start electronic commerce turn to Stronghold.

It's available at stronghold.ukweb.com. or www.c2.org.

Certificate authorities

Certificate authorities provide a way to vouch for someone's identity over the Internet. Imagine how difficult it can be to verify a person's identity in a medium where one is never seen nor heard in person.

A certificate authority, usually called a CA, essentially says, "Yes, you can trust Joe, I know him." Certificate Authorities issue *digital certificates,* which are something like online identification cards.

For more information, go to www.c2.net on the Web or see Chapter 15 in this book.

Zeus Server

Zeus Server is made by Zeus Technology (in the UK). It supports SSL and works with many versions of UNIX. Zeus Server small and high-performance, and it includes utilities for graphical site configuration and administration. It sells for about $900.

For more information, visit www.zeus.co.uk.

Server Software for Macs

WebSTAR is to-date the best known commercially available Web server software for the Macintosh platform. In fact, for those most familiar with the Macintosh platform, it's really the only viable solution currently available. Luckily, it's pretty good.

WebSTAR

WebSTAR 2.1 supports remote server administration using a browser, CGI programs written in C, Perl, or AppleScript, server-side Java applets that provide processing of HTML forms and database access, and secure electronic commerce transactions using SSL. It also supports the following features:

- Virtual interface servers for better traffic distribution and easier site organization.
- Proxy servers for better security and performance.
- Search engines on your site.
- Adobe PageMill for Web page development.
- Adobe SiteMill for comprehensive site content management.
- W*API, which lets you create server-side plug-ins.
- WebSTAR SSL Security Toolkit, which enables secure electronic commerce. The toolkit originally cost over $1,200 when first released.

WebSTAR 2.0, the previous version of this product, seemed a little slower than most other server products on the market, topping out at ten requests per second in CGI testing, according to *ZD Internet Magazine* (October 1997). This is not quite T1 speed. WebSTAR 2.1 offers significant performance improvements over the 2.0 version, due to the introduction of a file caching system that serves many static files from memory. WebSTAR 2.1 sells for about $499.

For more information, fire up your browser and head to www.starnine.com.

Apple server solutions

Apple Computer also offers server software bundled with server hardware as a complete package. These packages offer a significant opportunity for cost savings over some other Web server hardware/software combinations.

Several of the Apple servers come bundled with Apple RAID software for RAID 0 (striping) or RAID 1 (mirroring) to improve speed of access and reliability for your site. They also come bundled with basically all the other software you need for setting up and running a site. The Web software package available for the 9650 Workgroup Server includes the following:

- Apple RAID software
- Virex anti-virus software from Datawatch
- WebSTAR 2.02 server software
- BBEdit 4.0
- FireSite virtual domain manager, for setting up multiple "virtual Web sites" under one IP address on a single server (sometimes called *multihoming*)
- FireSite Speed Booster with a graphics cacheing function
- Skyline/Satellite Ethernet traffic analysis system
- Everywhere Tango Enterprise Server 2.11 for database integration
- Butler SQL 2.12 for database query speed-up
- GoLive CyberStudio
- Netscape Navigator 3.0
- Rumpus FTP server software for setting up your ftp host
- NetCloak for creating dynamic HTML pages
- Apple MacDNS for domain name services at your site
- Maxum PageSentry for making sure your connections (daemons) are still operating for http, ftp, smpt (e-mail), DNS, and telnet
- Stairways MacTCP watcher to show current TCP connections to your site (it can show packet routing and can test UDP (push) as well as TCP ports)

Chapter 6

Choosing Electronic Storefront Software

*I*n a physical store, you buy building materials, shopping carts, cash registers, and other physical items to put together the store. In an online store, you buy software to provide for the four operating parts of the store: the storefront, the customer shopping cart, the cash register, and the back room.

You have many types and brands of these electronic storefront packages to choose from; this chapter does some of the comparison shopping for you.

Opening the Door on the Electronic Storefront

The path through an online store inevitably falls in a certain sequence, which I use through this chapter as a sort of template to evaluate how each commercial electronic storefront product covered here serves you at each phase of your customer's shopping journey. The following sections describe an idealized scenario to keep in mind.

Entering the store

The customer enters your store. She browses through several pages and finds an item she likes. Many pages seem to be designed with her personal preferences in mind, such as color. To select an item, she clicks on it.

Picking up a shopping cart

When the customer selects an item for purchase, the item goes into her shopping cart. She selects another item, perhaps suggested as a "special of the week" to go with the item she just clicked on, which also goes into the shopping cart.

The shopping cart keeps a total of the items placed in it, automatically calculating any sales tax and shipping charges applicable for a selection of shipping methods.

At last the customer is ready to check out. She clicks the Buy button, which activates the cash register.

Stepping up to the cash register

The cash register accepts the customer's payment information, obtains authorization for the purchase amount, and carries out the transaction.

Your cash register may consist of a set of CGI scripts, a way to connect to a transaction processing service such as CyberCash, or both.

Peeking into the back room

In the back room, you handle customer data, ordering, and fulfillment. Here's an idea of what happens in the back room:

- ✔ Customer data for registered or repeat customers goes into a database for your own use.

- ✔ Ordering and fulfillment can be handled in whatever way is most comfortable for you and efficient for your product, most likely using another database to track orders as they arrive and go through the process of being assembled and shipped.

- ✔ The customer shipping address (from the fulfillment database) can be linked to your customer database, which is a nice way to create a list of what individual customers have ordered and get an idea of other products that may interest them.

It's a good idea to accept customer orders in as many ways as possible at your online store, not just through clicking items into a shopping cart. Ordering may include any or all of these options:

- ✔ By phone or fax
- ✔ By e-mail

✔ By printing a form from your site and faxing or mailing it to you

✔ By browsing through your online store, placing items in a shopping cart, and checking out at your virtual cash register

Altogether, these possibilities combine to create quite a few ways of ordering and paying, don't they?

While you visit the back room, you also want to take a look at your site statistics to see how many visitors you get and where they come from. That way, you have a better basis for targeting your ads or soliciting ad revenue from sponsors on your site. (For more information about tracking your site traffic and advertising revenue, please see Chapter 12.)

Basics of Buying Online

You want your customers to enter your online store through the electronic storefront "door" and plunk down their credit cards or hard-earned cash for your products and services. To enact these transactions, you need special software.

An electronic storefront product is a combination of everything you need to showcase your company's products, along with everything you need to actually sell those products. This usually boils down to the following items:

✔ HTML for product descriptions

✔ CGI scripts for the shopping cart

✔ Web-based forms for ordering

✔ A database for keeping track of your products and customers

The best storefront software provides utilities for things like tax calculation and shipping costs as well, possibly even support for different currencies.

Support for Java, Shockwave, and other technologies would be important in your electronic storefront software if you plan to use animation, video, and the like to describe your products. Support for CGI using Perl or other programming languages would be important if you want to use forms. (Ordering forms are usually provided with storefront products, but you may want to create any number of other forms, such as forms for customer preferences, forms used as part of promotions and surveys, and so on.)

The most distinctive part of electronic storefront software, to me, is the shopping cart, which usually is fashioned out of CGI scripts. It's the part that keeps a running total of items the customer has selected, and then conveys those items to the cash register when the customer checks out. Scripts for calculating taxes and shipping costs are usually incorporated into the shopping cart, although they're arguably part of the back room fulfillment services at your store. The cash register handles the details of conveying the customer's credit card information to the payment processor, obtaining authorization, and so forth.

You want to set up a two-part transaction system that works with your storefront's cash register. One part handles payment through your secure server or through an online payment processing service such as CyberCash, First Virtual, CheckFree, or Open Market (or others, as described in Chapter 16). The other part of your transaction system logs the transactions into your store's database, which tracks individual transactions for record-keeping purposes.

In the back room, you maintain your transaction records, maintain your customer information database, maintain an ordering and shipping system, and an inventory control database if needed. You also want to collect site statistics about who's visiting your site and from where, so you have a better idea of where you can gain site traffic by advertising with Web banners.

If you offer a truly complete and personable online store, include some facilities for customer service, such as e-mail support. And you could probably gain by offering chat rooms or bulletin boards where customers can talk about your products with you and with others. (Few electronic storefront packages help you out with these "advanced" store features, but several scripts are downloadable for free online. For more information about bulletin boards, chat, and where to get scripts, see Chapter 11 or the Internet Directory at the back of this book.)

Unfortunately, few if any electronic storefront products are Plug and Play. Most require hours, if not days or weeks, of customization and setup time with CGI. However, a couple of options for hosted storefronts are mentioned later in this chapter, which could provide you with immediate gratification — an online store in about an hour.

If you buy a Web server without integrated electronic storefront capabilities, you have some options to pick from:

> ✔ You need to buy a separate electronic storefront software product and install it on your Web server machine or your entire Web farm. That's what this chapter helps you do — select a separate storefront product.
>
> ✔ You can create all the transaction scripts yourself (or hire a programmer to do it for you).
>
> ✔ You can go out and hire a transaction processing service (such as CyberCash) to add commerce capabilities to your existing site.

Rolling Stone magazine made an interesting choice — they have a media-oriented Web site that's part of their magazine, not especially set up for commerce. To sell subscriptions, back issues, CDs, and so on, they use a *hosted storefront* (provided by a service called ViaWeb, covered later in this chapter).

The problem with electronic storefronts that aren't integrated into a server is that they require separate maintenance — sometimes a separate server program or process must be run, sometimes access permissions are problematic between the Web server and the shopping cart, sometimes the storefront's interaction with your server's search engines and database tools present another level of complication in the already complex task of managing an online store.

On the other hand, Web servers that come with storefront capabilities include Netscape Enterprise Server, Microsoft Site Server, Enterprise Edition (repackaging of the former Microsoft Merchant Server), Stronghold, or O'Reilly's WebSite Professional (see Chapter 5 for more about these software packages).

Factors that determine the costs include the price of your server machines, the price of any software you need, and whether you need to hire any contractors to set up your site for you, such as Web page designers, CGI programmers, database architects, or network administrators.

Storefront Software for Your Server

This section looks at some products on the market and compares how they support each part of your online store, from setting up the storefront displays, all the way through the back room.

Open Market

If you're seeking the top of the line in commerce software products, look no further. Open Market, headquartered in Cambridge, Massachusetts, has been in business since 1994. Its products are targeted at large and international businesses doing commerce online. Open Market's clients include Disney Online, Time-Warner, and AT&T. Open Market products are used in 21 countries.

Open Market has built a focused product line based on assisting three areas of online business: electronic publishing, retail sales of goods and services, and business-to-business sales. If cost is no object, Open Market would be a good way to go. Their Transact product adds commerce capabilities to existing sites, with all the bells and whistles including support for all standard currencies and international address formats.

Open Market's philosophy is that businesses are better-protected if the commerce transactions (in the back room) are completely separated from the content (storefront display) portion of a site. Therefore, Transact is designed to run on a physically different server machine than the site's content.

Transact runs on UNIX systems, including Solaris, HP-UX, and SGI Irix. It works with Netscape Enterprise Server and Microsoft Internet Information Server as content servers for the products sold using Transact. Transact also supports Sybase and Oracle databases.

Transact includes excellent facilities for online customer service including account statements, order credits, and disputed charge resolution. Transact supports advertising your products using push technology, as well as the more standard Web banners.

Open Market has a CommerceBot product that's a plug-in to Microsoft FrontPage. It lets customers use "Buy Me" buttons and discount coupons right in their HTML pages, and it checks to be sure that no errors are present before you upload the page to your site. CommerceBot stores information about the coupon's discount percentages, shipping charges, and other information associated with any of these coupons or digital offers (which is what it calls the "Buy Me" buttons).

For more information, visit www.openmarket.com.

Intershop Online

Intershop Online is a full-featured online storefront product created by Intershop Communications, of Burlingame, California. Its makers have done a good job of including everything you need to get your online store up and running. It's a lot easier than starting from scratch and may save you money on consulting fees if you have to hire the work out. The potential drawbacks for some are that

- ✔ The product relies extensively on Java scripting, which could be a cause for security concerns in some instances.

- ✔ It's not a product that lets you sit down and create a store in a couple of days, although it does provide templates and wizards that help you make appropriate choices for setting up your store, depending on the type of store you create.

For setting up your content pages, you can use the HTML editor that's included, or choose your own, which is a convenient feature.

Security is provided by SSL or SET (or both), which is nice because SSL lets you set up secure pages for transferring personal information other than just financial information (see Chapter 15 for more on encryption and security). Transaction processing scripts are included in the product, yet it also supports transaction services such as CyberCash and First Virtual.

Intershop Online comes bundled with a Sybase SQL Server 11 database, which is highly extensible — the program can import your existing databases from SQL, Excel, Access, and ODBC-compliant databases. Intershop Online can also run customized reports on registered shoppers, such as reports on their special interests and preferences.

Intershop Online runs on Windows NT and UNIX servers. It costs about $4,995 for the NT version, $7,995 for the UNIX (Solaris, HP-UX, AIX, or IRIX) version. For more information please see `www.netconsult.com`. You can download a free 30-day trial copy from the Intershop Web site at `www.intershop.com`.

Intershop Mall

Intershop Mall is a five-store version of Intershop Online (described in the preceding section) Intershop Mall can scale up to as many stores as you want. It's an excellent product for an ISP, or someone who'd like to rent out store space online. Also, Intershop Mall can be spread across a group of Web farm machines if needed, or it can reside on a single server machine.

Intershop Mall provides administrative utilities that let you open and close individual stores, back up store data individually, or back up the entire mall. Each store maintains its own ODBC or SQL database, which is helpful in maintaining customer privacy and security.

For a five-store mall, the NT server version of Intershop Mall costs $12,500, the UNIX version costs $15,500. Discount pricing is available if you'd like to create a mall with more than five stores. For more information, visit `www.netconsult.com`.

Merchant Builder

Merchant Builder, by The Internet Factory, comes in single-store and five-store versions. It's available for Windows 95/NT platforms and supports all major Web server software. Geared toward small businesses that want to run a store on their own, it's reportedly very easy to install, except for the need to tweak IIS to create virtual paths to the home directory.

The storefront includes templates. The display pages are created automatically from your database using Server Macro Language (SMX). It also supports Perl and CGI.

Security is provided by SSL. It supports CyberCash, First Virtual, and ICVERIFY for transaction processing.

Merchant Builder supports ODBC and SQL databases, and can import data using SQL. But to import data you have to have your database set up in Microsoft Access default format so that it matches Merchant Builder's fields. You can also enter SKU data by hand. Merchant Builder creates Web pages from your product database automatically using its own Server Macro Language (SMX).

Merchant Builder also has some built-in site statistics capability for information about customers, product sales, and regional sales. You can obtain other statistical information from your database using the SMX capability.

The single-store price is $1,495, and the five-store price is $5,000. For more information about Merchant Builder, please visit www.ifact.com.

The Vision Factory

The Vision Factory (www.thevisionfactory.com) offers a product that's ideally suited to businesses that want to move legacy databases online. If your company has an existing database in Oracle, Sybase, FoxPro, or a host of others, the Cat@log product is probably the one for you.

Cat@log has a basic template that creates rather plain-looking Web pages. It doesn't offer extensive templates as some other products do, so you may want to hire an HTML programmer or designer to help create your storefront pages. After creating the plain-vanilla pages, Cat@log does let you use any HTML editor you choose to edit them, giving them more sizzle if you like.

Cat@log supports CyberCash, First Virtual, and other transaction processing options.

The back room is where Cat@log shines. If you have a database, Cat@log can probably connect to it. Also, if you have several databases, such as a customer database, a product database, a database containing customer discounts, and so forth, Cat@log can bring together information from multiple databases at once onto your Web pages.

The Cat@log system, consisting of a site builder component that runs on Windows 95/NT and a commerce server that runs either on NT or on UNIX systems, sells for between $6,000 and $10,000. The exact price depends on your platform and the number of products in your store. Typically, a UNIX system has a premium of $3,000 to $5,000 over the NT version.

iCat

iCat (www.icat.com) Electronic Commerce Suite 3.0, Professional Edition is a very complete commerce solution for NT and UNIX platforms. It supports SET, SSL, CyberCash, and others. This product is highly regarded by some Webmasters in Silicon Valley because its commerce capabilities are very complete, and it's priced under $10,000.

Outreach Communications

Outreach Communications (www.outreach.com) has created a storefront product called Internet Store Manager that sells for $3,495. It runs on NT and UNIX platforms. If budget is your concern, but you need secure, real-time credit card transactions without a hosting service, this product is worth looking into.

Speedware

Speedware (www.speedware.com) is a Canadian firm that has specialized its product, OrderPoint 3.0, for business-to-business sales. This product ships with O'Reilly's Web site server product, but it works with any Web server for UNIX or NT platforms. Sold separately, the NT version is $420,000 and the UNIX version is $30,000.

Free, downloadable storefront products

As with server software for UNIX, some extremely good and popular products are available for free. These products offer the same features as some of the most expensive commercial storefront products you can buy. Your only up-front cost to use them would be for setup.

Selena Sol's Public Domain Web Store

Selena Sol's Public Domain Web Store is a full-featured electronic storefront for UNIX. You can find it at www.extropia.com. (Then click on Scripts and scroll till you see the link for Web Store.) On Selena Sol's site, there's a demo store called Selena Sol's Meme Mart. If you need a way to visualize some of the concepts talked about in this book, you may try visiting the Meme Mart. I especially found the Web Store Database Query Example entertaining when I searched for memes. Selena Sol's scripts are primarily written for UNIX machines, but many of them have been ported to other platforms, as well. Although the scripts come with no guarantees, a lot of people use them.

MiniVend

The MiniVend electronic storefront is freely distributed under the GNU General Public License. It runs on UNIX, the NT version is experimental. It has all the features you need to set up your store, including SSL, built-in credit cards transactions, and support for CyberCash processing. Like Intershop Online and Merchant Builder, it has mall capabilities as well. If you decide to get help in configuring MiniVend, Internet Robotics of Oxford, Ohio, offers to help you on the MiniVend download site (www.minivend.com).

ObjectNet iShopping Wizard

iShopping Wizard is designed for businesses who want to set up their own malls. The software for setting up the mall is free, and it's implemented in Java which means it's platform-independent. The only cost is a per-store registration fee, which the site points out can be charged back to your online tenants as the cost of setting up their storefronts for them.

A potential drawback of Java is that it can open up some security holes in your store. If you decide to use this product, pay particular attention to resolving security matters. Also, this product uses a proprietary encryption scheme, so you want to look at it closely.

The product includes Web Mall server software, shopping clients, two shopping cart interfaces built using Java Applets or CGI, a merchant store setup wizard, an order taking wizard, a product database search engine, a mall setup wizard, templates and samples, and 30 days free technical support. An extra year of tech support costs $299. Their site and a demo is available at www.objnet.com/webmall/webmall_isp_literature.html.

Hosted Electronic Storefronts

Two products, Cartalog, by Virtual Spin, and Store (a.k.a. LiveStore), by ViaWeb, provide a fulfilling combination of storefront-creation software and hosting service, so you can get your store running quickly (waste no time buying a server with these products!).

Cartalog

Cartalog is made by Virtual Spin, of Bellevue, Washington. When you use Cartalog, your store is hosted on the Virtual Spin server, which is a great solution for small start-ups or individuals because it requires little or no up-front capital investment in server equipment and software.

Quick and easy to set up, Cartalog provides a template for creating your content pages, and you can customize by entering your own HTML into the template fields. It lets you use any HTML editor you choose, and provides support for Java and ActiveX.

For transaction processing, you have to rely on a service such as CyberCash because transactions scripts aren't included, although CyberCash support is.

With Cartalog, you have support for SQL and Oracle databases as well as a native database format. You can import delimited files, Excel, Lotus, and EDI data.

One potential advantage of Cartalog is that the company plans partnerships with shipping companies such as Federal Express, UPS, DHL, and Airborne Express. Online stores that ship physical products have the advantage of direct assignment of waybill numbers and real-time calculation of shipping costs. By the way, it helps you calculate shipping costs using several different systems: base weight, flat cost, or as a percentage of dollar value of the product.

The price of Cartalog is based on the number of items in your store. For 150 items, the price is $49.99 per month. For more information, see www.virtualspin.com.

ViaWeb Store

ViaWeb Store is another option for getting your store up and running fast, because it is run by ViaWeb's hosting service. ViaWeb Store has won awards from ZD Internet magazine and PC Magazine as the best hosted storefront product. Its best selling points are its ease of setup — right from your browser, in minutes — and its great site statistics utilities. If you have a digital camera, you can even upload images in a few minutes and have them in your ViaWeb store. When you create a store with ViaWeb Store, you become part of ViaWeb Mall, which is advertised on their site as the Web's busiest mall, with over 8 million hits per day. Stores are accessible by category at the top level of the mall.

ViaWeb Store makes creating a store easy, because it lets you fill in forms using a wizard from your browser. It lets you use any form of applets on your pages to customize them.

ViaWeb Store provides security using SSL. ViaWeb Store doesn't include direct support for processing transactions online. Instead, you can log onto your Web site at ViaWeb and view your new orders, you can download them securely in a format that's importable into your local ordering database, or you can have your new orders faxed to you. Optionally, ViaWeb can provide live credit card transactions for you using CyberCash services, or it can pass the credit card information along to your site for use by a customized script.

ViaWeb Store supports ODBC, SQL, Oracle, and a native database format, and it can import your data in delimited files.

ViaWeb Store's site statistics package includes extremely valuable information like the referring URLs of visitors to your site, so you can figure out easily where your banner ads need to go.

ViaWeb 4.0 supports revenue sharing, which is becoming a popular business arrangement on the Web. Used by major sites such as amazon.com and CDnow, revenue sharing means paying money to sites that send you traffic.

You can try ViaWeb free for 10 days. You'd be in good company, along with *Rolling Stone* magazine, which hosts the storefront portion of its site on ViaWeb, and the Jim Henson store.

For $100 per month, you can have your store of up to 50 items running on the ViaWeb server in Cambridge, Massachusetts. Hosted versions are available for UNIX, Windows 95, and NT. For more information, please visit www.viaweb.com.

Chapter 7

Maintaining Your Site

. . . .

In This Chapter

▶ Looking at your maintenance goals

▶ Managing your pages

▶ Backing up your files

▶ Creating new log files

▶ Discovering the basics about network configuration for servers

▶ Looking into mirrors and virtual domains

▶ Confronting configuration options

▶ Using subnets efficiently

▶ Tuning your directory structure

. . . .

*M*aintaining a selling site on a daily basis is as important as the process of building it in the first place.

Some of the procedures suggested in this chapter are necessary for all sites, such as regular backups. Some tips, such as smoothing out the traffic, are needed more in larger sites than in small sites.

Regardless of the size of your site, this chapter shows you what you need to know about the behind-the-scenes aspects of keeping your site working well and looking good to customers — sort of like restocking the shelves, polishing the front windows, and sweeping the sidewalks around a physical store. You get tips about how to perform some of these tasks more effectively and thus to continuously make your site more attractive to potential customers.

Throughout this chapter, I show you some code examples to help get my points across. My examples are written for the Solaris UNIX operating system. By showing the examples in UNIX, I can explain at a basic level about what's going on underneath a GUI or other interface on a Macintosh or Windows NT server, these same tasks are performed, but with much more complex code.

By the way, many of these maintenance procedures are the basic tasks associated with operating a computer on the Internet, and the principles haven't changed much since the Internet began 30 years ago. You're in good company here!

Your Maintenance Goals

Basically, you want to make your site a place that readers come back to again and again. You can achieve this goal by making sure that your site runs efficiently and offers new content on a regular basis. At the same time, you want to make things easy on yourself and not drive yourself nuts about keeping your site up-to-date. Specifically, you want to keep the following in mind as you make your maintenance plans:

 ✔ Design your site so that it's easy to manage

 ✔ Make sure that customers get reasonable response time

 ✔ Back up your site often

 ✔ Create a regular schedule for site updates

Thinking of maintenance in these basic terms helps make it seem like a more manageable and worthwhile task.

Managing the Pages on Your Site

Handling all those intricately interlinked Web pages on a daily basis poses a serious site management challenge. It can be difficult to keep a picture in your head of all the pages and links, and how they change after you add something new. That's why many sites suffer from "404-Not Found" problems (signifying an invalid link) as they grow and evolve.

Unfortunately, not much commercial software exists to help you tackle this enormous problem. (The industry just hasn't gotten around to it yet — everyone is still focusing on Web authoring, and no one has thought about what to do with all those great pages after they are on the Web.) The ideal site management tool would accomplish the following tasks for you and your Web pages:

 ✔ Keep track of internal and external page links and automatically check them regularly to see that they are valid.

 ✔ Keep track of the site's page hierarchy and generate navigational elements automatically for each page.

 ✔ Offer search-and-replace features for easily implementing sitewide changes, such as filename and pathname changes.

✔ Watch the *greenroom* copy of the site for creation times and dates, and upload the latest versions automatically, at specified times or intervals, using FTP. (The *greenroom* is a repository for Web pages that are almost ready to be posted on your site.)

✔ Manage sites with several thousand pages of content.

✔ Let site developers use any HTML editor they choose to create the site's pages.

No single tool I've found performs all these tasks, although several tools can now help you out with portions of it, including the following:

✔ **Adobe SiteMill** (www.adobe.com): Very good at tracking links for sites of less than 1,000 pages

✔ **NetObjects Fusion** (www.netobjects.com): Very good at automatically generating navigation bars in headers or footers, but this feature works only with content that's been created with its own Web authoring features

✔ **Microsoft FrontPage** (www.microsoft.com/frontpage/): Although it is very MS-centric, some folks give FrontPage good marks for site management (particularly in the link management area)

Basic text editors often offer the best search-and-replace features currently available (I know several sites that use BBEdit to do this task). On the PC side, HomeSite is a good match for BBEdit on the Mac, and it has a great link verification tool. Also, Macromedia's new Dreamweaver program works with a repeating element library that lets you change one item and have the change reflected sitewide. Very cool.

Until site management tools get better (and they will), you need to give personal attention to all the items on the preceding list every time your site changes. Yes, it's "Webmaster as site management tool." That's another good reason to keep your site's organization simple, isn't it?

Even if site updates are a lot of work, you should really perform them regularly, perhaps every week. You must update your site often to keep people excited about your store and to keep them coming back. (Chapter 10 describes a good process for developing the material you use for updating your site's content.)

On the technical end, you may want to create some copy-and-replace scripts to make posting the updates content files to your site easier, and plan to run the scripts at regularly scheduled times. Scripts can automate at least one of your major site management headaches. If you can't write that script yourself, it's well worth hiring a consultant to do the task for you.

It's Dead, Jim! Backing Up Your Site or Server

The short answer: Back up. You never think it will, but disk failure eventually happens to almost every computer. Here are some tips for how to prevent agony:

✔ **Create a schedule for your backups and stick to it.** Most sites have a standard backup schedule and procedure for their server. Typically, you should perform a full backup at least once a month and an incremental backup every day. A *full backup* is just what it sounds like: every file on every machine. An *incremental* means a backup of just those files that have changed since the last full backup, or since yesterday if incremental backups are run daily.

Some large sites run a monthly full backup, a weekly incremental of the whole site, and small daily backups of certain key areas. You have some flexibility to find a backup schedule that works well for you and is reasonably convenient.

For your site, it depends on the number of files being created or changed daily and the overall size of your file system. The basic rule here is: better safe than sorry. When in doubt, back it up.

✔ **Keep two complete sets of backup tapes (including tapes for full backups, incrementals, and incidental daily backups), and alternate the tapes every month.** For example, if you call the tapes TapeSet 1 and TapeSet 2, you may use TapeSet 1 in September, TapeSet 2 in October, TapeSet 1 again in November, and so on. Having two sets of backup tapes gives you good protection in case anything should happen to one of the tapes — most files would have been backed up the preceding month and would be recoverable that way.

Figure 7-1 is a visual reminder of how you'd use this system of two sets of backup tapes.

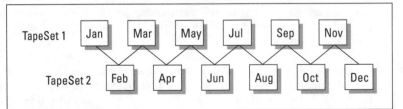

Figure 7-1.
Using two sets of backup tapes.

TapeSet 1   Jan   Mar   May   Jul   Sep   Nov

TapeSet 2   Feb   Apr   Jun   Aug   Oct   Dec

Several good software programs run your backups automatically, such as Retrospect Remote (at www.dantz.com/dantz_products/retro.html). If you have a set of machines running on a network, you can back up your entire local network from the server (in case your Web page designers inevitably forget to put something beautiful they've just created on their desktop machine onto the server for backup).

Backup programs can (and should) be set to run at light-usage times of day, such as 4 a.m. to 5 a.m.. A system backup, especially a full backup, is a reasonably intensive process, and it slows down your server's response time considerably, especially if you also have a lot of visitors.

As your site grows larger, you can add tapes to your backup set with little effort. Most backup programs are smart enough to continue the backup process across several tapes if needed, because they carefully enumerate the files and file sizes before they start writing the tapes; that is, the programs know ahead of time just how much space your files need.

Creating New Log Files

Your Web server software automatically generates site log file. The files contain information about who visited your site and when.

You should rename your log files every day for ease in sorting out your site statistics. You can set up a script to rename your log files every day at midnight, if you like, by following these steps:

1. **Rename the existing log files.**

   If you set up a script, you can use a date or other function call to generate the new name automatically.

2. **Give the** sighup **command to create the new day's log files.**

   Because the old files have been renamed, the sighup command works to create the new log files; if the system finds a log file it appends to it, but if no log file exists with the name it expects, sighup creates a new one and then starts writing into it.

If something goes wrong, run the top command to see what processes are using the most system resources. If the root process has blown up, it shows up in top.

Keeping Up with Your Server

Regardless of what type of server hardware and Web server software you have, you face similar site management and configuration tasks. In this section, I tell you how to handle this basic piece of your site's hardware. (By the way, if you haven't picked out your server hardware and software yet, you can find more information about those tasks in Chapters 4 and 5.)

When I give examples of server maintenance, I use the syntax of the UNIX operating system (used by the Sun Solaris). UNIX has no graphical user interface, allowing UNIX to show the nature of the task more clearly. The commercial site management tools that provide you with an interface are just glossing over the underlying tasks, which, for good or bad, UNIX does not.

The basics of setting up your server

Before you can get your server up and serving content to your customers, you need to look at three distinct tasks:

- ✔ Installing your server software
- ✔ Getting an IP address
- ✔ Editing your hosts and hostname files to reflect your site's configuration

Conscientious follow-through on these tasks can help you avoid server problems in the future. After you complete these tasks, your site is up and running — and connected to the Internet. As your site grows, you can look at some special options for configuration, such as mirroring, virtual interfaces, or round-robin DNS (described later in this chapter).

Installing your server software

If you download your server software from the Web, follow the instructions given at the site or in the software's Read Me file. If you use one of the server software programs on the CD that accompanies this book, follow the installations given in Appendix A. If you purchase commercial software, follow the instructions given in the documentation for installing the software product.

Before installing software, back up your existing files. You never know when something may crash during an installation because of unforeseen incompatibilities. It never hurts to have an extra backup.

Getting an IP address

An IP address identifies a computer on the Internet, so you can't really do much with your server until you get an address.

Major Internet sites, including Internet Service Providers, have a range of IP addresses assigned to them by a central Internet authority. Your Internet Service Provider gives you your IP address. (By the way, the fellow who assigns the IP addresses to your ISP, the top dog, is Jon Postel, an Internet old-timer who's been doing that among other things for 15 or 20 years.)

Sometimes your IP address is assigned to you permanently, sometimes you get one that's assigned from a pool, depending on the type of access you need. Your ISP is an expert at this process and can help you through the steps to tell your server machine its IP address.

Editing your hosts and hostname files

Your host and hostname files must contain the IP information for your machine or your local network.

You must configure your server to know its own IP address, and probably also to know the addresses of the other machines it talks to most frequently. You need to make entries for each IP address and domain running on your server(s).

Although the examples here are given for UNIX, the same principles apply to servers running other operating systems: Your machine has to know its address and the addresses of any other machines on your local network. Network system administration tools contain utilities for setting up IP addresses in NT, MacOS, and other operating systems.

Setting things up especially for your server

After you take care of the basics of installing your server, getting an IP address, and editing your host and hostname files, you can take care of server needs that are specific to your site, including the following:

- Setting up mirror hosts and adding them to round-robin DNS (which is a way to share the customer load among several servers automatically)
- Configuring virtual domains (*virtual domains* are another way to distribute customer traffic in a balanced way across your site)

Understanding Internet configuration

If you have a Web farm or other local network, you need to know a little bit about network configuration so you can set up or troubleshoot your site. (See Chapter 3 for more information on Web farms.)

The process of telling Web server machines their addresses is called *Internet configuration,* or sometimes more generally, *network configuration.* Every computer on the Internet (including your server) has to know its own

IP address so the computer knows whether any of the data flowing by is intended for that computer. Each time a machine is rebooted or reconnected to the Internet, it needs to find its IP address all over again. Rather than having a system administrator sit there and tell the machines their addresses all day long, several automated ways have been created for network machines to find out their own addresses.

Basically, the process goes something like this:

1. **A machine is restarted or reconnected.**

2. **It needs to find its network address, so it looks in a file it keeps called a *hosts file* or *host configuration file*.**

3. **If the information isn't in the file, the machine sends out a data packet on the network saying "Hey, does anyone out there know who I am?"**

   Usually on every network there's a computer called a *DNS server* (domain name server, or nameserver, for short) that keeps all the information about the names and addresses of the computers in its domain. The DNS server responds to the machine that requested its address. (But this takes time, so it's better to have a hosts file on each machine.) That's why when you apply to the InterNIC for your domain name, you have to have a host machine with an IP address ready to go. Each domain name has to match an IP address, and vice versa.

If you have trouble getting your network machines to boot properly, or if you run out of local IP addresses, you probably want to hire a professional network administrator or Webmaster to help you out.

Maintaining Windows NT servers

NT servers are popular, and they're growing more popular as Microsoft improves the tools available for building and managing NT-based Web sites. Nevertheless, or perhaps for this very reason of their growing popularity, I thought it worth repeating a few points about NT Web servers, which I heard from an experienced computer programmer whose job it is to set up NT and UNIX servers for customers of a large corporation.

The current state of Windows NT server administration is precarious at best. Although a sizable suite of server management tools are available for administering NT-based servers, NT servers currently leave a lot to be desired in terms of selectivity of administrative access and resulting security holes. (You have to grant mostly all-or-none administrative access to your server, which means you could have inexperienced or even unfriendly people poking around areas of the server where you don't want them to be.)

Microsoft is working to improve the administration tool situation with a product called Microsoft Management Console (MMC); however, some of the problems remain with the server itself.

Security is a very serious issue for NT servers at present. The kinds of security holes that hackers are finding in NT servers are the kind of holes hackers were finding in the UNIX system 30 years ago. There's just no way NT can catch up quickly, either, because the NT source code is proprietary.

NT and UNIX

My conclusions: Windows NT servers are most successful today at serving small to medium-sized sites, medium-sized workgroups (up to 150), and corporate intranets. They're an unbeatable starting point if you're already familiar with the Windows environment. However, as your site grows large, you should seriously think about moving to a UNIX server. Why?

UNIX machines grew up on the Internet. The UNIX operating system, by its very nature, is just full of mysterious and wonderful *daemons* (background processes) waiting to talk to networks. By contrast, the NT operating system has been stretched toward its limits by the addition of all the complicated processes and tools required for operating in an Internet environment. The required network processes have at best been "grafted on" to the NT operating system. Microsoft is doing its best to make the system work, but at present, UNIX may offer the best options for starting your selling site.

Why is my super duper 4-processor NT machine still so slow, Mom?

Another factor to keep in mind for maintaining NT servers at larger sites is the difficulty NT has in operating over a network with a multiprocessor machine, particularly a 4-processor machine. In a multiprocessor environment, NT's operating system runs all of the I/O (input and output tasks) through one processor while the other processors handle the remaining tasks. It sounds like a good idea at first blush, but any computer geek knows that "a machine becomes I/O-bound long before it becomes compute-bound," which translates to: "A computer runs out of speed and space for handling user requests — such as reads and writes to databases or downloads of files into Web browsers — long before it runs out of capacity to process any other type of task." When running an NT server, this fact has some serious consequences: One processor usually bogs down while the others wait for it, so your Web server still gives substandard performance to your customers. To counteract this problem, Netscape Navigator for NT actually has a special code built in for NT systems running on multiple processor machines: It finds out which processor is handling I/O and avoids it.

One thing that's going to make it possible for NT Webmasters to consider moving toward UNIX server platforms as their sites mature is the fact that Apache, probably the most widely-used server software on the market, will be available soon for NT and (has already been available for some time) on UNIX. The opportunity to retain familiar server software while switching the underlying operating system may make the idea of migrating seem palatable. And by the way, NT server lovers, don't pout. I'd say the same thing to a Macintosh administrator.

Managing Your Site Traffic

Site traffic is the constant stream of visitors to your site, sort of like traffic on a freeway (you hope!). It's a good idea to pay attention to your site traffic, keeping it balanced, so that all your customers get good response time when visiting your online store. For example, some areas of your site may attract more visitors than other areas. You can use several techniques to make those frequently visited areas more accessible to your customers. One method is called *mirroring,* which means creating a duplicate of a heavily trafficked area. Another method involves creating virtual domains, which amounts to creating a special URL that gets people to that part of your site quickly. (I tend to think of a virtual domain like a "mother-in-law entrance" to an apartment — a separate doorway to a self-contained unit.)

Mirror, mirror on the server

Mirroring involves setting up more than one server machine that contains duplicates of all the files on your site (or a heavily-used part of your site). Mirrors for Web server machines are just like when you look into a mirror — an exact image. Selena Sol's site (www.extropia.com) makes use of mirror sites in a way that you may find interesting. Often, you can't tell when a site is mirrored; you just notice an improvement in response time on parts that were slow.

Knowing when to set up mirrors

Mirroring is a subjective thing, a judgment call, in most cases. One test you can try is visiting your own site during a busy time. See how long it takes you to connect and get to the page you want, say a few layers deep into your links. If you get impatient, maybe your customers are, too. If you are really lucky, some caring customer sends e-mail telling you that your site is too slow. Don't get mad, get mirrored!

Do you have to buy a server just like the one you already have to use as its mirror? No, the thing that is mirrored is the content of the site, not the actual hardware. Can I use that old Mac I have in the closet a mirror to my ultramodern Mac server or Windows NT server? Yes, by all means — some mirroring usually is better than none, especially if your customers are getting bogged down in frustration.

Keeping your mirrors in synch

Some site management tools include features that update mirror sites automatically. However, in some cases you need to do some copying and uploading of updated HTML or database files by hand. Be sure to develop a checklist of every place that needs to be updated.

Mirroring your database

Plain and simple: Don't mirror your database. If your site is slow, try mirroring everything else instead. Why? Databases are so complex and they change so often that it would most likely become a management headache within about three days. (I would also try adding a software utility that keeps several database connections open at all times; database connections usually are the culprits that bog down traffic. One I know of: the Apache server has an extension that lets you perform this task with an Informix database.)

Making mirrors transparent to your users

Sometimes the mirrors are obvious to customers, because you tell them to try another URL if one doesn't respond. Sometimes the mirrors aren't obvious; you can set up your site so that visitors are transferred to a mirror site automatically when the primary site has reached its capacity. Generally it's easier just to set up a duplicate site at another URL and direct customers to click on a link and go there if they get impatient. However, it's nicer for the customers if they don't have to know whether they're at the "original" site or the "mirror."

To make mirroring transparent to your customers, probably the best technique you can use is called *round-robin DNS.* In round-robin DNS, a process automatically parcels out connections to each of your Web farm machines, in rotation and according to which machine is most heavily loaded. (Ask yourself: Which machine on your local network (a.k.a. Web farm) suffers most during peak times of customer usage? That's the machine to mirror.)

You maintain round-robin DNS by using two sets of files that match IP numbers with names and, inversely, names with IP numbers. (For more about IP numbers, see the "No more addresses?" sidebar later in this chapter.) For example, a file entry in the first file could look like this:

```
www.mysite.com IN A 207.46.37.11
```

In the other file, you put a corresponding entry, something like this one:

```
207.46.37.11 IN PTR www.mysite.com
```

Each file has multiple entries of this form, and each entry matches an Internet IP address with a domain name.

Round-robin DNS is performed automatically by a relatively new version of a program called BIND (which stands for *Berkeley Internet Name Domain*). The version must be 4.9.3 or newer. If a machine runs an appropriate version of BIND, the computer is thus round-robin "aware," meaning that it accepts multiple matches between domain names and IP numbers. (That is, it reads multiple entries in host files and stores them for its own use.) It then performs the round-robin tasks itself. If a machine is not round-robin aware, your server machines perform the issuance of names and IP numbers and send them to the requestor, one by one.

To add a new machine (or interface) into round-robin DNS, you add an entry to each of your two round-robin DNS files. On Solaris/Apache, DNS filenames look like this:

```
/etc/named.conf/db.mysite (on one nameserver machine)
etc/named.conf/db.38.217.84 (on the other nameserver)
```

Notice that one filename matches the domain name and the other matches the IP address.

To select a new IP address for a machine that you are adding (as long as it's within your allotment of IP addresses from your provider), look at the last entry in the file and choose a number sequentially higher. For example, if the last IP number ends with .67, choose .68 as the last portion of your new machine's IP number. Remember to enter the new name and number in both files.

After changing these files, you need to stop and restart the `named` (name server daemon) process on the server. To stop the `named` process on a UNIX system, you can use the `ps -ef` command to get the Process ID (pid) of the named process. Then perform a `kill -1` command using that `pid`. Even easier, use the following command:

```
kill -1 'cat /etc/named.pid'
```

Notice the use of backquote, which causes the system to substitute the result of the `cat /etc/named.pid` command into this command line. (The result of that command is the Process ID of the named process, because that `pid` is stored in the file `named.pid` in the directory `/etc/`.)

Finally, if you have primary and secondary DNS servers at your site, to keep them consistent you must change the timestamps of these files. To change the timestamp, here's what to do: In the second line of each file (or so), you see a 12-digit number representing the number of seconds since 1969 (or something like that). That number is the file's timestamp.

At the command line, use the following command:

```
date +%s
```

This command returns a new timestamp value; then copy and paste the result into the file instead of the existing 12-digit number. Do this for both files. Otherwise, the DNS servers will be out of synch by several hours.

Virtual domains

Sometimes you can't divide your Web site traffic by creating one or more duplicate mirror sites. For example, sometimes your budget simply doesn't allow you to purchase the additional servers you need to set up a mirror.

If your budget is limited, you can still manage your site traffic a little more efficiently. You can set up a *virtual domain,* which is a kind of subdomain under your primary domain, on the same server. In effect, you make it look like you have more than one server for the purposes of relieving the traffic burden on your top-level domain server.

You can set up virtual domains on a single machine or across several machines (on a local network or Web farm). Virtual domains tend to special- ize the content areas, rather than duplicating them. Basically, a virtual domain parcels out the traffic you receive across major subject areas of your site, and groups the areas within your site's content by category or subject matter. Thus, if I sold greeting cards online, I may set up a domain for friendship cards (mysite.friendly.com), a domain for sympathy cards (mysite.condolences.com), a domain for congratulations cards (mysite.congrats.com), and so on. I may also set up a special domain for seasonal or holiday cards, too. It depends on what areas are getting a lot of traffic and how you conceive of your content fitting together.

UNIX offers the most flexible type of virtual domain hosting, because it lets the Webmaster associate multiple domain names with one IP address, or multiple IP addresses with a single domain name.

Under the Solaris operating system, a system administrator can use a command-line interface to set up virtual domain names that look, to the user, like separate (virtual) host machines. Some commercial server software has adapted this capability as well.

By using virtual domains on logical interfaces within a single server machine, your site can avoid the significant delays associated with DNS propagation through the Internet. (Or if you are an ISP, you can run more than one customer's online store from a single server machine, effectively splitting the machine into parts.)

Virtual domains can be shut down and brought up with one-line commands on UNIX. Using this capability, UNIX system administrators can bring down a domain on a machine that is overcrowded and bring it up simultaneously on another host machine, thus evening out the traffic among the site's host machines in a way that's invisible to users.

The examples given in this section uses the command syntax specific to the Solaris version of UNIX. However, most UNIX system administrators recognize the commands and adapt them easily to their own flavor of UNIX. Even if you don't have a UNIX server machine, you may want to peruse this section. Why? The GUI interfaces provided for Windows and Macintosh site configuration are just glossy finishes to the nuts-and-bolts operations of managing an Internet site. When you look at these UNIX configuration how-tos, you really look under the hood of your GUI configuration tool and learn more about how the Internet works.

Interface cards

To set up a virtual domain, you need a network interface card (NIC) that connects your machine to the network. Actually, any machine connected to a network needs one of these.

Typically, every machine on your local network (for example, your Web farm network) already contains an Ethernet card (or another type of network interface card), and your local network is then connected to the Internet through a router and firewall of some sort. (Routers and firewalls are discussed more fully in Chapter 3.)

Each virtual domain on your local network is associated (using your machine's configuration file) with a specific network interface card within a specific machine on your network.

The role of the logical interface

By setting up logical interfaces on a single network interface card, you can divide one interface card into "many" and share it — one logical interface for each virtual domain. That's a good thing, partly because some computers (server hardware) have limited expansion slots for adding new cards and such, including new network interface cards.

A logical interface is like a piece of a physical network interface card. A virtual domain uses a logical interface in a one-to-one correspondence.

At least one popular firewall, the Raptor Eagle, doesn't support logical interfaces. If you use a Raptor Eagle and want to set up virtual domains, you need to consider another firewall product.

Configuring your virtual domain

For purposes of configuring your site, a virtual domain is defined by

- ✔ The physical Ethernet card with which it is associated in its host machine
- ✔ Its number among all the logical interfaces operating on that physical card

For example, a logical interface on an Ethernet card named le0 (which is typically the first Ethernet card on a machine) would have the prefix le0 followed by a colon and its interface number. Thus, the second virtual domain that's set up on a machine with one Ethernet card, named le0, would use an interface called le0:2.

You can use more than one physical Ethernet card on a machine. Several types of Ethernet cards have different prefixes, such as qe, be, and hme. For example, a card that can deliver 10MB and 100MB Ethernet has the prefix hme0. You see these names in your site's configuration files, so now you can understand what you read.

Moving a virtual domain to another machine

Here's an advantage of setting up your site using virtual domains: When traffic is too high on one area of your site, or on one machine of your local network, you can move that virtual domain to a machine that's less crowded. (Among UNIX Webmasters, virtual domains are often referred to by the name of the logical interface rather than the virtual domain name — there's a one-to-one correspondence — so I use the term *interface* in this section.) Moving an interface involves bringing that interface down on the old machine and bringing it up on a new machine. Here are some steps:

1. **Be sure your Web server machine has been reconfigured to accept connections on the new IP address.**

   That means be sure your hosts and hostname files are up-to-date— select a new IP address if needed.

2. **Type** `ifconfig -a` **on the old machine to show all interfaces.**

3. **Find the interface that you want to take down and type** `ifconfig <your interface number> down.`

   For example, to take down the interface `le0:2`, you would type `ifconfig le0:2 down.`

4. **On the new machine, see which interface names or numbers are in use by typing** `ifconfig -a.`

5. **Configure the new interface by typing** `ifconfig <new interface number> <IPaddress> netmask + broadcast + -trailers.`

   Notice the spaces between `netmask` and its following plus sign and `broadcast` and its following plus sign. You need to type those characters in.

   As an example, to configure a new interface called `le0:3` at IP address `208.7.7.7,` you would type `ifconfig le0:3 208.7.7.7 netmask + broadcast + -trailers.`

6. **Type** `ifconfig le0:3 up` **to bring up the new interface.**

If you want to make your new interface come up each time you boot the machine, you need to edit each machine's configuration files — that is, the hosts and hostname files — to show the new interface running on the new machine, and delete it from the configuration files on the old machine.

Bringing up an interface

This procedure works to bring up a physical interface card or a logical interface (with its associated virtual domain):

1. **Type** `ifconfig -a` **to see all the interfaces running on the machine.**

2. **Type** `ifconfig <interface number> up` **to bring up the interface.**

   For example, to bring up an interface called `le0:3`, you would type

   ```
   ifconfig le0:3 up
   ```

Bringing down an interface

To bring down a physical interface card or a logical interface and its associated virtual domain (for example, when you don't want your customers to have access to it, after it's up and running on another, less-crowded machine) just follow these steps:

1. **Type** `ifconfig -a` **to see all the interfaces running on the machine.**

   In response to this command, you get a list of records like the following:

   ```
   <interfacename>    <options> <status>
   <IPaddress>, <netmask>, <broadcast>
   ```

2. **Select the interface you are looking for and bring it down.**

   For example, to bring down the interface called `le0:2`, you would type

   ```
   ifconfig le0:2 down
   ```

When you bring down a logical interface, your customers can't see the virtual domain that uses that logical interface. It's off the network at that point.

Editing the hosts and hostname files

Each time you change the way your local network is configured to improve the traffic flow, you need to alter your network configuration files to reflect the new situation.

On UNIX, these files are called `/etc/hostname` files and the `/etc/hosts` file.

Or, you need to edit these files after adding a mirror site or after bringing up a new virtual domain, especially if you want your new mirror or domain to be set up each time a machine is booted.

Editing the hosts file

To update the `/etc/hosts` file, enter a line with the IP address and name of the new domain. For example, you could type the following:

```
208.7.7.7        www.mysite.com
```

Or, suppose your site has three mirrored server machines (M1, M2, and M3), each running a virtual domain called `www.mysite.com`. This virtual domain has a different IP address on each machine. For example, in the hosts file on M1 may be an entry like this:

```
208.7.7.10       www.mysite.com
```

In M2, a similar entry appears, with a different IP address, such as

```
208.7.7.11       www.mysite.com
```

In the hosts file on M3, you find yet another similar entry, something like this:

```
208.7.7.12        www.mysite.com
```

With these entries, each host machine is telling itself that it answers to the domain name www.mysite.com (among others). When the DNS server later initiates its round-robin DNS services, all these machines respond to domain name requests for www.mysite.com. (But they have different IP addresses, which means that they are each individually connected to the Internet, thus spreading out the communication load among them.)

Creating and deleting hostname files

Every domain hosted on your server machine must have its own individual hostname file. For example, if you add the logical interface le0:3 to a machine, you must create a new hostname file, called /etc/hostname.le0:3. That hostname file should contain one word — the name of the associated domain (virtual or otherwise) that uses the interface (logical or otherwise), such as the word "holidays" (no quotes).

The easiest way to create that new hostname file for matching a virtual domain (in this case called holidays) and its logical interface (in this case le0:3) is to type the following command:

```
echo holidays>/etc/hostname.le0:3.
```

To get rid of the hostname file containing the interface le0:3 on the old machine, you type the following:

```
remove /etc/hostname.le0:3
```

That command deletes the file, and that hostname (virtual domain name) is no longer recognized by the machine, which means that the machine no longer responds to network requests for information provided by that domain.

When you reboot, a host machine must translate each defined domain name into an IP address. It checks its hosts file (/etc/hosts) to get the names and IP addresses of the domains that run on it. If it doesn't find the information it needs in the hosts file, it then asks the DNS server for the information. Your goal is to have the machine not have to ask the DNS server for the information, because that takes longer. That's why each machine always should have its own accurate hosts and hostname files.

Dealing with the httpd Process

A number of things can go wrong with your server, even in the best-run sites. Sometimes a process goes haywire, and sometimes even though the machine is up and running fine, no HTML pages reach your customers.

When Web pages aren't reaching your customers, usually the *httpd process* (the process on your server that responds to requests for information over the Web) is at fault.

Starting an httpd process

The most common cause of pages not being served is that the httpd process was never started. Because this situation is so common, you should run a script called `check.httpd` about every minute on your server.

If the httpd process is not in fact running, you experience a 59-second maximum delay while the process starts. The `check.httpd` script also sends e-mail notifying the *webmaster@yoursite.com* about the occurrence.

If `check.httpd` fails, type `webhttpd start` to start an httpd process.

Killing httpd processes gone bad

Your server won't serve up pages if the `httpd` (HyperText Transfer Protocol Daemon) process didn't terminate properly the last time it executed. It needs to be killed and restarted.

Use `ps -ef` to look for errant `httpd` processes and kill them individually by using the `sighup` command.

Why Web processes turn bad

A Web process occasionally "explodes," which means that it quickly grows to use a lot of CPU and a lot of memory. You can use a script, `killWildHttpd`, which runs once a minute to get rid of Web processes that have exploded.

The current theory is that Web processes can explode when a user cancels a request in the middle of transmission, because many browsers don't handle cancellation cleanly. They ought to send a "never mind the rest of this transmission" message.

In general, you have three ways to kill a process on a UNIX system:

- sigterm, which means "execute a normal process shutdown when you get around to it"
- sighup, which means "hang up" and "reread your configuration file"
- sigkill, which means "I don't care what you are doing, stop now"

If you give a sigkill (kill -9) command, it kills the process without killing any of its children. Thus, if you give a sigkill to the root httpd process, its Web httpd children are left on their own and hard to get rid of.

Just in case of that eventuality, a script called killemall takes a regular expression as an argument, and then uses that expression to search and destroy selected processes. Needless to say, this script must be used with care, because killemall * can create a disaster.

Killing the root httpd process

If the root process has blown up, use this command to kill the root process:

```
kill -9 'cat /web/httpd/httpd.pid'
```

The string in backquotes tells Solaris to look in the file web/httpd/ httpd.pid and get the process id (pid) of the root process; the rest of the command says to kill the process with that pid. Thankfully, the pid of the root process has not changed, even though it has blown up.

Using Subnets Efficiently

You should put your machines that talk to each other frequently on the same subnet, such as your Web farm's database server and top-level Web server machine (from which customers enter database requests). Talking directly on a subnet means that the packets are sent from machine to machine over a local network, such as an Ethernet, without using the router.

If your local network is configured by splitting it efficiently into subnets, you get two major benefits:

- Your overall network traffic can be reduced by avoiding a lot of local broadcast traffic, because the machines can be configured to talk directly.
- Because Class C address space is hard to come by, your allotment of IP addresses lasts longer.

When you send Address Resolution Packets (ARP) packets or other special-purpose packets, you can often save bandwidth on your local network by talking directly over the subnet.

Fortunately (or perhaps unfortunately), routers can help make up for poor subnet configuration, because they usually know what packets should come to them and can respond to network broadcasts on a LAN as if they were a machine.

To determine whether two machines are on the same subnet, the configuration server daemon performs two logical AND operations, as follows:

- Address of the broadcasting machine AND subnet mask
- Address of the destination machine AND subnet mask

If the results match, the two machines are on the same subnet. If your machines aren't on the same subnet and you want them to be, you must reconfigure the hosts files to assign IP addresses that put the two machines on the same subnet, such as 255.255.255.012 and 255.255.255.013.

Tuning Your Directory Structure for Fast Access

One site in San Francisco that sells greeting cards online, Greet Street at `www.greetst.com`, made a great marketing deal and suddenly the traffic on its site increased about seven-fold in a day. The servers were all bogged down, strained to the limits (UNIX systems running Apache, at that). What were those servers doing? Searching the directory structure for files, finding the files, and downloading the files into the wonderful Greet Street customers' browser windows.

It was a desperate situation. See, each of the greeting cards was stored as a file. Each time a customer ordered a card, that file had to be located from within the site's directory structure.

No more addresses?

The Internet is running out of IP addresses! The designers never anticipated the unprecedented amount of growth the Web has experienced over the last few years. There's a plan in the works to expand the available number of addresses on the Internet so that it could theoretically include everyone, every machine, and every appliance on the planet.

The problem? The tree was too deep, not wide enough, so most of the searches had to travel too many steps down the tree before they found their card of choice to download. Those steps take a long time and tie up the processor.

The solution? Create a wider directory structure for the whole site (well, the part with the cards, which is most of it). If customers can find any card within two steps on the tree, the servers have a lot less searching to do.

If you want to set up your directory structure for quick, searchable access to lots of small files, make it wide and shallow, rather than narrow and deep. If fast searching is not your priority, a deep structure often works well for making your links faster.

Part III
Creating Selling Content

The 5th Wave   By Rich Tennant

@RICHTENNANT

"I have to say I'm really impressed with
the interactivity on this car wash Web site."

In this part . . .

Your store's content determines your financial success. Spend some time in this part and find out how to use text, images, and interactivity to make your site stand out among online stores. I also talk about keeping your content consistent by regular and thorough site maintenance.

Chapter 8

Giving Your Text Some Character

*Y*ou can find many great books on the shelf about how to write Web pages using HTML, so this chapter doesn't go into the details of HTML. Instead, this chapter tells how to use HTML templates to make your life easier, and it gives some tips about great tools for HTML development on your chosen platform.

After reading this chapter, you can spend less time worrying about your site's text and more time planning your next big marketing campaign. (For tips on planning that great campaign, read *Marketing Online For Dummies,* by Bud Smith, published by IDG Books Worldwide, Inc.)

Good Ol' HTML: Gateway to the Search Engines

The basic files that display your products or talk about your services are written in HTML. If you don't already know HTML, you may want to pick up *HTML For Dummies,* written by Ed Tittel and Steve James, published by IDG Books. You can also find several good sites that show you the basics of HTML on the Web. (See "The *Selling Online For Dummies* Internet Directory" for more information about those sites.)

You should put some time into your HTML files so that your site shows up well on the big Internet search engines, and so that your time spent developing HTML is as efficient as it can be.

The better and more organized your site looks, and the more often it shows up on a search engine site, such as Yahoo!, the more sales orders you're likely to receive. And the less time it takes you to accomplish all of that, the better. (Chapter 1 contains lots of information about how to make your site well-organized and appealing.)

A few points to remember about selling online and HTML:

- **Page titles make a big difference.** When your site shows up on a search engine, the engine priorities matches according to the page titles. Make sure the main name of your product or some crucial descriptive words appear in the title.

- **Add metatags.** If you don't already know what a metatag is, I'm pleased to tell you that they are special HTML tags that invisibly store information within your file. Metatags also help your page show up better in Web searches. Spend an extra five minutes to add descriptive keywords in some metatags for each file.

  When you fill in your metatags, it may be tempting to put in the same keyword a lot of times, like 100 times or so, to give your pages even more chances to show up in a search engine. *Don't do it.* The search engines are aware of this trick, and they throw out pages that use the same keyword an unreasonable number of times.

- **Keywords, words that succinctly describe and categorize your product or service, should appear frequently in the actual text customers see on your site.** It's only natural — of course your text talks about your products and services, right? Be sure to use some of the same keywords you used in the title and the metatags, because search engines frequently estimate "goodness" of a search string match using frequency of word occurrences within an HTML file (that is, on a Web page).

Why use templates instead of starting from scratch?

A template can remind you about your metatags and make it so, so easy to fill them in. An HTML template (such the one you find in this chapter and on the CD that comes with this book) contains a lot of niceties for you, so you don't have to remember to include things, like company logos, each time you start a new file.

A template provides a place to paste in new text, so that every page on your site looks similar from the outset. For more information about templates, please see the section called "Looking at a Sample HTML Template, " in this chapter.

The template that's included in this chapter incorporates all of these elements (and more) for you. It helps you make sure you're taking advantage of all these ways your site's HTML files can help you reach more potential customers (especially through the search engines) and sell to them once they arrive. Figure 8-1 shows the template included on the CD before you paste any text or graphics into it.

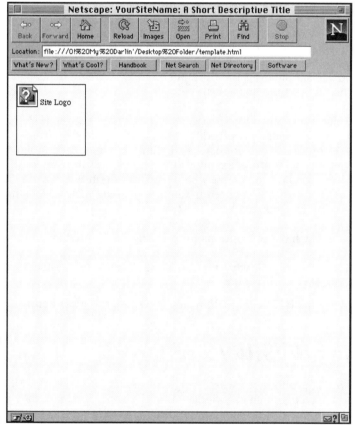

Figure 8-1:
The unadorned template.

Every page is a possible entryway to your site. Don't assume that people will come in at the page you consider the top (usually your `index.html` file). Give every page some navigation buttons, especially one that points to the top of the Web site. Navigation buttons provide helpful assistance to anyone trying to find their way around your site.

Help your potential customers quickly gain context about your site and your products by putting a little contextual information on each page that gives them a sense of "You Are Here." Navigation links within the text may read something like this: "For more information about prices, please visit our newest Pricing Sheet" (where the words "Pricing Sheet" are a link).

Choosing the Right Tools

A good HTML editor can make your life a lot easier. Lots of tools are available now that automatically turn the text you type into HTML. Other tools let you use simple drag-and-drop positioning to create pleasing Web page designs that include images and text.

Some electronic storefront software comes with a built-in HTML editor and won't work with just any ol' editor. Other electronic storefront software lets you use any editor you choose to create your pages, then molds them together into your store. Examine any electronic storefront software package you're considering to see what HTML editors it works with. (Electronic storefront software is covered in Chapter 6, along with various products that work with HTML editors.)

You basically have two options for creating the HTML files for your site:

- Use a WYSIWYG (what you see is what you get) HTML editor, which is easiest
- Write the HTML yourself, which gives you the most control

Using WYSIWYG editors

WYSIWYG (pronounced whizzy-wig) editors let you create HTML files without needing much knowledge of HTML basics. Instead, they provide visual cues about how your page looks in a Web browser (leading to the term What You See Is What You Get).

Particularly for a beginner, placing text and graphics with these tools is much simpler than hand-coding. The drawback of these products is that they control many aspects of the page's appearance for you. They usually produce Web pages that look alike, so it could be hard to create a different look for each area of your site with these tools.

Lots of electronic storefront products come with WYSIWYG editors. (Electronic storefront products are described in Chapter 6.)

WYSIWYG editors provide a great way to get started, but you probably want to go beyond what these auto-generated pages have to offer fairly quickly.

Writing your own HTML

If you use a text editor or a specialized HTML editor (non-WYSIWYG) to create HTML files for your selling site, you can use any text-editing program you like, and any type of operating system: UNIX, PC, Windows, or Macintosh.

Many UNIX programmers use the standard UNIX editing programs, such as Emacs, to develop HTML code. The other "native" UNIX alternative is a text-editing program called FrameMaker, which offers a feature for generating HTML files automatically from your text files.

If you know HTML fairly well, Microsoft Word also makes reasonable choice for HTML development, especially for the PC/Windows platform. Other good tools specifically designed for HTML editing on Windows and Mac platforms include HotDog, HotMetal, and HTMLed Pro.

Putting your HTML to the test

HTML is really only plain text with some special codes in it that tell the computer things like, "Make this text boldface." For every boldface command, another command has to be inserted that says, "Stop making this text boldface."

Because writing HTML can be a repetitive task, mistakes are common. In fact, one of the most common mistakes is leaving out a command that tells the computer to stop putting the displayed text into boldface; thus the rest of the file shows up, unintentionally, in boldface.

You can save yourself a lot of time searching for HTML errors by routinely checking your HTML files before you post the files on your site. Lots of HTML editors, such as BBEdit and HotMetal Pro, let you check your HTML with a mouse click, sort of like a "spell checker" for HTML. If all else fails, just load the file into your browser — any HTML mistakes usually become painfully clear at that point.

Microsoft Word is a fine text and HTML editor for the Mac, too, and it has the advantage that Word files are relatively compatible across Mac and Windows versions of Word. However, to make creating HTML on the Macintosh a lot less work, I recommend BBEdit 4.0, because it has a practically indispensable feature that automatically checks your HTML code for you.

For the Mac, BBEdit 4.0 or better has a "Check HTML" button. When you click that button, BBEdit counts how many errors your file has and shows them to you, one by one. When your file has no more errors, you get a nice smiley face as a reward. That smiley face can be addicting! Other text-editing programs (such as FrameMaker for UNIX and Word for Windows) are adding HTML-checking functionality, too.

The Macintosh has great development tools such as BBEdit for HTML, Photoshop for images, and many other Web design tools available, and graphic artists often prefer to use Macs. If you have a choice of platform, you may want to consider using the Mac as your site's content development platform, even if you are using another platform as your site's primary Web server. (You always move the files onto your Web server anyway for viewing by customers on the Web.)

What are the most popular tools for creating your online store? Among the market's most popular Web page editors, most products are compatible with the Windows platform. Table 8-1 shows you a list of products you can find at your local computer superstore.

Table 8-1	Popular HTML Editors
Product Name	*Made By*
HotDog	Sausage
Navigator Gold	Netscape
HoTMetaL Pro	SoftQuad
Internet Assistant	Microsoft
BBEdit	Bare Bones Software (Windows version coming)
PageMill	Adobe
FrontPage	Microsoft
HTML Assistant	Brooklyn North Software Works
Web.Designer	Corel

Setting a Standard for Your HTML

You want to keep your HTML development time to a minimum, so you have more time to spend on developing your products and advertising your site.

To help keep your development time and costs in line, write down a few site HTML standards to make sure that you remember them as you develop your pages. If you have more than one person working on your HTML, make copies of these standards and pass them around.

I find the following standards especially helpful while working on HTML:

- ✔ Put all your HTML tags in ALL CAPS. That way, they're easy to spot within the rest of the text.

- ✔ Make sure each file has a header telling what version of HTML it conforms to. It's amazing how long some of those files stay around, and as the HTML standard develops, some of your old files will start to look strange in the browser window. They'll need to be updated occasionally. Also, some browsers don't handle some versions of HTML as well as others, so that header that tells what version of HTML was used to create this file can help you save time in diagnosing errors.

- ✔ Make sure each file has at least one metatag that includes a brief description of what the file is supposed to contain, who last edited it, and the last date it was edited. (See "Good Ol' HTML: Gateway to the Search Engines" for more information on metatags.)

- ✔ Name all the files for your Web site in lowercase letters without spaces or special characters. Many FTP programs automatically convert filenames to lowercase, which means the names would be changed if you upload them to your server using FTP (which is common practice, especially if your site is hosted or co-located). In that case, the file named MyHomePage.html would end up with the same filename as myhomepage.html. This change could cause lots of problems, because browsers are case sensitive when it comes to reading images and links.

When you have a standard for your HTML files, making major changes to your site becomes a lot easier. Think you won't be making any major changes once you get it all set up? Guess again. After you get started, you can always be able to find new ways to make your site more attractive and more appealing to your customers.

Assigning HTML tasks piece by piece

If you have more than one person working on the HTML for your selling site, assign responsibility for each line of the HTML to some person or department. That way, everyone knows what to edit, and what not to change.

For example, the following organization worked quite well for the team that constructed the template you find on the CD that comes with this book:

✔ HTML authors create the body text and links that fill up the BODY section of the template. That's the "meat" of the Web page your customers will see.

✔ Editorial staff fill in the metatags.

✔ Design staff create the overall appearance of documents that uses this template, and for the appearance of any graphics, such as logos or image files that are linked to from within the text.

✔ Technical staff write the CGI scripts that put the headers, footers, and advertisements on each Web page.

See how one little template can call a whole company into action? Of course, if you are a small business, you may be doing most or all of these things yourself. Still, it's useful to visualize all the different hats you wear, so it's easier to separate them as your business grows.

Don't forget that if several people are editing the same file, you need some way to "check out" the file so that changes aren't lost if two people edit the file at the same time. One way to accomplish a checkout procedure is by using a good old-fashioned routing slip. If only the person with the routing slip can edit the file, changes will be made sequentially. Fancier technical solutions are available as well, but a routing slip can get you up and running fast.

Looking at a Sample HTML Template

If you use a template to create your documents (which means just paste your text into the template and you're done!) you can spend a lot less time wondering why your HTML doesn't work right, and a lot more time refining your sales pitch.

Using this template (or one a lot like it), you can easily set up a consistent look and feel across your site. Your site's unique look and feel is important. It gives your customers a sense of corporate identity and personality that embellishes your products and services — in short, it is part of your brand.

Simplifying with the template

You can ignore or delete anything in this template you don't need, or you can substitute a simpler element.

Simplifying the SSI in the template

If your store doesn't need to generate the (header and footer) navigation and advertisement portions of your site "on the fly," you can substitute simpler HTML links for these SSI parts of the template, which run CGI scripts on your server.

To simplify the ad portion, put in some basic HTML links to image files that contain your sponsors' Web banners instead of the SSI given in the template, which calls an ad script. (An ad script lets you set up a situation where ads appear on each Web page dynamically, according to a rotation system.) What's the difference? The same Web banner ad appears on your page every time it is served, instead of a variety of ads. That may mean you have to update your pages by hand more often to change the ad links.

To simplify the navigation portion, you can create some GIF images that look like buttons, such as "Previous Page," "Next Page," "Back to Home Page," and so on. Then you can easily make those buttons into working links using basic HTML. (And, of course, if you use ALT text properly in your image links, as any good HTML book can tell you, you end up with text-based buttons even if the image files can't be found for some reason. Nice.)

Not all Web server software includes capabilities for running server-side SSI. (Server software is covered Chapter 5, including information about which servers can handle SSI.) SSI files have to (generally) be specially named: the extension must be .shtml, not just .html. Also, SSI sometimes requires special handling by the Web server administrator to get everything working together correctly. The good thing about SSI is that it gives you a lot of ability to customize your site's pages. For example, if you decide you want to use SSI scripts to set up an ad rotation, or to let the navigation bar on each page work as a map to show your customers dynamically where they are on your site at any given time, you may want to hire some professional help. This template shows how you'd plug in those dynamic elements to get them working on your pages.

Simplifying the table in the template

The table I use to display the site logo is not necessary. Some Web designers prefer to use tables for these sorts of elements because they can exercise finer control over the placement of the elements on the page. I include the table to show you how to use one — it's a solution you may use if you can't get the logo to show up precisely where you intended.

You could eliminate the table elements altogether and come up with pretty much the same results, as long as you don't care where the logo appears — you may think, "I'll be happy as long as it's at the top." In that case, cut the table and substitute a link to the image file (probably a GIF) that contains your company logo.

Good titles, good metatags, and good use of keywords within your page's text can help you generate more sales by making sure your site shows up in Web searches. A template such as this one helps you remember these important aspects of your HTML by showing you good places to insert your keywords.

Filling out the template

In this section I show you a sample HTML template and explain each part of the template in detail. You can decide what pieces of the template (if any) your site needs, and simplify accordingly if your site is simple. Because this template is on the CD that comes with this book, you can just copy and paste the parts you'd like to use:

```
<!DOCTYPE HTML PUBLIC "-//W3C//DTD HTML 3.2//EN">
<HTML>
<HEAD>
<TITLE>YourSiteName: A Short Descriptive Title</TITLE>
<META NAME="description" CONTENT="a sentence about this page
          or site that contains less than 200 chars.">
<META NAME="keywords" CONTENT=" YourSiteName, yoursitename,
          and keywords that add up to less than 200 chars">
</HEAD>

<BODY BGCOLOR="#FFFFCC" LINK="#0000FF" VLINK="#663399"
          TEXT="#000000">
<BASEFONT SIZE="3">

<!-- here the dynamic header for each page is inserted with
          SSI-->
<!-#include virtual="/scripts/header.html"-->

<P>

<TABLE CELLPADDING="2" CELLSPACING="2" BORDER="0">
<TR>
<TD VALIGN="top">

<!-- go get the GIF file for the site logo and put it here-->
<IMG SRC="/images/logo.gif" ALT="Site Logo" WIDTH="100"
          HEIGHT="100" BORDER="0"><BR>
</TD>
```

```
<TD ALIGN="right">
<!-- ad script called here to rotate an ad onto each page
         using SSI, basic rotation -->
<!--#exec cmd="/web/ads large basic border=0"-->
<BR></TD>

</TR></TABLE>
<!-- Finally, you can put your main body of text here -->
<!-- Here is the footer, dynamically inserted on the page
         with SSI. -->
<!--#include virtual="/scripts/footer.html"-->

</BODY>
</HTML>
```

 For those who don't know much HTML and who are really in a hurry, here's a short cut: Copy this template from the accompanying CD, type in your site's name in the title tag, put in the pathname to a file containing your company's logo instead of /images/logo.gif, fill in the blanks under description and keywords, paste in your sales text, and you're up and running. You won't have any headers, footers, or advertisements, but you can add those later.

 If you want your site to show up well in Web searches, don't use frames. Web search engines don't like frames; that's why this template doesn't use them. Wait to use frames until your site is already well-known. Also, Web search engines don't like pages with a lot of graphics, so try to keep graphics minimal on most pages of your site. Graphics look nice, but like anything else, you can create too much of a good thing.

You may be wondering what all that HTML code does. Relax and read on. It looks complicated at first, but each piece is simple when you break it down.

The first line

The first line in the file reads

```
<!DOCTYPE HTML PUBLIC "-//W3C//DTD HTML 3.2//EN">
```

This line is just a declaration that this is an HTML document that conforms to the HTML 3.2 standard. The customer doesn't see this part — it's for your use when maintaining your Web site.

The title definition

The next three lines are just HTML for defining your site's title:

```
<HTML>
<HEAD>
<TITLE>YourSiteName: A Short Descriptive Title</TITLE>
```

It's a good idea to keep your site's title to two or three words. Also, if you sell used cars online, remember that the title "Welcome to my store" isn't as effective a title as "Great Used Cars."

Give each page of your site a title that's dynamic and related to your company's product or service. Titles are an important element that Web search engines look for when performing a search.

The metatags

The next lines are metatags that give some additional information about the document for anyone working on the site or anyone searching the site by keyword:

```
<META NAME="description" CONTENT="a sentence describing this
            page or site that contains less than 200 chars.">
<META NAME="keywords" CONTENT="YourSiteName, yoursitename,
            and other keywords that add up to less than 200
            chars">
</HEAD>
```

The metatags are followed by the standard HTML tag that closes the HEAD section of this HTML file.

Remember that the customers won't see the metatags when they browse your site. Metatags are for your use and for the benefit of the search engines which crawl the Web looking for new sites to classify.

The body tag

Within the HTML body tag, you use BGCOLOR to set specific colors in which the text is displayed on the screen, including the colors of the link text:

```
<BODY BGCOLOR="#FFFFCC" LINK="#0000FF" VLINK="#663399"
            TEXT="#000000">
```

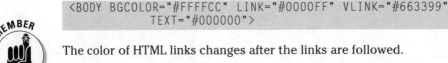

The color of HTML links changes after the links are followed.

The basefont tag

You may want to set up a standard font size for screen display to insure consistency in the appearance of all your site's files.

After this basefont is set up in the following tag, you can make text larger or smaller by using increments such as SIZE="+1" or SIZE="-1". (By the way, the HTML default value for the basefont tag is 3.) Using a basefont gives additional control over displayed text size, it's more precise than using the header tags (<H1>, <H2>, and so on).

```
<BASEFONT SIZE="4">
```

Comments and a header

In the following lines, comments surround a call to a CGI script that displays a header on each page of the site. (Remember, if your Web server software doesn't support SSI, or if you don't want to use dynamic navigation headers, you can substitute a simpler header constructed of "hardwired" links to related pages. It's just a little more work to check and maintain those links whenever you update your site.)

Sometimes headers are actually advertisements, and sometimes they can be navigational aids for the customer. You can use the header space in whatever way best suits your site's needs.

```
<!-- here the dynamic header for each page is inserted with
        SSI-->
<!--#include virtual="header.html"-->
```

A table for the logo

The paragraph break is followed by lines that set up a table. The table displays the company logo along side an advertisement. You don't have to use a table to display your logo, it just gives you a little better ability to place the logo precisely where you want it on your Web page. If you don't need that much precision, you can get rid of this table and put in a link to the image file that contains your company logo (or another image you want to display prominently on your page).

Your logo says a lot about your company or your product. If you don't already have a logo, look into designing one.

```
<P>
<TABLE CELLPADDING="2" CELLSPACING="2" BORDER="0">
<TR>
```

The following lines build a table cell containing the site's logo:

```
<TD VALIGN="top">
<!-- logo begins -->
<IMG SRC="/images/logo.gif" ALT="Site Logo" WIDTH="100"
         HEIGHT="100" BORDER="0"><BR>
<!-- logo ends -->
</TD>
```

The advertisement

The following HTML aligns an ad GIF within a table cell created for it in the previous lines.

Notice that ads are placed within this cell by an ad script, which is a dynamic element within an otherwise static HTML page. The ad script is called by a #exec command, which is a Server Side Include (SSI) command.

In the following example, the script calls an ad from the "basic" ad rotation for the site:

```
<TD ALIGN="right">
<!-- ad script called here to rotate an ad onto each page,
         basic rotation -->
<!--#exec cmd="/web/ads large basic border=0"-->
<BR></TD>
```

If you got rid of the table in the last part, you can still put in an ad rotation. Delete the other lines and keep just the line that says

```
<!--#exec cmd="/web/ads large basic border=0"-->
```

If you don't want to use an ad script at all (or if your Web server software doesn't support SSI), you can just create a link to the file that contains the banner ad you want to display on this page of your site. Then when you want to change the ad on this page, you'll have to edit the file to change that link by hand.

You can use different ad rotations for different areas of your site. (For more information about ad rotations, please see Chapter 12.) Ads can be an important source of revenue for your site, so try to fill up the ad space on each page with sponsorships. (If your site doesn't have sponsors yet, you won't need to use this part of the template.)

End of the table

The following standard HTML tags close the table:

```
</TR></TABLE>
```

If you don't want the table, delete these lines.

The main body of text

After the table (or at least, at this point, if you decided not to use the table), you can insert the main body of your text, whether it's product information, promotional material, or what-have-you. (See Chapter 9 for tips about putting images on your site.) If you don't a WYSIWYG editor to create your HTML text, refer to a basic HTML book to tell you how to make the text look the way you want, with section headings, boldface, big text and small text, and all the other elements that make text more appealing. (*HTML For Dummies,* by Ed Tittel and Stephen N. James, published by IDG Books, provides great HTML hints.)

Use keywords about your product, sprinkled throughout your text body. But make sure any keywords you use actually are contained within the flow of your text, for example, as part of the product decription. Don't make the mistake some "creative" Webmasters have made of typing in loads of repetitive keywords and making the text color the same as the background color so they don't show up in the browser window.

```
<!-- Finally, you can put your main body of text here -->
```

The footer

A footer facilitates navigation through the site. Provide a method of navigation on every page of your site, because customers won't always enter your site from the home page. (Remember, customers may follow a link from another site that bypasses your site's main *index.html* file.)

Every page in your site should include at least a "Return to Home Page" link. Some sites like to put this link in the footer (that is, at the bottom of the page). others swear it should appear in the header (that is, at the top of the page). I don't mean to start any religious wars by including it as part of the footer.

```
<!-- Here is the footer, dynamically inserted on the page
        with SSI. -->
<!--#include virtual="/scripts/footer.html"-->
```

End of the template

Finally, the following tags conclude the HTML template file:

```
</BODY>
</HTML>
```

And that's all there is to it! From this template, you can use whatever parts you need to create your own template.

If every document you create for your site starts as a template, you make it easier to manage your site's files over time. Then you have more time to focus on marketing and selling your products, instead of on HTML errors.

The template gives your files consistency — in your customer's browser window, consistency of look and feel makes your company look well-organized, dynamic, and efficient.

Chapter 9

Images, Anyone?

· ·

· ·

*I*mages can help you show off your products and enhance your corporate image. This chapter shows how to create good images and use them effectively for selling online.

The possibilities for using images on your site are almost endless. With the tools available now, you can convert photographs into images for the Web and then modify them if you like. You can even convert bitmaps and video frames into animations for your site. Or why not go all out and make a movie for your customers? Or even a whole new reality? I tell you what you need to know about each of these possibilities.

Using Images Effectively on Your Site

One picture is worth a thousand words. This old chestnut is no more true anywhere than on the Web. It just plain makes sense to use images, sounds, or whatever techniques you need to give your customers a good impression of your products and services online, where they can't see or touch them. Images increase the chances of a sell.

Although pictures appeal more to customers than text, many customers still have relatively slow Internet connections. To accommodate these slower connections, create several alternative ways to describe the products you show at your site. For example, don't eliminate all descriptive text and pictures when you add a link to an animation or a movie, because some customers have equipment that's too slow to appreciate movies on the Web.

Scanner or Digital Camera?

You can acquire images of your products for your Web site in two ways:

- ✔ Using a digital camera
- ✔ Taking pictures with a regular camera and then scanning the pictures to create your images

Which produces better results? Which is least expensive? Either option can produce excellent results for you. I discuss the pros and cons of each option in the following sections.

Old reliables: Scanners

Until recently, a scanner was definitely the way to go for small and medium-sized sites (and for many large sites, as well) because of the prohibitive cost of digital cameras (which I discuss in the following section).

It may take a while to get used to scanning — to select an acceptable resolution that doesn't take too much disk space, to calibrate your scanner to your screen colors, to figure out how to save scanned files in appropriate formats, and so on. However, after a little practice, you should be able to quickly scan a photograph and use it online. You may want to consider purchasing a bigger hard disk to hold the images (but the same is true for images from a digital camera — they can also be large files).

If you have an old computer sitting around doing nothing, consider putting it to use as a scanning workhorse. I use a Macintosh IIci that I happen to have sitting around, set up with an older program called Ofoto, to scan my images — it's my dedicated "scanning station." I find that it improves my productivity to keep scanning separate, because I can work on something else while the scanner merrily chugs away. Also, it keeps more disk space free on my main computer (scans usually make big files).

To scan images at high resolution, I recommend a *flatbed scanner*, which resembles a photocopier — you can lay the original document on the glass face (or *bed*) of the machine. However, several types of scanners exist: sheetfed scanners, hand-held scanners, photo scanners, and others.

Besides the scanner hardware, all scanners require software that performs the scan and saves the images to your hard disk (this software is usually bundled with the scanner when you purchase it). Some of these scanners include *optical character recognition* (OCR) software, which actually reads text from the pages as you scan them and turns the image into text that you can edit in a word processor. (Traditionally, OCR has not been terribly accurate; however, it's getting better.)

You may find that the following scanner products fit into your budget:

- **Apple:** For Macintosh computers, the Color OneScanner has at least two models available, priced from about $600 to about $900. The Color OneScanner offers great quality and includes OCR software.

- **UMAX:** For Mac or Intel platforms, UMAX offers several scanner models, available from about $250 to about $1,400. UMAX scanners have a reputation for reliability in their price range.

- **Hewlett-Packard:** The company offers three or more ScanJet models ranging from about $400 to about $900. HP makes great quality scanners.

- Other great vendors with a range of scanner products and prices are Epson, Agfa, LinoColor, Nikon, and Microtek.

The scanning software that comes with the scanner is almost as important as the scanner itself. If you shop around, you can get a great deal — many manufacturers offer scanner and scanner software bundled together with other software. Some scanners even include image processing software that let you enhance and adjust the quality of the images you scan.

In contrast, you can find several lower-resolution, light-duty *sheetfed scanners* to help with scanning business cards or for filling up a database more quickly from paper-based customer information. (A sheetfed scanner can be especially convenient if your database is built from the information available on business cards, right?) These scanners also require software, which usually comes bundled with the scanner itself. Like their flatbed cousins, some of these scanners include optical character recognition (OCR) software, which reads your pages as you scan them and turns them into editable text (sometimes with questionable accuracy).

You can find the following light-duty flatbed scanners currently in stores — check them out if you consider purchasing a scanner:

- **Visioneer PaperPort:** With PaperPort software (I love the name) and OCR, you can pick up this scanner for about $300.

- **Mitsubishi MCA Color Document Scanner:** With OCR, this scanner lists for about $300.

- **HP ScanJet 4S scanner (grayscale only):** With PaperPort software and OCR, the ScanJet 4S runs about $200.

Of course, you need to remember copyright laws when you find yourself with this much scanning power. You may be tempted to scan images for your Web site from magazines, or from other sources that someone else holds the copyright to. Ummm — that's copyright infringement. (For more information about copyrights, please see Chapter 17.)

Cool stuff: Digital cameras

Some Web designers I know swear by the digital camera because it can get images onto a Web site so quickly. Take a picture of a new product, and five minutes later, you can place the image on your Web site to advertise a special.

Until recently, digital cameras have been notoriously expensive. A digital camera used to cost as much as $30,000 or more, and a so-called mid-range digital camera could cost between $3,000 and $7,000. With the price of digital cameras coming down, this option looks better all the time — several rather modestly priced cameras are now available.

Well-known manufacturers such as Sony, Konica, Nikon, Fuji, Canon, Olympus, Agfa, and Kodak all make digital cameras now in the $300 to $700 price range. Features vary a lot from camera to camera; some shoot and store a lot of low-resolution images, while some top-end models (such as the Kodak Digital Science DC120) can shoot very high-resolution images, up to 1280 x 960 dpi (but only a few at a time).

You can expect to store up to 48 images in low resolution from one of these cameras, and about 24 images in normal resolution (same as a standard 24-exposure roll of film). If you shoot high-resolution images, the camera may store only about ten images. However, some models contain extra memory *(flash memory)* for storing images, so you can shoot more pictures before you need to download some to your computer's hard disk. (The flash memory is often found on PCMCIA cards that can be read directly into a laptop or a desktop Smart Card reader.)

Some cameras (like the Sony Digital Mavica MVC-FD7) can store images directly to a floppy disk as "film" in JPEG format, which is great for convenience and portability.

Some other feature you can expect to find in digital cameras include the following:

- ✔ Many cameras download images to your computer over a serial port.
- ✔ Many come with bundled digital image processing software.

✔ Some digital cameras can connect directly to your TV so you can view your images.

✔ Some have a built-in LCD display, which lets you see your images right away and take new ones on the spot if you aren't pleased.

Think about the following factors before you decide to buy a digital camera:

✔ Digital photographs often contain color *artifacts,* which require a bit of image processing to lessen or remove. (Artifacts are things that appear in your images that weren't there in the real picture, such unusual color effects caused by translating the picture into digital dots.)

✔ Most photographs taken with digital cameras tend to be slightly more "soft" (blurry) than photos taken with a regular 35mm camera, because of optical filtering in the camera that's intended to reduce color artifacts.

✔ Photographs taken with digital cameras often have stubborn *jaggies,* which are jagged edges along which the pixels are clearly visible. (The more technical term for jaggies is *aliasing.*)

You can make up for these shortcomings of digital photos with the judicious use of a digital image processing program, such as Photoshop, but it does require some time (and budget). However, it may be that the time saved by being able to download the pictures directly from the camera onto your hard disk makes your processing time worthwhile. Also, over time you could save some money by avoiding the processing costs for normal film.

Slightly more-expensive digital camera models sometimes include a small LCD screen that lets you see your images instantly. This feature helps eliminate some of the glitches in digital photographs, such as color artifacts. (You can sometimes avoid artifacts by a slight refocus or change of angle.)

Before you work on one of your digital images, make a copy and work on the copy. That way, if you make a mistake during the processing, you won't have to take time to go back to the camera and download the image all over again.

Processing Your Digital Images

Digital image processing is such an integral part of designing Web pages that no self-respecting Web site can get along without at least one image processing product.

Adobe Photoshop

Most people who do desktop publishing have at least heard of Photoshop. It's been around for years and is pretty much the undisputed leader. It's not cheap, because it may well be the premiere product in its field. Due to the expense involved, many vendors create add-ons, generally known as Photoshop filters, to help sell the program.

Photoshop (about $895) runs on Macintosh and Windows platforms. For more information, see www.adobe.com.

A less expensive option than Adobe Photoshop is Adobe PhotoDeluxe. It sells for about $99, and it offers the basics of digital image processing for photographic effects.

Photoshop filters

Photoshop filters enable your basic Photoshop program to achieve effects that are otherwise next to impossible (if not impossible). For truly professional results, try adding some of these currently popular offerings to your software menagerie:

✔ **Andromeda Series 4 Techtures 1.0:** By Andromeda Software, Techtures retails for about $120. You can use the product to create interesting textures, blending created textures with your original image.

✔ **ColorSync 2.1.1 Plug-ins:** ColorSync technology maintains true colors as you switch your images among media. For example, your Web site may become so successful that you decide to capture a lot of it in a book. You want to maintain the original vibrancy of the screen color in print media, which is more difficult than it sounds. Photoshop already converts those screen colors that your output device (such as a color printer) can't reproduce into their nearest printable equivalent — but that sometimes isn't too close. ColorSync Plug-ins scales the color of the original image into the printable repertoire of the output device. (You can download ColorSync for free at colorsync.apple.com.)

✔ **EyeCandy 3.0:** By Alien Skin, EyeCandy retails for about $200. It was the first tool that easily let you create drop shadows and embossing effects that take a lot of work in Photoshop.

✔ **Extensis Phototools 1.0:** By Extensis, Phototools retails for about $100. The program offers a solid set of filters for setting text and creating drop shadows, bevels, glows, and so forth. The interface makes this program easy to use, too.

- **Kai's Power Tools 3.0:** By MetaTools, Kai's Power Tools retails for about $200. These tools have become so popular among Web designers that the trade magazines often just refer to them with a nod as *KPT.* KPT let you manipulate images in unusual ways, sometimes creating fantastic effects and sequences.

- **Kai's Power Tools Convolver 1.0:** For about $200, you can purchase this tool to add sharpening, color-balance, and contrast effects.

- **Paint Alchemy 2:** By Xaos Tools, Paint Alchemy retails for about $100. Paint Alchemy has a "brushing engine" that lets you turn your images into anything from oil paintings to etchings. (GalleryEffects filters in Photoshop can give you similar effects, but perhaps a shade less rich.)

- **PhotoSpot CT 1.0:** This plug-in helps Photoshop handle spot-color separations better. It lets you create additional color plates to intensify certain CMYK colors (about $595).

- **ScanPrepPro 3.4:** By ImageExpress, ScanPrepPro retails for about $700. ScanPrepPro is an "autopilot" for Photoshop that creates excellent pre-press color separations before your eyes for a number of output processes. It can operate on existing images, or it can operate a scanner or a digital camera for you.

- **Terrazzo 2:** By Xaos Tools, Terrazzo retails for about $200. Reportedly the easiest way to create seamless images for things like Web page backgrounds.

Processing tools for Windows 95 and NT

Looking for digital image processing tools especially for Windows 95/NT? Try these products, which include nice features like built-in GIF animators and automated wizards for creating beveled buttons and rules:

- **Fractal Design Painter 5.0** ($449; `www.fractal.com`): Great painting filters. (This one is available for Mac as well as Windows.)

- **Ulead PhotoImpact 3.01 with Web Extensions** ($139; `www.ulead.com`): Great tools for creating GIF and JPEG images for the Web.

- **Corel PHOTO-PAINT 7** ($495; `www.corel.com`): Chosen by *Internet World* magazine as best all-around editor, August 1997.

- **Micrografx Picture Publisher 7** ($99; `www.micrografx.com`): A bargain with great special effects.

Making Your Graphics Web-Compatible

Web graphics are an important part of your site's content because they offer your customers some visual interest. Your graphics are the place to display your products, you company's logo, and whatever else seems helpful in creating an appealing and identifiable shopping environment for your customers. They help create the unique presence of your online store.

Before you can use graphics, photographs, and other images on your Web site, you must save them in one of the formats I tell you about in this section.

Save line drawings in GIF format and photographic-quality images in JPEG format, wherever possible.

CompuServe GIF format

GIF is probably the most popular Web graphics format. Some people even refer to any Web graphic as *a gif*. (The widespread use of the GIF format has created some legal controversy. CompuServe and Unisys disagree over who has the right to license GIF. As a result, some Web sites are looking for alternatives to GIF for their Web graphics.)

Creating GIF files for your Web site is easy, because almost every commercially available illustration tool currently supports GIF format. Just create a drawing in almost any drawing tool, such as Illustrator or CorelDRAW. Then choose Save As and select the GIF option. The software saves your picture automatically in GIF format, ready to go up on your Web site.

PNG format

The World Wide Web Consortium (W3C) format, called Portable Network Graphic (or PNG, pronounced "ping"), offers an alternative to the controversial but popular GIF format.

PNG is royalty-free and, like GIF, it is compact. Unfortunately, PNG doesn't support animation at this writing; however, rumor has it that animation may be added in the future.

PNG allows some nice improvements over GIF format. Table 10-1 shows a point-by-point comparison of GIF and PNG.

Table 10-1	Comparing GIF and PNG Graphics Formats
GIF	**PNG**
8 bits per pixel	Up to 48 bits per pixel
256 colors	16 million colors
Two levels of transparency (zero or 100%)	254 levels of transparency in an image (effective shadows and shades)
Little or no error checking	Complex checking to see if image is corrupted
May look different on different platforms	Looks the same on any computer that's been color-calibrated
One type of compression	Different types of compression, whatever produces the smallest file size
Animation	No animation

For creating PNG files, Photoshop 4.0 handles GIF and PNG, and older versions of Photoshop can save in PNG format with the help of some plug-ins. Also, Paint Shop Pro (available at www.jasc.com) is an excellent shareware program that supports both formats.

The PNG format isn't supported yet in some Web browsers, and many customers who visit your online store still use older versions of browsers anyway. (Wait a while before relying totally on PNG for your site's images.) Microsoft Internet Explorer 4.0 supports PNG images. For older versions of MSIE or for Netscape Navigator, you need a plug-in. Try the NGLive plug-in from Siegel and Gale, at www.siegelgale.com/png for Windows 95. For the Mac, try Sam Bushell's PNG plug-in at iagu.on.net/jsam/png-plugin.

JPEG

JPEG (which stands for Joint Photographics Expert Group) is another popular format for creating Web graphics. JPEG is popular because it *compresses* the images and thereby makes them a lot smaller to download, smaller than most GIF files.

You should use JPEG to put photographic-quality images on your site. JPEG makes your enormous photo-quality images more manageable for the average browser.

Ordinary JPEG images appear in the browser from the top down, so you don't "get the picture" until you download the whole JPEG. A relatively new format called Progressive JPEGs makes a low-resolution image form as soon as the page starts to download; the image gets, well, progressively clearer as more of the JPEG image loads. Progressive JPEG is supported by all the major browsers. (Netscape Navigator has supported it since the 2.0 version, and Internet Explorer supported it starting with the 3.0 version.) For a demonstration of Progressive JPEG, visit www.in-touch.com/pjpeg2.html.

Using the Safe Palette for Your Images

The Mac and Windows operating systems each have a *system palette,* which is the default set of colors that a computer can ordinarily display. The system palettes on the Mac and Windows platforms each contain 256 colors, but the individual colors in the two system palettes are not quite the same. The *safe palette* contains only those colors that are the same in both the Macintosh and Windows system palettes, which is 216 colors.

Without the safe palette, Web pages designed on a Windows platform usually look bad on the Macintosh platform, and vice versa. When you use the screen display colors in the safe palette, your Web pages maintain their quality across Windows and Macintosh operating systems and in different Web browsers.

To see a safe palette, you can check out Lynda Weinman's wonderful and informative Web site at www.lynda.com/hex.html.

Selecting colors from the safe palette is easy, once you know a little trick. First, you need to know that all screen colors are designated by 6-digit hexadecimal numbers, 000000 to FFFFFF inclusive. Those numbers give Red, Green, and Blue (RGB) values for each unique color you can see on your screen. How so? The leftmost two numbers, taken together, specify the amount of Red, the middle two numbers together specify the amount of Blue, and the rightmost two numbers specify the amount of Green. This designation system lets you represent any screen color.

In the safe palette colors, the numbers representing Red, Green, and Blue must be multiples of three. Clear as mud? As an example, 000033 would be a pure, safe blue color, but 000044 would not. The color 336699 would be safe, but 224466 would not. Also, 363636 would not be a safe color, because the two digits in the columns that represent Red, Green, and Blue must be the same.

Test your graphics on several browsers to see what they look like. Even using the safe palette, variations can be noticeable. Among the browsers you should test are Netscape Navigator 2.0, 3.0, 4.0, Microsoft Internet Explorer 2.1, 3.0, and an AOL browser. For more information about testing on different platforms and browsers, please see Chapter 10.

Creating Web Animations

Web animations can add significant visual appeal to your site. (Pick up a copy of *Web Animation For Dummies,* by Renée LeWinter and Cynthia Baron, published by IDG Books Worldwide, Inc., for basic info on web animation.) A well-planned, well-placed animation makes the viewer's screen come alive. For example, I personally like the shooting stars in the Netscape Navigator browser; they let me know that the system is at least trying to reach the site I select. And somehow it makes Netscape feel "alive" to me. It breathes.

On the other hand, gratuitous animations create a sense of visual clutter or distraction for your customer. Lots of sites now display spinning globes, blinking cursors, and other animations that rapidly become annoying. Remember when the Macintosh made multiple fonts easily available within a document? Say no more.

For some animations, bandwidth can become an issue. Each frame of a Web animation must be downloaded to the viewer's machine. If the files are large, lots of visitors will leave your site instead of waiting to see your darling animation on display.

As a general rule, viewers dislike waiting for a file larger than 75K to download, especially as an animation or animated banner advertisement. Many Web wizards recommend keeping files far below that size, as small as 35K.

A majority of Web site developers currently rely on GIF format for their Web animations. GIF animations technically are known as GIF89a, but who's counting? Nearly all the animations on the Web use this format, which was released by CompuServe, yes, in 1989. GIF89a offers several advantages:

- ✔ GIF animations are small, which means they download faster than some other formats and help keep your customers at your site instead of clicking somewhere else in frustration.

- ✔ Most programs used to create GIF animations are freeware or shareware, which keeps your budget low.

- ✔ GIF animations are no more difficult to use in an HTML file than a regular, nonanimated GIF file.

A popular software tool for developing GIF89a animations on the Windows platform is GIF Construction Set, created by Alchemy Mindworks (www.mindworkshop.com). The GIF Construction Set was released in 1995, and some people say it has been used for up to 80 percent of the GIF animations on the Web. If you try GIF Construction Set and you like it, the cost of the shareware is $20.

An alternative to Alchemy Mindworks' GIF Construction Set is the Microsoft GIF Animator, although at this writing it is available only for Windows 95. GIF Animator is available free from the Microsoft Web site (www.microsoft.com/imagecomposer/gifanimator/gifanin.htm).

Microsoft says that GIF Animator will eventually become part of FrontPage, a Microsoft Web page building tool that is available either in Windows or Mac format for $149.

For building animated GIF files on the Mac, GIFBuilder freeware, created by Yves Piguet, is a good choice (iawww.epfl.ch). Released in January of 1996, GIFBuilder offers sophisticated features such as wipes and fades, and the files it produces are readable by any browser that has features similar to Netscape 2.0 and higher. Overall, GIFBuilder offers much more than its Windows freeware equivalents, true to the Macintosh tradition of excellence in desktop publishing.

For Macintosh and Windows platforms, Adobe Photoshop contains a built-in tool called GifBuilder that is good for creating animations.

Conceptually, you follow these steps to create a GIF animation:

1. **Draw or otherwise create an image for each frame of your animation.**

   These frames create a sequence of poses that "add up" to a recognizable action. For example, they can be cartoon drawings or photographic-style images of a person waving hello.

   If there's only one portion of a picture you animate, such as blinking eyes, you can cut out that portion and animate only it (to make your downloads as fast as possible). You can use a table to reassemble your picture with the animated portion in the right spot.

2. **Compress each frame of the animation individually, as necessary.**

   Keep the total size below 40K.

3. **Use your animation-building tool (such as one suggested earlier in this section) to establish the sequence and duration of each frame, and of the entire loop.**

4. **Post files appropriately on your site.**

5. **Put the links to your new graphics files into your other site files.**

6. **Admire your work.**

Keep it simple! Remember that line art downloads a lot faster than fancy graphics, and it's still a 28.8 world out there, at least for the moment.

Extra, Extra: Movies and Music

This section talks about some options available for creating more sophisticated visual and audio presentations on your site. It includes discussion of technologies like QuickTime (for the Macintosh), VRML, QuickTimeVR (which is VRML for the Macintosh), and music data formats such as MIDI files. This section gives a basic description of video and audio streaming technology.

QuickTime movies

QuickTime movies are popping up everywhere on the Web. Besides QuickTime, which is a Macintosh-based movie format, two other movie formats popular on the Web are AVI (Video for Windows) and MPEG.

The task of creating movie files from video can be exhausting. However, after you have the movie file ready, it's easy to link to it just like any other file on your site, using a tag something like this:

```
<A HREF="movie.mov">Click here to see our product in
          action!<A>
```

When including a movie on your Web page, it's a good idea to include a thumbnail, some text showing how big the movie file is, and even include a link to a viewer.

Music

You can embed music files in your Web page just as you would embed any other file (such as a GIF file containing a graphic). Just use a link to a file that contains your music.

Most music files on the Web are MIDI files. MIDI stands for Musical Instrument Digital Interface. A MIDI file is a data file that stores musical notes as digital information, so that the music is playable by computers equipped with MIDI sound cards, such as the Sound Blaster card by Creative Labs. The HTML command to embed a MIDI file looks something like this:

```
<EMBED SRC="my_midi_file.mid" HIDDEN=TRUE>
```

To make a MIDI file play automatically (on browsers like Netscape 3.0 and others equipped with the proper plug-in), you can take advantage of the `<EMBED>` tag, like this:

```
<EMBED SRC="my_midi_file.mid" HIDDEN=TRUE AUTOSTART=TRUE>
```

For more information and other options, check out the Netscape LiveAudio Syntax page.

Video and audio streaming

Video and audio streaming are a bit of a twist on the usual ways to get your images and sounds onto your customer's browser screen over the Web. Here's the difference in a nutshell:

- Normally, a video or audio file must be downloaded completely to the local computer (that is, to your customer's computer hard disk) before it can be viewed or played. That's why you see so much advice telling you to keep your image and sound files small. That advice is especially good for files in JPEG, GIF, AIFF, and WAV formats. (The average customer won't wait longer than it takes for a 75K file to download before clicking away in disgust.)

- Streamed audio and video start right away and download the rest of themselves in the background, while you already see or hear the beginning.

What a great idea. Someday your grandchildren may ask you, how did streamed video and audio get started, grandma? Here's what to tell them: Well, Johnny, the first major departure from the "usual" way of getting files in front of a customer (all at once, that is) came with *interleaved GIFs*. An interleaved GIF downloads the picture a little bit at a time, so the customer starts seeing something right away. The GIF image is downloaded "in passes," so the effect is as if a blurry picture is coming into focus. It's a lot more satisfying than a regular GIF when you use a 14.4 modem, believe me. Yes, Johnny, they had modems that slow back then. (Software tools are available that help you create interleaved GIF files.)

Programs such as Macromedia's Shockwave went a step further by delivering animations and sound using streams. That means a Shockwave animation starts playing as soon as the first part arrives at a customer's machine, and the rest of the animation keeps downloading in the background while the first part is playing. Any sounds that go with the animation arrive in the same manner.

Then some products became available to create streamed video, which is yet more complicated than streamed animations. Think of playing a movie within a Web browser — there's a lot that has to happen behind the scenes. The video player has to know how to keep the video and audio tracks in synch, for example, by dropping out video frames when it can't keep up, rather than by skipping parts of the music. And, of course, the huge video/audio files are stored on disk in a compressed format, so they have to be decompressed as they stream. Just as an example, over a 56K modem (which you know seldom really operates at 56K, right?) a reasonable benchmark to achieve would be 15 frames per second (movies run at 30 FPS) in a 320 x 240 pixel display window (not exactly Cinemascope). Once this minimum sort of "acceptability" standard had been achieved, Discovery Channel, CNN, and Hollywood Online started to make use of video/audio streaming technology.

By the way, Microsoft bought a company called VXtreme that had developed the technology to stream HTML and Java applets along with video, and they bought ten percent of another company called Progressive Networks that created products called RealAudio and RealVideo. Using some other related technologies along with these, they created their Active Streaming Format (ASF). So Johnny, that's why we can watch movies on our computers today. You know, when I was a kid, they used to have these crazy things called televisions. . . .

Virtual Reality on Your Site

Would you like to have a product catalog on your site that lets your customers pick up your products and look at them from all sides, see a panoramic view from the balcony of your hotel, or take a ride on the roller coaster at your amusement park? Or would you rather have the same old boring brochures and product catalogues with flat photographs you always had, just translated onto the Web?

VRML basics

VRML stands for Virtual Reality Modeling Language. With VRML, you can build 3-D environments, called "worlds" that are limited only by your own imagination and ability. VRML acts as an intermediate, descriptive language that communicates with your browser so you can build chat rooms, games, 3-D animations, or whatever suits your fancy. For example, you can program visual fly-by sequences, or you can make sound files and video clips that play whenever a user takes a specific action within a game. Or perhaps customers can "try out" a product configuration on line with VRML before they buy it.

VRML was created in 1994 by Tony Parisi and Mark Pesce. Since then, big companies such as Netscape and Microsoft have become interested, and several small companies have formed to make products based on VRML. SGI has a VRML browser for Mac and Windows. Netscape and Microsoft are reportedly building support for VRML into their browsers, which will do a lot for the popularity of VRML in the next few years. Up until now, you had to download a 6MB plug-in before you could view a VRML banner ad. (Just to name one, WorldView 2.0, created by Intervista Software, is a Netscape Navigator plug-in for VRML 2.0, also licensed to Microsoft for integration into MSIE.)

The VRML 2.0 specification has gained the nickname "Moving Worlds," because for the first time VRML lets you program animation into your worlds by controlling cameras and objects that move. Previously, a user had to click on an object to make it move. And VRML 2.0 includes a Java API and JavaScript support. Before the VRML 2.0 standard was achieved, there were versions of VRML from Microsoft, SGI, and Sony, among others. Now that the specification is stable, VRML will be able to move into broader use. ISO is adopting VRML as a standard, too.

VRML is about interactivity. A customer can come to your site and see a physical simulation of your product, see a 3-D visualization of your data, have a teleconference, or take a class in a 3-D "classroom" online. I decided to include the information here because, to me, it fits best among all the different ways you can use images to help your site and your products make a big impression on your customers, with one caveat: Not many Web browsers among the general Internet population currently have VRML plug-ins or enough memory to support VRML, so right now it's mostly good for "special effects." Wait a year or two before you think about building your whole online store using VRML.

VRML trivia

It's been reported that VRML coinventor Tony Parisi prefers the spelled-out pronunciation "V-R-M-L" over the sometimes-heard "ver-mal" pronunciation. "Verm" is German for "worm." Not a great association for a great technology.

VRML for the Mac

VRML development has been behind for the Macintosh platform until recently, even though some of the technology for VRML began at Apple. Only a few VRML development packages currently exist for the Macintosh. Here are a few possibilities:

- ✔ **Virtus 3D Website Builder** (`www.virtus.com`): This software lets you place and modify premade VRML objects, using drag-and-drop.

- ✔ **FreedomVR** (`www.honeylocust.com/vr`): This freeware lets you create photographic VR worlds from your own photos (but no fancy cameras or photo stitching), using a Java applet. Can be seen by anyone with a Java-capable browser with no VRML plug-in required.

- ✔ **Virtual Home Space Builder** (`cosmo.sgi.com/products/homespace/vhsb/`): Good, but it doesn't support spheres and curves.

- ✔ **Infini-D** (`www.specular.com/products/infini-d/infini-d.html`): Some reported problems with export capabilities.

Try these VRML browsers for the Macintosh:

- ✔ WorldView 2.0, by Intervista (`www.intervista.com`)
- ✔ Netscape's Live3D Plug-in (`home.netscape.com/eng/live3d`)

General VRML resources

These sites offer VRML information, specifications, and tips for users of VRML on all platforms:

- ✔ The VRML Consortium (`www.vrml.org`)
- ✔ VRML Newsgroup (`comp.lang.vrml.newsgroup`)

QuickTimeVR

If you do your site's content development on a Mac, you may be interested in QuickTimeVR (QTVR). It can create stunning 360-degree panoramas and interactive movies. To make a panorama, you take photographs with as precise a rotation as possible (that is, use a tripod), digitize the photos, "stitch" the digitized photos together into a 360-degree image, edit the image, create any links you need to other scenes as "hotspots" in your panorama, compress, and finally, convert the scene into a playback file.

You could also create "synthetic" photographic panoramas using 3-D graphics tools that offer a Save as QTVR option. The good news is that these synthetic images won't need to be stitched. Another type of movie you can make is an "object movie," which is a view of an object from all angles — again, stitched together from photographs of the object.

If you need inexpensive solutions, you can convert your images into a regular QuickTime movie; then drag and drop your movie onto Apple's free Make QTVR Object tool. That's the only tool you need to make object movies. You end up with a movie that lets your customers manipulate the objects.

Just like regular QuickTime movies, QuickTimeVR movie files use the filename extension .MOV and can be added to HTML files using the `<EMBED>` tag. To view your QTVR movies, customers will need the following:

- The QuickTime plug-in
- Either QuickTime 2.5 or QuickTime for Windows (available on Apple's QuickTime site at `qtvr.quicktime.apple.com`).

QuickTimeVR movies can be played back on the Mac 68040, PowerPC, or on Windows 3.1 and Windows 95 computers.

Video compression basics

Like any other kind of image or sound on the Web, video data must be compressed to make it downloadable in real time to a browser window. Two popular video compression formats are available: MPEG and Cinepak.

MPEG

MPEG, which stands for Moving Picture Experts Group, is an industry-standard video compression format for video files. The MPEG group meets and establishes the standards as part of the ISO (International Standards Organization) worldwide. Many corporations worldwide work together to create the MPEG standard. Only one of MPEG's uses is on computers, many are in the broadcast industry. MPEG is not a platform-dependent format, so MPEG files can be read on any computer system with the proper viewer.

If you use video files on your site, you definitely want to use some type of compression, and MPEG is a great choice. Because MPEG compression is so sophisticated, MPEG files are much smaller than any other video files while maintaining the same quality. When creating files in MPEG format (which is not simple), it's a good idea to keep the screen size of your movie small so that playback will be smoother. Files stored in MPEG format have the filename extension .MPG.

MPEG trivia

Did you know that MPEG is a nickname? The official name of MPEG is ISO/IEC JTC1 SC29 WG11 (International Standards Organization/International Electro-technical Commission, Joint Technical Committee 1, SubCommittee 29, Work Group 11, moving pictures with audio). I think that beats supercalifragilistic-expialidocious. No wonder they wanted a nickname! For lots more trivial and not so trivial information about MPEG, try looking at `www.crs4.it/~luigi/MPEG/mpeggeneral-1.html`.

What tools compress video into MPEG? Software tools called *MPEG encoders* are available now, although for years MPEG had to be encoded by hardware boards that cost around $10,000. MPEG decoders (that is, players) are also available, because MPEG is such a good format for use on the Web. Hardware MPEG decoders are still used in products such as TV set-top boxes.

For UNIX systems, free MPEG encoders are available at Stanford (`havefun.stanford.edu/pub/mpeg` or `ftp.arc.umn.edu/pub/GVL`) and Berkeley (`mm-ftp.cs.berkeley.edu`). It's quite a complicated process to create an MPEG movie. There's a document on the Web at `www.arc.umn.edu/GVL/Software/mpeg.html` that tells how to create an MPEG movie for UNIX systems.

If you make or acquire an MPEG movie for your site, it's also a good idea to put a link to a site with an MPEG viewer available for download, or even to post the viewer on your own site for convenience. Here are some sites that have free MPEG viewers:

On the Macintosh, MPEG videos are played using a utility called Sparkle, which is available at `ftp://ftp.ncsa.uiuc.edu/Mac/Mosaic/Helpers/sparkle-245-hqx`.

For Win32 machines, there's a utility posted at the same location called MpegPlay. Also, the Microsoft ActiveMovie player is an MPEG player.

Many companies make MPEG-related products, this section is designed just to give you a feel for what MPEG is and how to investigate it further.

Cinepak

Many computing and gaming platforms can play Cinepak movies. For example, Apple, Microsoft, Atari, Sega, and Time Warner all are Cinepak technology licensees.

Cinepak movies can be created using digital video streams from popular personal computer add-on boards such as the Truevision Targa 2000 and miro's DC-20 (high end), or even the VideoSpigot series of boards (low end). The original video for a Cinepak movie can be shot with a Betacam, Hi-8 or S-VHS camera (and should be for best quality at the end). Cinepak takes a lot of video editing, even frame-by-frame editing in Photoshop sometimes, to eliminate noise and artifacts caused by digitization, and thereby to create good quality movies.

The process of making Cinepak movies, however tedious, seems more straightforward than making MPEG movies, because the video doesn't have to be split into separate Y, U, and V stream files as when making MPEG movies (whatever those are!). However, the overall quality of the Cinepak images will be a significant step down from broadcast-quality MPEG.

Information about Cinepak is available at www.squeezebox.com.

Chapter 10

Testing Times Three

A successful testing process for your store's content will win friends and influence people. Not only does testing help you fix broken links, correct typos, and double-check your facts, it helps you get information about the *usability* of your site. Usability is what makes your site comfortable for your customers and profitable for your business.

Testing with Multiple Browsers and Platforms

The first rule of testing any site for use on the Web is to test it with as many Web browsers as you can. As you know, your site looks different depending on what type of browser your customers use. By testing your site on as many different browsers as possible, you increase the chances of catching every flaw that your various customers may see.

Some older versions of Web browsers may not be easy to obtain from their company's Web sites. Because vendors want to encourage users to upgrade, they don't keep older versions around for downloading. If you can't find the browsers I mention in this section on the Web, don't despair. Here are some options for getting copies of older browsers for putting together a "testing suite" (that's a fancy name that quality assurance (QA) engineers call groups of software like this, used for testing):

✔ Ask your friends and associates which browsers they use. You'd be surprised what old browsers they have lying around.

✔ Run a "send us your browser" promotion on your site. That way, you could get copies of the browsers that your customers actually use. However, stipulate that you only want copies of browsers that are distributed as freeware.

TIP

Keep these browsers around to test your site's appearance and functionality. Lots, and I mean LOTS, of people still use these older versions:

✔ **NCSA Mosaic** (hoohoo.ncsa.edu): It's the great-grandma of all Web browsers, and some people still use it.

✔ **Netscape Navigator 1.0** (www.netscape.com): Versions of Netscape Navigator older than 2.0 don't support frames, some kinds of tables, or plug-ins such as Shockwave. To play well on these browsers, you want to make sure your ALT text for images files and your text navigation links are working.

✔ **Netscape Navigator 2.0** (www.netscape.com): Netscape Navigator 2.0 is the first browser to support frames and tables. It's a good solid browser that lots of Web surfers still use, so it's an important one to test.

✔ **Netscape Navigator 3.0 and above** (www.netscape.com): These browsers support some specializations of HTML that may not be compatible with other browsers, such as Microsoft Internet Explorer.

✔ **Microsoft Internet Explorer 3.0 and above** (www.microsoft.com): Like the Netscape browser, MSIE 3.0 and above supports specializations that may not be common to all browsers. For example, the Java version supported by MSIE is a little different than standard Java.

✔ **AOL Browser 2.7** (www.aol.com): Tends to be slow, but reliable. Still in use on some older machines that can't run AOL Browser 3.0.

✔ **AOL Browser 3.0** (www.aol.com): Larger to load than the AOL 2.7 browser. I've had trouble loading and running it sometimes on some PowerMacs, for no obvious reason. Otherwise, it seems reliable, if slow. Too big to run well or at all on older machines with small amounts of RAM.

✔ **WebTV** (www.webtv.com): WebTV has some interesting requirements because of the lower resolution of TV screens. Test to ensure that you can read your font sizes on a TV screen, for one thing. That means making them larger, because the TV screen has less resolution than a computer screen, in general. (WebTV is a product, a "black box" that plugs into your TV set. There's no browser to download. If you're serious about testing for WebTV, it means buying one of these boxes, which currently sells for about $199. See their Web site at www.webtv.com.)

Remember, Netscape Navigator 4.0 and Microsoft Internet Explorer 4.0 are on the CD that accompanies this book. Sooner or later you'll want to test those, too.

Besides testing on several different browsers, you should test on different operating system platforms to find out crucial information about your site's performance. If you have access to Windows NT, UNIX, and Macintosh platforms, test on all three and compare the performance times for different operations, such as following a certain set of links. That way, you have an idea what parts of your site may present problems (or just appear slow) for users of different operating systems. (Another scary example, sometimes your Web server can fail in such a way that users of one kind of operating system can't get access, while others have no trouble at all. It's rare, but it could happen. In that case, you're likely to need a Webmaster to help you figure things out.)

Using the safe color palette helps your images look more similar on all browsers. You can read more about the safe color palette in Chapter 9.

Planning Your Test-O-Rama

Commercial software goes through rigorous, well-defined testing before it's released for public use. In contrast, testing for Web sites tends to be pretty informal and haphazard.

But this doesn't have to be the case. A Web site development plan should include a written plan for testing your site's HTML content, as well as your CGI scripts (which actually are computer programs and should be tested as such).

For every test, keep a record of who performed the test and the date it was performed. If someone reviewed the test results, keep a note of who did it. That way, if questions arise later about exactly what failed and what worked, you can talk to the person who was "eyewitness" to the test. Keep a file of comments about what worked well and what needs work before the next update. Remember that the more errors you find and fix, the fewer errors your customers find for you.

Remember, your files should be available on their server already. The Web browsers that you want to test (mentioned in the preceding section) should be loaded, too. Most sites keep these browsers loaded all the time for testing, adding new ones as they become available.

Testing your links

When you test your site, click through every page and follow every link. Clicking every link actually accomplishes two things for you:

- ✔ You verify that your links work the way you want them to work.

- ✔ Your trial run shows you how a customer may use your site. By using the site yourself, you may get ideas about how to make the site smoother, faster, and easier for your customers to use.

If you rename a file when updating, that small change could affect a lot of links. Be sure to test every link that could possibly have been affected by the change, including the following:

- ✔ Any pages with links that pointed to the old page

- ✔ Any pages with links that should point to the new page

- ✔ Any pages that the old page pointed to (are they lost in Cyberspace with nothing pointing to them?)

- ✔ Any pages that the new page should point to

Get used to thinking in terms of what points to what else on your site, because you can't just think one-dimensionally when you're running an online store.

You need to retest your links when you move files around on your site, even if nothing on the page itself changed. Why? Many of the directory names may change, especially if you specify filenames by including all the names of the directories and subdirectories within which the files are stored. (These filenames are called *full pathnames* because they trace the name of the file by recounting a path, starting from the top level of the file system and following the directory tree all the way down to the name of the file itself. Not that you actually need to know that.)

Testing your forms

Enter normal data in every field of your Web page forms. Then enter bad data in every field and see what happens. For example, try putting letters in a field where you know numbers should go. Make sure something reasonable happens in every case — if the resulting error crashes your browser, or worse, your desktop computer, you have a problem that needs to be fixed. Get help if you need it.

Have someone who hasn't seen the forms before use them and give you some feedback about them. Is it clear what data is desired in each field? Be sure to actually try submitting the form, because scripts often fail at that point if some data is missing. (*HTML For Dummies,* by Ed Tittel and Stephen N. James, published by IDG Books Worldwide, Inc., offers great tips on creating winning forms.)

Checking your files

Proofread and fact-check all files before you upload them. You may be amazed at what inaccuracies can sneak in at the last minute.

Using a style guide to help prepare your HTML pages should put you in good shape in this area (see the following section for more information on using a style guide). Also, you can look at simple design factors, including the following:

- ✔ **Text:** Does the text show up well against the background? Many pages on the Web are hard to read because they use too much color.

- ✔ **Links:** Does the color of the links that have been followed stand out against the background? Is that color easily distinguishable from the color of the rest of the text on the page?

- ✔ **Balance of text and images:** Are your images well-placed and balanced with your text on the page? Are the images clear, not distorted or dithered? (*Dithering* occurs when the computer has to choose between two nonoptimal colors because the graphic asks for an intermediate color that the computer screen can't display. Dithering distorts the lines and shading of the picture.)

- ✔ **Font:** Are the fonts readable? Too large? Too small?

Keeping the design of your display pages simple and calm makes them easier to test. (Also, your pages become more intuitive for your customers to use.)

Bringing in the Style Police

Every site needs at least one editor. The editor is responsible for "policing the style" of your site, which means setting and maintaining the tone and character of what appears on the site.

Going to the Web for info

You can find tons of resources for designing better Web pages online. The Internet Directory portion of this book has a section that lists Web resources with tutorials, tips, and tricks for creating better Web pages.

When you (or your editor) use a well-defined procedure to police style issues, your site and your customers aren't plagued by bad links, typos, and other distractions when they arrive to purchase your products and services — and new information gets onto the site in a timely manner.

When you put your business online, you're a publisher. Just like in any other publishing company, everything you put on your site needs to be copy-edited and fact-checked. Just because you can put things up onto the Internet quickly, don't let yourself get sloppy! Everything on your site reflects on you, your product, and your company. Create a good production plan, one that's as simple as you can make it *but no simpler,* and stick to it. Don't worry — I tell you everything you need to know to get started.

A style guide is a set of guidelines that tells people how to prepare content for your site, helping you to maintain your overall corporate image and business objectives. (If you're working on the site all by yourself, the style guide helps you remember your style decisions.)

Create your style guide early and stick to it. Forget the idea of going back and bringing things up to a standard "later," because you will never find enough time to fix it later if there's not enough time to do it right in the first place. For example, finding every occurrence of the words "email," "electronic mail," "Email," and so forth throughout your site and changing them all to "e-mail" can cause headaches, if not nightmares. At best, it's a time-consuming and thankless task. Better to let all your writers know in advance that the preferred usage and spelling is "e-mail."

A style guide usually uses a well-known published style guide as its basis. Then you can customize the rules, and add new ones, to fit the needs of your site.

Besides preferred words and usages, which fall into the general category of "editorial standards" for your site, your style guide should include guidelines about the following areas that pertain to creating professional display content for your store:

- ✔ Conventions that you use for HTML, including filenaming conventions and conventions about what to put into metatags.

- ✔ Locations of standard HTML page templates or other standards that you use for page layouts, page lengths, or default window sizes. If your site uses templates, include an explanation of each part of the template and how it should be used. (An online style guide can accomplish this excellently using links.)

- ✔ Guidelines for use of images, video, and sound, including maximum permissible file sizes for your site.

- ✔ Sitewide navigation standards, such as where to find navbar files, whether to include text links as well as image-based navbars. (*Navbars* is short for *navigation bars,* which are text or images that combine a group of standard navigation links, such as forward and back, together on your Web page. That's different than the browser's navigation buttons.) Navbars can go at the top or bottom of each page, or both.

- ✔ A sitewide directory structure and naming conventions, including instructions about what types of files belong in which directories.

- ✔ Policies at your site for allowing linking to your site and to other sites, and conventions for creating crosslinks within your site. For example, would you require full pathnames for links to other files on your site or just the unique parts?

- ✔ Guidelines for proper use of your company's logo, fonts, exact corporate colors (and online equivalents), and other trademarks. (Sometimes people call these items *corporate image guidelines.*)

- ✔ Legal guidelines about where and how to use copyright notices, legal disclaimers, and so on.

- ✔ Guidelines for reviewing new content or any other procedures your site needs.

- ✔ Any other general guidelines you need about how to achieve overall consistency in your site's "feel." For example, you may want to include information about who originally designed each element; if you hired a freelancer to design an element, you can hire the same person again to keep the look and feel consistent.

Include as much information as possible in your style guide explaining each style decision. Doing so saves you a lot of rethinking time after the original designers have moved on.

The more the pages of your site look similar, the easier it will be for customers to identify your site no matter where they may enter it, and the more comfortable they will feel there. The consistent look and feel of your site creates a brand advantage, and it could serve as a legal advantage should anyone decide to copy your ideas illegally for their own use.

Keep your style guide online, in the development area of your server (not where the public can see it) so that it's easily available to everyone working on the project. In addition, an online style guide allows you and your designers to copy and paste preferred spellings, phrases, logos, and disclaimers, rather than retyping them.

Got a Plan? Get a Plan!

To make information easy for your customers to find, you need to promote consistency in the content of your site, both in terms of text wording and a progression of themes. A production plan can help you achieve these goals.

If you use your product's keywords consistently throughout your text, your site has a better chance of showing up in searches by Internet search engines.

Similarly, setting up a consistent progression of related themes — whether it's educational articles related to your products and services, or a series of promotions and contests — helps you generate search engine results along with continued customer interest in your site.

For example, Tripod, Inc. (a large media site located at `www.tripod.com`), always has a six-month projection of what will appear on the site and who will be responsible for it. The site's plan can change radically, but there's always a plan in place.

Updating your site often encourages customers to return often.

Defining the production process

The production process means the process of developing a piece of content for your site from start to finish, including its associated text and nontext elements. Content for your site may include any or all of the following items:

- Articles related to your product or service
- Pages that let your customers make a purchase
- Text from chat rooms

✔ Q&A files

✔ Anything else that your customer sees online

Usually, the production process for any Web site involves an editor and a designer. The editor handles the text-related elements of a page, including the following:

✔ Creating the technical wish list and making specific requests for graphical elements and overall appearance

✔ Getting help from another editor for proofreading and copyediting

The designer handles the non-text-related elements of a page, including the following:

✔ Creating the visual appearance of the page

✔ Getting help from production with HTML troubleshooting as needed

Behind the scenes: Developing your site

When many people work on your site, you need an orderly way for them to use and store the files so that everyone knows where things can be found.

One good way to create an orderly process is to create a layered development directory structure that you use for content development. (Remember, content development is just a name for the process of getting the HTML pages ready to go up on your site so they can be seen on the Internet.)

The structure you use for making your content development go smoothly is different than the way you structure your site to make it well-organized and snappy when customers visit it.

I want to tell you about the production process at a hypothetical media site I call BigWebsite. On BigWebsite, a little bit like at the theater, the site is set up so there's an OnStage-site, which is the area that customers actually see. Behind OnStage-site, you find a Greenroom-site area for things about to be posted on the live site and a Rehearsal-site area for parts of the site under development.

Your business may resemble BigWebsite in many ways; for example, you may have a current product and price list on your equivalent of Greenroom-site, and a price sheet for a sale that starts tomorrow on your OnStage-site area. On your Rehearsal-site area, you may have a draft version of an announcement for a product or service you want to launch next month.

You get two advantages when you use this type of layered structure for your online business site:

✔ You have a built-in backup in case any files from your main site are lost, damaged, or deleted, because a previous version (perhaps lacking only a few details) will remain in your "offstage" areas. For example, your "Greenroom" will have a version very similar to the one your customers are actually seeing on your site.

✔ You have a better chance of catching last-minute errors because you get to see your new material "complete," before it's posted for the world to see.

Adopt a layered structure that suits your site's needs. Depending on how big your site is, how many people you have working on the files, and how much disk space you have, you may want to have only two areas. Unless you already have a large Web-site staff, it's fine to start with two areas, such as a Live-site and a "Greenroom"-site, and add an additional area if you need it.

With two areas, for example, you can duplicate all the files from your OnStage area on your Greenroom area, and then add updates from there, in the Greenroom. Then move the updated Greenroom files back onto your main site when you're ready. You can always expand your site's directory structure to include a (third) Rehearsal-site area when your customer base, your staff, and your resources grow!

Looking at a sample production process

If you have a small site, you may be able to streamline this process a bit. For example, at your company, the writing, editorial, design, and production staff may be the same person. But you may want to think of those three jobs as separate, for later when your business grows.

About 14 days before you go online

Approximately 14 days before a new piece is scheduled to appear on your site, you should do the following:

1. **The assigning editor receives the text in the template from the writer or topic editor. The assigning editor then**

   • Checks that there is a good URL, text, and the basic HTML for the piece. The piece should exist electronically somewhere on the Rehearsal-site at this point.

- Fills out a routing sheet, prints the text of the piece, and starts the paper routing process for editorial purposes. (Proofreading and copyediting usually are done on paper.)

- Sends the URL to the designer (or assigning designer) to start the design process for any graphical elements needed.

2. **The copy editor gets a paper version of the piece with a routing sheet on top so everyone knows who has seen it and who else will see it. The copy editor then**

- Checks for good links, completed META tags, completed TITLE tags.

- Reviews the piece, deep or shallow as needed. Notes any spelling or grammar errors. Proofreads, possibly checks facts.

- Returns the copy on paper to the assigning editor.

3. **Upon return from the copy editor, the assigning editor does the following:**

- Approves changes as appropriate, delivers paper routing packet to production.

- Sends a second heads-up to design saying that the copy is done for the piece. (The design could be done already if only simple artwork is required.) If it's a templated piece, there may be no design involved.

- Pastes the copy into the template and makes sure the anchors are good.

About 7 days before going online

Here's what should be happening about 7 days before a new piece is scheduled to appear on your site: Testing! (You also need to finish the design, if needed.) Testing is especially needed if technical staff's help is involved in creating the piece. Special technical needs, such as database lookups, should be incorporated and treated as fully functional at this point. Errors should be reported as bugs.

The piece should be viewed and clicked using different browsers and different versions of browsers, using different operating systems, using AOL, and so forth. (See "Testing with Multiple Browsers and Platforms" in this chapter for a list of the browsers you should test your site on.)

The day before going online

Follow these steps one day before your site's scheduled debut on your site:

1. Move the piece from Rehearsal-site to Greenroom-site.

2. Production receives the final piece if changes have been made by the copy editor. Hopefully production has it complete already by this time.

3. Production staff performs a few final tests of HTML, graphics, text, and links, and any other technical stuff that needs to be looked into.

Launch day

At last the day has arrived. Follow these steps to get the new piece onto your site smoothly:

1. Production staff moves the piece to OnStage-site around midnight (or whatever normal update time you set for your site).

2. Alert production or technical staff to move any other required files, such as CGI or Perl scripts, to OnStage-site at the same time they move the HTML for the piece onto OnStage-site so things will work as planned.

Chapter 11

Interactivity 101

• •

In This Chapter

▶ Defining interactivity

▶ Looking at uses for animation

▶ Getting familiar with plug-ins

▶ Using chat to get in touch with your customers

▶ Sparking interaction with a message board

▶ Programming your site for interactivity

▶ Using other technologies to encourage interactivity

▶ Understanding push technology

• •

Creating interaction with your customers lets you get to know them better, which is very good for business. In this chapter, I suggest a few ways that you can encourage interaction at your site and get to know your customers better.

Understanding the Advantages of Interactivity

Interactivity creates a sense of connection between you and your customers. Animation, music, and video clips often add a sense of interactivity to your site, because they offer your customers more than a set of static Web pages.

In addition, interactivity makes your site seem more real. You may be familiar with interactive video games in which you feel like you're "really there" in another world as you play the game. Similarly, creating an interactive element for your site draws your customers into your store and makes them feel more at home.

Interactivity also encourages a sense of loyalty about your site (and hopefully about your products). As you respond to their input, your customers begin to feel more like participants in your business, which after all they should, because you literally couldn't do it without them!

Getting Animated with Dynamic HTML and Layers

Animation can add quite a bit to your site — as long as it doesn't get in the way of your site's performance or of presenting your products and services clearly.

In addition to the sheer enjoyment and esthetic value animation can bring to your site, animation can also help you sell better by making your product descriptions more enticing. For example, if you sell seeds and garden tools, you can create an animated garden that blooms, fades, and loses its foliage. Or, if you sell your own brand of clothes, you could use animation to let customers try on clothing in your online boutique, choosing different colors and styles by dragging and dropping.

Adding animation to your site

The Web and HTML are continuously evolving, and likewise new ideas about creating animation are evolving. For example, with the upcoming HTML 4.0, both Microsoft and Netscape promise a new technology called Dynamic HTML (the Microsoft product) and Layers (the Netscape product). Both of these new technologies offer animation capabilities within HTML itself. They both work through the creation of layers that are placed and removed in the browser window. Both technologies offer this functionality without downloading any plug-ins or large files.

Microsoft and Netscape offer their own, mutually incompatible and competing HTML syntax to support layers, but their functionality is similar. A layer is like a sheet of cellophane placed over your browser window. You can use HTML to draw elements on this cellophane layer, which can be transparent or opaque. Using scripting, you can even move the layer around. These movable layers are called positionable layers, which are supported by the Worldwide Web Consortium's (W3C) draft syntax for positioning HTML via cascading style sheets (a win for Microsoft, whose dynamic HTML is based on style sheets). Netscape's simpler <LAYER> tag builds on existing standards by taking HTML scripts and making them dynamic.

It pays to investigate new Web technologies as they come along, but keep in mind that simpler technology and simpler appearance often proves effective when selling online. You know who your customers are and what technology they feel comfortable using. For example, if you sell software to other software developers online, they may have all the latest gizmos and gadgets. If you sell widgets to mom and pop with a 2400 baud modem, they may appreciate a simpler interface.

Not everyone using the Web has a fast modem or even a color monitor. To create a site that can be visited by as many customers as possible, you may have to forego some fancy design elements. Or at least offer visitors a text-only alternative, if you can't resist fanciness.

Exploring dynamic HTML on the Web

For additional information on adding animation to your site with Dynamic HTML and layers, visit the following Web sites (you need the 4.0 versions of Netscape Navigator or Microsoft Internet Explorer to see the demos at these sites):

- ✔ Overview of Dynamic HTML by Microsoft: `www.microsoft.com/ workshop/prog/aplatfrm/dynhtml.htm`

- ✔ Overview of Netscape Layers: `developer.netscape.com/library/ documentation/communicator/layers`

- ✔ W3C Cascading Style Sheets, Level 1 syntax: `www.w3.org/pub/WWW/TR/ REC-CSS1`

- ✔ W3C Positioning HTML Elements Syntax for layers: `www.w3.org/pub/ WWW/TR/WD-positioning`

Another variation of HTML, called XML, is fast gaining interest within the online business community. It promises to offer modular capabilities for setting up electronic commerce at your store. For more information about XML, contact CommerceNet at `www.commerce.net`.

Playing with Plug-Ins

Plug-ins are extensions to a browser's software that give the browser special capabilities. For example, if you want your customers to hear music while they shop your site, you can offer a plug-in at your site that ensures they have the technology to hear the music. (Or you can offer a link to another site where they can download the plug-in, with permission from that site.) Plug-ins let you create a pleasing environment for shopping, which may encourage your customers to stay longer and buy more at your site.

Your customers need to download each plug-in before they use it the first time, which can take a while. Afterwards, they have the plug-in every time they load the browser.

Plug-ins allow for great flexibility and variety in what a browser can do. They have their good points and their bad points, however:

✔ Many customers don't want to take the time to download a plug-in, even if it's free.

✔ Many machines do not have enough memory to run a browser with several plug-ins. For example, at home I used a Macintosh Quadra 840AV with 16MB of memory for several years. Finally, my system began to crash when I tried to run the Shockwave plug-in with Netscape 2.0. The crashes tended to happen especially when I had just used another application, such as Microsoft Word 6.0. The machine just ran out of memory. Eventually, I bought a Power Mac to alleviate the problem, but you can bet that your customers won't go out and buy a new machine just to view your plug-ins. The moral of this story: Keep plug-ins to a minimum.

In the following tables, I list a few (among the hundreds) of the free browser plug-ins that you may want to try. I include only those plug-ins that work on at least Mac and Windows platforms and Netscape and MSIE browsers. I consider these "market-strength" products because they reach the greatest number of potential viewers.

Table 11-1	Multimedia Plug-Ins	
Plug-In	*URL*	*Why You Want It*
Macromedia Shockwave	www.macromedia.com	Many sites include Shockwave animations these days, using them as splash screens to introduce the site or as animation files to describe a product.
Macromedia Flash	www.macromedia.com	Great for seeing tiny animations, like buttons and logos.
RealNetworks RealPlayer	www.realaudio.com	Plays video and audio in synch and fast. Works on UNIX, too.

Plug-In	URL	Why You Want It
Apple QuickTime	`www.quicktime.apple.com`	The de facto standard in real-time video (looks like TV) on the Internet.
VDOnet VDoLive	`www.vdo.net`	Multicast and broadcast audio and video over a dial-up or LAN connection.

Look@Me, produced by Farallon (`www.farallon.com`), is a great communications plug-in. You can use it to view another user's desktop over the Internet in real time, including documents, spreadsheets, business presentations, and what-have-you. Use Look@Me for meeting online with your potential customers or with far-flung contractors and employees.

Table 11-2	Virtual Reality (VR) Plug-Ins	
Plug-In	**URL**	**Why You Want It**
Apple QuickTimeVR	`www.quicktime.apple.com`	Photorealistic views in 360-degrees. Over 5,000 Web sites offer QTVR scenes; you may want to join them if your product suits QTVR.
OmniView PhotoBubble Viewer	`www.omniview.com`	Panoramic video in proprietary format.

When you prepare your Web site, remember to plan for your plug-ins. Sometimes that availability of the appropriate plug-ins affect how you develop a page or an image.

Table 11-3	File Reader Plug-Ins	
Plug-In	**URL**	**Why You Want It**
Adobe Acrobat Reader	`www.adobe.com/acrobat`	Reads Portable Data Format (PDF) files. Converts almost any color or black and white document to PDF format, zoom.

(continued)

Table 11-3 *(continued)*

Plug-In	URL	Why You Want It
Tumbleweed Software Envoy	`www.tumbleweed.com`	Embedded hyperlinks (for viewing multiple pages easily) and a great zoom feature.

These plug-ins let customers read documents you create, but they can't edit them easily. File reader plug-ins are great for simple documents like downloadable product documentation.

Table 11-4	Windows-Only Plug-Ins	
Plug-In	URL	Why You Want It
Big Bits Software PhoneFree	`www.phonefree.com`	Phone conversations over your computer — talk to your customers using the Internet.
OnLive!Traveler	`www.onlive.com`	Create chat room fun for customers.
Visdyn Software Jutvision	`www.visdyn.com`	Virtual realities can be viewed with this one, which is great for game products.
Microsoft Power-Point Animation Player	`www.microsoft.com/mspowerpoint`	Reuse those old marketing PowerPoint presentations on the Web.
Visual Components Formula One/Net	`www.visualcomp.com`	Put Excel documents on the Web, which could help you put up price sheets quickly.
Netscape Media Player	`www.netscape.com/comprod/mirror/media/downloadmplayer.html`	Provides audio streaming, which plays great music or gives demo talks online.
Microsoft NetShow	`www.microsoft.com/netshow`	Audio and video using ActiveX lets your Web pages and products come alive.
Intervista Software WorldView	`www.intervista.com`	Virtual reality in your customer's browser window.

Net.Medic is a Web management plug-in for your browser (Navigator or MSIE) that helps you diagnose your Windows 95 and NT servers. You can get Net.Medic for about $50 from VitalSigns (www.vitalsigns.com). Use your browser with this plug-in to connect to your own server to see how well your server handles visitor load. As you connect to a server, say one of your own, Net.Medic indicates the health of the server (in terms of load, at least) on an icon with red, yellow, and green. It can compare your current connection to your past connection performance, and it tells you the speed with which you retrieve information.

If you run a media site, or any other site that posts updates frequently, on a Mac, try Lari Software's Electrifier plug-in. (For Netscape and MSIE running on Power Mac System 7.5 or better.) This plug-in lets you display large graphic files and animations with very small file sizes. Pick up at www.electrifier.com.

Let's Chat

A recent report by Jupiter Communications, a New York-based market research company, projects that 30 percent of the people online will utilize chat for social reasons by the year 2002. I recommend chat for your business because a lot of your customers have heard of chat and like to use it. Chat is becoming a great asset in terms of improving customer service and promoting cross-sell opportunities. Chat also builds up a customer's sense of loyalty and connection with your site. (Turn to Chapter 14 for more information on how Chat can improve your site's customer service.)

Figure 11-1 shows a typical chat room, in this case a personal chat room on Tripod. I was in the chat room all by myself to get this picture for you, so it's not very interesting. If more users were in the room, you would see more people talking!

If you plan to include a chat room on your site, keep the following tips in mind:

- ✔ To get your chat sessions going and to let your customers know about them, provide instructions on how to chat, including how to log in, how to participate in chat, URLs where chat is held, and times for special chat sessions. A good way to notify people about upcoming chat is to post a note about it on the first page of your site. You can also send e-mail with the pertinent information, sort of like an invitation to a party.

- ✔ Establish a topic for a chat session ahead of time. Even with well-defined topics, chat often goes off onto various digressions based on the moods of the participants. A moderated chat, that is, a chat with a host or hostess (usually you, the proprietor), generally is preferable to unsupervised chat for this reason.

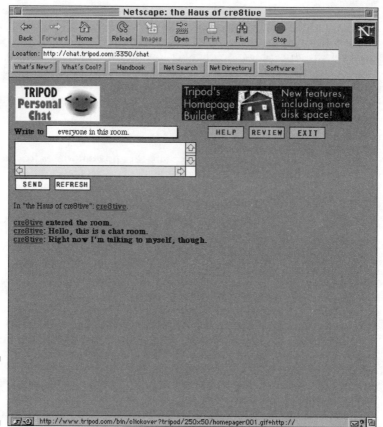

Figure 11-1.
A typical
chat room.

No matter what the site or the topic, you often get someone in your chat room who's trying to sell something or who is generally obnoxious. One of the most valuable commands to know, unfortunately, is the command for how to boot someone out of your chat space.

✔ Schedule a celebrity or an important person in your company to "meet" with your customers. Advertise the chat on your site (and elsewhere if you like). When the big day arrives, the hostess can conduct the chat as an "interview with an audience," a forum in which she interviews the guest while others watch, or an open session in which the guest handles questions from one and all. If a guest is not familiar with the Internet and chat, be sure to have the hostess at hand to help her guest throughout the event.

If you're not familiar with Internet chat, you can try it out at a popular spot called Chat Soup at www.chatsoup.com.

Using a Message Board on Your Site

A Web-based message board allows you to bring people together to discuss a topic of mutual interest. Your commercial site can benefit from message boards in the following ways:

- ✔ You can perform quick surveys about new products among your customers or run a focus group.

- ✔ You can disseminate information (maybe about a new sale) quickly to your customer base.

- ✔ You can establish interactive message boards that create a true sense of community at your site. (See Chapter 14 for information on using a message board to improve your customer service.)

Web-based message boards have two basic characteristics:

- ✔ Messages can be posted and read using a Web browser.

- ✔ All messages are stored on the Web server, so you can use them or refer to them later.

Aside from those two qualities, Web-based message boards can differ remarkably. Some have separate areas for separate topics of discussion; some require a password; some keep an archive of old messages (and some don't).

Threaded message boards

Hopefully, many people want to post to your company's message board. The number of messages can quickly pile up and become overwhelming, unless you divide and conquer.

Set up separate areas for separate *threads,* which are major discussion topics. That way, you can easily manage the message board, and the discussion will be easier for newcomers to follow.

Many freeware and shareware programs can help you set up message boards and create threads. For example, you find freeware programs at Selena Sol's site (www.extropia.com) to give your site threaded discussion capabilities.

Message board security

If you post information about your business on the message board, such as budgets or planned product announcements, or members-only discounts, you may want to require some sort of membership and password arrangement for people who have access to the message board.

Commercial software packages for building message boards let you establish a security level for your message board: You can make information public, registration-required, or private. You can read more about two such packages at WebCrossing (webx.lundeen.com) and Facilitate.com (www.facilitate.com).

Setting up a site message board on Windows

You can find Perl scripts on the Web as freeware to set up and run a message board on an NT server, but that requires some programming experience. If you want to try, you can start at Yahoo! (www.yahoo.com) and then follow the links through these subject areas in order: Computers and Internet: Internet: Programming: CGI. You arrive at a page or more of links to free CGI scripts, some of which are NT-specific.

Not-so-fluent programmers should purchase a commercial software package, such as Allaire's Cold Fusion (www.allaire.com). The program offers a handy Web-to-database product that has accessories for setting up threaded bulletin-board style discussion and chat rooms.

Setting up a site message board on UNIX

For UNIX-heads, a search through the links at Yahoo! (www.yahoo.com) yields close to a million freeware message board and chat room scripts. Almost all the scripts are aimed at UNIX servers. Many scripts can be downloaded, un-Tar'd, un-zipped, compiled, and away you go.

Setting up a site message board on a Mac

You can get a simple message board up and running in 10 or 15 minutes, all because a fellow named Lars-Olof Albertson at Lund University in Sweden wrote a Hypercard-based free CGI program called Hyperconf. Just follow these steps:

1. **Download Hyperconf from** `www.lu.se.info/Editor/`
   `HyperCgi.html`.

   The download is a single file, called Hyperconf.cgi. Put the file at the
   top level in your Web server folder.

2. **Open the Hyperconf.cgi file by double-clicking.**

3. **When you see the main Hyperconf window, select Edit List Head
   from the Hyperconf menu.**

   You see the HTML at the top of each list of messages on your message
   board.

4. **Put in the name of your message board, your e-mail address, and the
   other appropriate information by replacing some bullet characters
   (•••) you see.**

5. **Customize the footer by choosing Edit List Foot from the Hyperconf
   menu and typing in your information.**

6. **Customize the record form by choosing Edit Record Form from the
   Hyperconf menu and entering your custom information.**

7. **Start your Web browser and open the right location, something like**
   `www.yoursitename.com/Hyperconf.cgi`.

   You see an empty, customized welcome page with no messages on
   it (yet).

8. **Send a couple of messages and see how they look.**

   Check out the built-in search engine. You can look through the message
   board for any topic you want more information about.

9. **Customize the appearance of the HTML pages by adding your
   company's logo, adding some links to other parts of your site, or
   whatever strikes your fancy.**

Apple's Guestbook CGI, available at `applenet.apple.com`, also helps you
set up a message board on a Mac server.

Programming Your Site for Interactivity

I want to tell you about some general-purpose Web development technologies that can help you create interactivity for your site. Actually, some of
this stuff is pretty techie — you may have to hire a programmer for some of
these, but hey, it keeps down the unemployment rates among software
engineers. And after reading this section, you won't have to run away
screaming in fear when your hired programmer starts talking about the likes
of CGI and Java.

CGI — Not a secret government agency

CGI stands for *Common Gateway Interface.* Web site developers first used CGI to add interactivity to their sites for things like order forms and online payments.

CGI commands are commonly grouped into entities called CGI scripts. CGI scripts can be written in any of several programming languages, including most commonly C, C++, or Perl. In fact, Perl is the "traditional" language Webmasters use to create CGI scripts. (Perl is a programming language that runs on UNIX, Windows, and Mac.)

Essentially, a CGI script calls up your server's regular operating system and says, "You there, run this program for me, will ya?" Then the CGI script can run any program that your server machine could normally run.

The primary limitation of CGI is that it requires processing time from your server machine. It also consumes your Internet connection's bandwidth as the information passes between your customer's browser and your server. Limit usage of CGI to what you really need. That way, all the customers experience better server performance at your site.

Any programming language that can run on your server machine can be used as a vehicle for CGI scripts, and those programs can perform any function your machine can normally does, including writing to disk, deleting files, and so on. For example, CGI commands let you generate and process forms that your customers fill out on your site, such as registration forms. You can gather the answers they give and store them into your database. You can give feedback to your customers, too, using CGI forms, but it's not as immediate as some newer methods of interactivity, such as JavaScript. (Java and JavaScript are covered in more detail later in this chapter.)

You may not want to allow CGI scripts direct access to your system or your database, because doing so involves some security risk. You can protect your site somewhat by setting appropriate directory protections, requiring password authorization, and so on. If you worry about security, the Web offers freeware and commercial programs that let your customers enter information into a form that's then e-mailed to you. For starters, try the freeware security program at Matt's Script Archive, `www.worldwidemart.com/Scripts/formmail.shtml`.

You can find all kinds of cool CGI-related stuff, including scripts for credit card verification, logging site visits, and setting and retrieving cookies, at the following Web sites:

✔ **Matt's Script Archive** (www.worldwidemart.com/Scripts/): Although Matt's Script Archive provides pretty good documentation in the form of readme files, you may need some programming expertise to get CGI scripts like these running on your server. Some of the Perl CGI scripts you find at the site require Server Side Includes to be part of your server software's capabilities — but many do not.

✔ **Selena Sol's Public Domain CGI Script Archive and Resource Library** (www.extropia.com/): Like most freeware, the programs at Selena Sol's are aimed at UNIX platforms. However, a number of programs are being adapted to run on Windows 95/NT machines, so keep looking.

Java

Since its introduction by Sun Microsystems in 1995, Java has been hot. It's actually an object-oriented programming language, related to C++ (which is object-oriented C), so you may need to hire a programmer to take advantage of Java's capabilities, which are many. Java was designed to increase a programmer's efficiency (so that the poor programmers can keep pace with the astounding industry-wide developments in processor capability).

You may have seen Java on the Web in the form of bouncing balls and animated logos, which are cute. However, Java is powerful and well-suited to creating HTML tools and interactive areas on your site, such as chat rooms and interactive advertisements. More than just being cute, these uses for Java can actually help sell your products.

To see a big collection of applets you can download and use at your site, check out Gamelan, which is the official directory of Java, at www.gamelan.com.

Java tools for beginners

If you decide to use Java on your site, but you're not a Java programmer, take heart. Recently, some new tools have become available that make Java more accessible to non-programmers. For example, Jamba, which has been called "Java for the rest of us," is a visually-oriented Java programming environment that lets non-programmers put together simple Java applets. You can find out more about Jamba at www.jamba.com.

Another such environment is Studio J++ by Microsoft, part of Microsoft's Visual Studio suite of development products. It supports Microsoft's Java implementation, which is a little different than standard Java, so watch out for compatibility issues here. (For more information, visit the Microsoft Web site at www.microsoft.com.)

JavaScript

JavaScript resembles Java in name, but JavaScript is lighter in capabilities. For brief, simple animations or other simple tasks like site redirections, in JavaScript you don't have to use (and clients don't have to wait for) a separate Java applet.

JavaScript code can be included right in the body of your Web pages, because it just extends the capabilities of HTML. It can also speed up your site's performance if you need interactivity such as animations.

Want some good news? Netscape Navigator and Microsoft Internet Explorer browsers handle Web pages enhanced by JavaScript. For sample code, visit the Microsoft JScript page at www.microsoft.com/jscript.

Because JavaScript is part of an HTML page, loaded only into your browser, it has no access to your system outside the browser software. If you experience any security problems with JavaScript, errors in a browser extension, a plug-in, or similar problem may cause them. JavaScript doesn't write directly to your hard disk (without telling you), because no commands in HTML do that.

Other Java products

If you're psyched about Java and JavaScript development, you may want to try the following products:

- ✔ ActionLine (Interactive Media; www.imcinfo.com): Allows you to create dynamic Web pages without typing a line of Java code. (The Internet needs more tools like this to make Java more accessible.) However, due to Java compatibility problems, ActionLine runs only on Macs at present.

- ✔ Visual Café Pro (Symantec; www.symantec.com): Designed for rapid application development (RAD) of Java and databases, Café Pro includes a Java compiler, a local SQL server, a browser, a Webserver, and middleware such as Symantec dbAnywhere Workgroup Server and ODBC drivers. It also includes Sybase SQLANywhere, Navigator Gold, and Netscape FastTrack Server.

If you want to read more about the fundamentals of Java, pick up a copy of *Java For Dummies,* by Aaron Walsh, published by IDG Books Worldwide, Inc. Or surf to the JavaSoft home page at www.javasoft.com.

Pushing the Outer Limits

Clearly, the trend on the Web is toward more active use of the Web's basic capabilities. A great example of this trend is push technology, which has been hot since it cropped up in 1996. (Just recently, the ardor for push technology has seemed to cool slightly. Time may determine the right "niche" for push and other highly innovative Internet technologies.)

Push technology is a new model for obtaining information from the Web. The most common model for using the Web may be called a "pull" technology model, by contrast. That is, as people think of the Web now, a customer typically uses a browser to traverse the Web and click on items of interest. The click is essentially a request for the information to be delivered, so the customer is, in effect, pulling in items of interest through the browser interface.

Conceptually, push technology is closer to a traditional cable television or radio broadcasting model for distributing information. In push technology, a customer selects "channels" that specify an area of interest, something like tuning in the "Arts and Entertainment" channel on your cable TV. From that point on, items of interest are automatically delivered to the customer's computer through the channel. You could use push technology to get stock quotes or other time-sensitive information on a continuing basis.

Push technology can be very helpful to your business. You can get the latest information over a newswire, or you can send out good news that boosts your business, such as new product announcements, increases in earnings, and so forth, to your most interested listeners (such as the press). However, push technology can be a complicated thing. Although some server software and HTML page builders come with push technology capabilities (see Chapter 5 for more information about server software with push capabilities), you want to hire a programmer to use push technology for sending information out from your online store.

The two best-known makers of push technology products are a company called Marimba (www.marimba.com) and a company called PointCast (www.pointcast.com). As of 1997, Marimba's Castanet product was the market leader in this area. Microsoft also offers a push technology called Channel Definition Format (CDF), and Netscape's offering is called NetCaster.

Several Web-page building and HTML tools now offer push technology options for the pages you build. Among these is an editor called HotDog Pro (Version 4), which runs on Windows 95 and NT. HotDog Pro 4 supports three of the common push media standards: Microsoft's CDF, Netscape's Netcaster, and PointCast. Another plus: Like BBEdit for the Macintosh, Hot Dog Pro has a built-in HTML syntax checker for HTML versions up to 3.2. You can read more about Hot Dog Pro at `www.fourthnet.co.uk/hotdog`.

Microsoft's FrontPage 98 HTML editor also lets you create channels on your Web pages by adding a small CDF file to your HTML. It lets you add "Subscribe to this channel" as a button on your site.

Part IV
Keeping Your Web Site Strong

The 5th Wave   By Rich Tennant

SCHOOL OF ENTOMOLOGY

PEARSON BUG EXTERMINATOR

"You'd better come out here — I've got someone who wants to run a banner ad on our Web site."

In this part . . .

What good is your store if no one knows about it and your merchandise? This part shows you how to get the word out about your store — both online and offline. I also tell you about gathering statistics about your customers in order to keep them coming back, and about keeping your customers happy by giving them better customer service than they could get at an offline store.

Chapter 12

It Pays to Advertise

*T*his chapter lets you in on the best ways to get people to visit your site, including customers who buy products and sponsors who buy ad space. I look at advertising from two sides — I discuss how and where to advertise your site and how to get sponsors to purchase ad banners on your site.

You also get a quick tutorial on how to put up a Web banner on your site, if you must do it yourself. In addition, I suggest some questions you should ask before selecting an agency to develop your advertising campaign for you, should you choose to go that route.

Getting People to Your Site

Everyone who gets online wants to know how to make his or her site a success. Getting people to visit your site — and to return again and again — is really a simple thing in concept, but it's not necessarily easy to do. It takes a little work, but it can be a lot of fun.

The number one best way to create excitement about your online store is to make it a place worth visiting. That's worth repeating:

Make your site a place worth visiting.

How not to bring people to your site

At some point, you may be tempted to wire into a Usenet newsgroups to talk about your product. Posting a written advertisement for your product or service would be considered closer to spam than to a welcome suggestion. Although, if you want to advertise your online store on a Usenet group, your best bet would be to politely and intelligently answer posted questions related to your line of business, without unduly mentioning your products.

The Internet community has a characteristic way of finding outstanding sites and telling everyone about them. The popularity of those sites seems to grow like wildfire.

You can find so many ways to make your site worth visiting; the basic ingredient is well-done content, with perhaps a sprinkle of something unique and refreshing about it. (To obtain this ingredient, apply a liberal dose of your own imagination and creativity.)

Your site seems most worthwhile to your visitors if she feels she can accomplish one of these things with each visit:

- ✔ Discover something new
- ✔ Gain something
- ✔ Contribute something

After you create a great site, you can use the strategies, tips, and techniques described in this chapter to make your site easily accessible. Then you can believe your online business will be a winner. After all, as they say, word of mouth is the best (and cheapest) form of advertising.

Establishing Your Site Traffic

To sell banner ads that increase your site's revenue stream, you need to demonstrate that your site generates substantial site traffic (see "Building a Better Banner" in this chapter for more information on banners). Much like the way advertisements in newspapers and magazines are priced on the basis of circulation (number of subscribers), advertisements on Web sites are priced according to the traffic that reaches your site. (You might hear terms like *impressions* or *clickthrough* used to describe the pricing for online advertising. These terms describe the act of seeing ads online, sort of like people turning pages in a magazine or newspaper and seeing the advertisements there.) In addition, ad sponsors look for sites with a lot of site traffic, or they look to reach a specific demographic, so they know that their advertising dollars are well-spent.

To substantiate your claims about how many people could see a particular ad, you need to gather some reliable site statistics about the number of people visiting your site. The best way to build your site's credibility is through a third-party audit report. Good idea. But before you invest in such an audit, you may want to take an informal read of your site's traffic, just to see if the audit is worth the expense.

Gathering informal data

Your site may still need to grow a little before you pony up the big bucks for an external audit. Usually you can get some basic information about who's visiting your site from reading your server's log files. In this section, I tell what you need to know to get a rough idea of how much traffic your site generates.

Your Web server software creates log files for you, which constantly monitors your site and stores statistics such as the IP addresses of visitors and the pathnames of files that visitors request. That information can help you a lot when you try to measure your site's success in terms of site traffic. (Chapter 7 tells more about managing your logfiles, such as how to create new ones each day to keep your site's records straight.)

Hits

Every time your server serves a file, it records a *hit* in the logfile with that file's pathname. However, the number of hits you record does not necessarily reflect the number of visitors at your site. Each HTML page your server serves usually produces several hits, because each graphic, MIDI recording, Quicktime Movie, or other piece of media associated with that page is contained in a separate file (and linked into the main HTML text).

Although hits are a good form of baseline data, they aren't the best measure of how many people are seeing your Web pages. A hit is just a measure of how many files a visitor accesses.

Server software that uses proxy servers employs caching to speed up server response, but it does interfere with hit counting. Also, browsers such as Netscape employ caching that also defeats the hit counting mechanism. If your server uses caching, you can bet that you have a lot more hits than your log file shows.

Impressions

Impressions are roughly equivalent to page views. A reasonable rule of thumb is that about ten *hits,* which are download requests for files on your server, equals one impression. (Each Web page typically comprises several individual files, such as images, calls to CGI scripts, and so on.) Most people talk about impressions in association with selling banner ads.

Your server log doesn't actually contain a measure of impressions, only hits, and it's a little bit complicated to calculate impressions based on hits. (Thus the need for the rule of thumb that ten hits equals one impression, more or less.) Actually, the relationship between hits and impressions also has to do with the timing with which a group of individual files are served — files with related pathnames served within a short timespan are highly likely to be part of the same impression.

Measuring hits and impressions

You can install products on your site to help you see what your customers are doing when they visit your store. Based on entries in the log file, these programs can create some pretty good guesses about who visited your site, how long they spent, and what they saw. Those guesses are important when estimating site traffic to impress some potential sponsors. The following software makes reasonably accurate estimates of site visits and ad impressions:

✔ **APS SiteTrack:** By American Productive Services, Inc., (wwwapsinc.com/) SiteTrack is an add-on to Netscape's server. SiteTrack lets you track how customers enter, move through, and leave your site. SiteTrack can completely trace the paths they follow in your online store. SiteTrack also has features that let you adapt the pages of your site dynamically, using CGI, SHTML and customized HTML elements, based on the information it has gathered about users. The SiteTrack system is compatible with SGI and Sun computer systems (UNIX).

✔ **Interse Market Focus:** Manufactured by Interse Corporation (www.interse.com), Interse Market Focus software uses algorithms to reconstruct the actual visits of users and organizations based on hit data. Using Interse Market Focus, you can find out where your visitors spend the most time on your site, how many clicks it took each user to reach your sales order page, and which Web advertisements attracted the most visitors. Interse Market Focus is a Windows 95/NT product, and it's compatible with Microsoft SQL server databases.

✔ **NetCount:** Created by Digital Planet (www.digiplanet.com), NetCount was recently acquired by I/Pro, which is a good step forward in standardizing the industry's systems of Web site tracking. (The two systems had been competing, but complementary, for some time.) The NetCount tracking system provides detailed analysis and reporting of how your customers use your online store. The statistics it provides resemble Nielsen's — a universally recognized rating system with information broken down by page, day, and hour. NetCount can monitor traffic on your site, and (uniquely) among specified external sites as well; thus it can verify which ad banners are bringing traffic.

Checking IP addresses

Visitors are potential customers. Your log file can help you identify your site's visitors by the IP address of their domain (or their company's IP address, or their ISP's IP address), and possibly of even the address of their individual machine, which is stored in the depths of their Web browser software whenever they are connected to the Internet.

How do you count visitors? Your server's log file records the IP address to which it sends requested data. You can generally assume that data (impressions) sent to the same IP address within some pre-established time limit, say 15 minutes, is sent to the same visitor.

Measuring visitors via IP addresses isn't completely accurate because of the arbitrary time limits set on visits. For example, what looks like one long visit by a single visitor could be several short visits by different individuals, using the same machine. Alternatively, if a customer dials in and visits your online store from several different service providers, you see several different IP addresses in your site's log files, but all will be from the same person.

Backlinks

Backlinks help you determine, at least unofficially, how well you're reaching your intended customer base. (Backlinks are links from other sites toward yours.) You use search engines to check backlinks.

Wired's Hotbot (www.hotbot.com) lets you type in the name of your site, then select "links to this site" directly from a "Look for..." menu.

When you're little and just starting out, trading links with other sites helps you get those first few backlinks. Find a few sites that share a common theme with yours, or ones that offer complementary products and services. Ask them to trade a link for a link with you. If you like, set an expiration time for the link, such as in a month or two, similar to the duration of a banner ad.

Server software products for ad management

You can verify your site's activity informally using software that gathers statistics for you. One good option, called AdServer, comes from a company called NetGravity (`www.netgravity.com`). AdServer is a high-performance database coupled with scheduling software for handling advertisements on your site: placing them on pages, rotating them around to different pages so the customers don't always see the same ad on the same page, tracking which ads get the most clicks, targeting ads to specific customers or specific areas of your site, and reporting the overall success of individual ads and specific sponsors on your site.

If you have a Solaris, Windows NT, or SGI Iris machine, you can install and run NetGravity AdServer on your site that

✔ Keeps track of ad inventory available for use on your site.

✔ Delivers a guaranteed number of ad impressions for advertisers on your site.

✔ Delivers ads according to keywords, such as on a search page. For example, if your customer searched your site using the keyword *cars*, and if Valvoline was a sponsor of your site, NetGravity delivers an ad related to motor oil on that page, rather than an ad for financial services. (Delivering an ad means displaying an ad on a Web page. All advertisers hope this will happen at the "right" time on the "right" page to the "right" customer.)

✔ Schedules maintenance of your ad system automatically.

✔ Targets your ads to a specific demographic profile.

✔ Produces customizable reports about your site's activity, including analyses of your site's traffic, and publishes the statistics directly to the Internet where your potential advertisers have easy access to them.

The statistics produced by AdServer are approved by Nielsen I/Pro. Nielsen offers an additional product called I/Audit Advertiser Insert that works with AdServer to let you provide a third-party audit of the statistics for specific ad banners on your site, including

✔ Ad views per day.

✔ Ad clicks per day.

✔ Comparisons among advertisers on the site, without compromising confidentiality.

✔ Standard reports you can furnish to third parties about your site's ad usage.

The ability to audit ad statistics may help you, because a few proven successful ads will draw more sponsors to your site.

More and more good products for monitoring site traffic pop up every day. For the Macintosh, StarNine (www.starnine.com/) offers a companion to its WebStar server that can perform site traffic monitoring.

External audits

Third-party site auditing companies offer you an objective report about your site's activity. These reports differ from reports you may receive from your own Internet Service Provider (ISP), because your ISP has a vested interest in seeing your site traffic numbers as high as possible: They can charge you more if you have more traffic.

The reports from your ISP alone won't be good enough to attract big advertising dollars to your site. The informal reports you can gather from your log file won't do, either. To sell bid banners, you need to shell out the clams for a third-party audit.

A third-party audit of your site can yield the following statistics, which can help you sell your ad space:

- ✔ Number of visits per month
- ✔ Number of pages visited
- ✔ Average visit length
- ✔ Visits categorized by day of the week and time of day
- ✔ Most frequently requested files
- ✔ Visitors listed by state and country
- ✔ Visitors listed by organization name

Many companies can do one of these audits for you, including the following:

- ✔ Audit Bureau of Circulations (www.accessabc.com)
- ✔ BPA International (www.bpai.com)
- ✔ Nielsen Media Research (www.nielsenmedia.com)

Third-party auditing reports are not currently standardized, so you need to ask, "What's included?" Talk with several third-party auditing firms before making a selection. That way, you're likely to find a solution that works best for you, and you may get a better deal on the cost.

Most third-party auditing firms require that you make some small changes or install special software on your site; take into account the time and cost of any alterations you must make to obtain the reports, and add that expense into your budget for the project. Some auditors actually visit your site and examine your server machines; others don't.

Building a Better Banner

Banner ads are small rectangular ads displayed on other sites that link directly to your online store. Banners allow you to get visitors to popular sites to see your name and to have the opportunity to visit your online store instantly, if they so desire.

To illustrate the potential advertising powers of banners, imagine you have an ad on a site that gets a million hits per day. If you get only 1 percent of those visitors to click on your ad, you have 10,000 visitors per day. Better look into bigger network connections when you take out an ad like that, yes?

Banner basics

If you're familiar with offline advertising in general but not with online banner ads, here are a few differences to remember:

- ✔ Unlike television and magazine ads, which become more comforting and familiar to the viewer and therefore more effective in generating sales after several viewings, online banner ads become annoying to the customer with repetition.

  Because online advertisements "behave" so differently than advertisements in traditional media, it's extremely important to produce a constant stream of new banner ads, and to vary the location of your banner ads often.

- ✔ Unlike television ads, which increase the customer's propensity to buy after several viewings, banner ads are most effective the first time they're seen. If a customer hasn't clicked on a banner ad by the time they've seen it five or six times, they're not likely to.

✔ Television and print based-advertising generally has a ramp-up period of a few weeks to a few months before it begins to affect sales. Internet ads begin to affect sales essentially immediately, and cool off just as fast.

✔ Generally, online advertising is much more centered on the user, anticipating needs and questions, rather than projecting a message as traditional print and media advertising does.

Actually saying "click here" as part of the ad text increases the response rate considerably.

Buying banner ads

Naturally, when you buy a banner ad, you want to get as much as possible for your money. Ad prices on the Internet right now usually are based on *impressions,* measured in CPM (which is a throwback to old copy ad jargon, but now generally means "cost per thousand impressions"). Some pricing is based on clickthrough, which is favorable toward the sponsor who's buying the ad.

You can expect to pay about 2 cents to 15 cents per impression for an ad banner on a reasonably popular site. For example, the pricing of one major search engine at this writing for 500,000 or more impressions (site-wide, not just on the search engine part) is $20.00 net cost per 1,000 impressions, which works out to about $10,000 for an ad banner there, at 2 cents per impression.

The placement of your ad on the site also is important. Would you prefer an ad on the first page of the site, or buried somewhere in the back?

Make sure your ad is placed on a portion of the site that's related to your product or service. For example, if you own an accounting firm, get your banner ad on a page of financial information or stock quotes.

Banners for sale

A new startup in San Francisco, called FlyCast (www.flycast.com), automates the process of buying and selling Web banner ads. It maintains Open Network, a real-time ad buying and selling market. Advertisers and Web content providers can conduct transactions in a way similar to financial market trading.

Another company, NarrowLine (www.narrowline.com), acts as an expert "matchmaker" to help you place your banner ads in front of the most suitable customers by finding the sites they visit most often.

Ad rotation, which means varying the pages on which a specific ad appears, guarantee your ad sometimes appears in a highly-visible portion of the site, even if other times it appears in a back corner someplace.

Some sites do offer the opportunity to buy an ad on a specific page of the site. In that case, either negotiate to get your ad in a place it's likely to be seen, or be thankful and accept a bargain-basement price. (Many sites now use ad engines that set up categories of ads and rotate them through only the most relevant parts of the site. Better ask about that.)

Don't forget that as your own site grows larger, you can put ads for your own products or services onto the more highly-trafficked parts of your site. You can use this method to bring customers into the less-traveled parts of your site, or the special areas where maybe you have something waiting for them, such as a promotion or survey with a free gift.

Selling banner ads

The marketplace has a lot to say about how much you can charge for ads on your site. Top sites, those with perhaps a million page views per month, naturally, can ask and get more for their ad space. A going rate for ads at a top site is about 10 cents per impression. Sites with fewer visitors often charge less, perhaps 3 cents per impression.

Ads sold per impression may get a lower rate, but ads sold on clickthrough are only paid when a user actually clicks on the ad banner and visits the sponsor's Web site, and you can't control that directly. You *can* however control how often the sponsor's ad appears on *your* site and where it appears.

Ad engines help you, the ad seller, create value for your sponsors. Ad engines let you set up and maintain multiple ad rotations, so no ad has to be relegated strictly to the back room. Your ad rotations control how often and where a particular ad appears on your site, based on how much the advertiser has paid you.

Who to give your money to

A recent survey asked Web surfers how they found out about most of the Web sites they visited. An overwhelming 71 percent of the surfers reported that they used search engines to find out about other sites. Based on that information, it sounds like dollars spent buying banners on search engines can prove extremely effective.

You can rotate the ads so that every sponsor's ad appears prominently on your site some of the time. Thus advertisers pay you more because of higher traffic on those areas of your site. (In fact, you can specify approximate percentages for each ad to appear prominently in the ad rotation.) It's also good to rotate the ads on your sponsor's behalf so they don't "wear out" as quickly for the customers, which banner ads tend to do much faster than television or print media ads.

Alternatively, it may be worth more to your sponsor to have their ads appear only in parts of your site where people are likely to be looking for that product or service. You can set up ad rotations designed for specific areas of your online store. For example, if you have a site that sells red and white wine, you could set up an ad rotation so that beef ads appear with red wines and chicken or fish ads appear with white wines.

The sponsors buying ads like to see them at the top of the page, but your site's visitors usually prefer ads at the bottom of the page, where they're out of the way. (That way, the ads don't make the visitor have to scroll the browser window so much — of course, if they don't scroll the browser window, they don't see the ads at the bottom of the page, and you don't get much clickthrough, which is another problem.)

Ad placement on a page is a constant balancing act between what the sponsors want and what the customers want. For that reason, some sites place ads at the bottom of the page, but in a frame, so the ads are always visible. That's a fairly unsatisfactory approach from a customer's point of view, because the screen space available for displaying the rest of the page's contents is diminished considerably by the ad frame.

Some sites place ads in a pop-up JavaScript window. Using JavaScript, an ad appears the first time the page is visited, in a separate and smaller window of its own (you can read more about JavaScript in Chapter 11). The customer can close the pop-up window and not see an ad again until a new page is loaded. Besides preserving real estate in the browser window, the pop-up approach also works well because it actually brings attention to the ad as the JavaScript window pops up onto the screen. Of course, this method is hard to implement (at present) unless you have programmers on staff. However, as Web site products become more sophisticated, expect to see innovative ad techniques like this one become more widely available.

Making linkable banners

After you sell some ad space to a sponsor, you have to get down to the work of actually constructing a banner for their ad. The technique I show you produces a very simple banner that gets you started. It also works for a smaller site that's still handling a few ad placements by hand. (When you don't use an ad server to set up an ad rotation, you have to edit the HTML code of each Web page to create a link to the image file (probably a GIF) that contains your sponsor's ad banner. That takes a lot of work if you have more than a few ads and more than a few pages on your site.)

Because Web banners are just GIF files, you can place them on your Web pages just like placing any other image on your Web page. To create a linkable banner, surround the tag that calls up your GIF image. (Of course your graphic designer has already made one, or your client has given you one, right?) For example, you could surround this tag

```
<IMG SRC="my_clients_banner_ad.GIF">
```

with a link tag, like this:

```
<A HREF><IMG SRC=" my_clients_banner_ad.GIF " border=0></A>
```

Now your GIF file is a clickable, linkable banner. (Without a default blue border surrounding it.)

Here's a more complete specification of the example link. To make this link work on your site, you just replace the sitename given with the real name of the site you want the link to connect with.

```
<A HREF="http://www.gotothissitename.com/">
<IMG SRC="my_clients_banner_ad.GIF" border=0></A>
```

And that's all you need to get one, simple banner working on your site. You're ready for your first ad.

Getting the Word Out: Your Offline Advertising Plan

Your customers aren't always online! But people who connect to the Internet, are well educated as a group — which means they probably read lots of publications when they're not online.

I don't suggest that you beat the bushes offline to find clients that have never used the Internet before. That's a hard sell. But I do have a couple of tips about how to bring otherwise Internet-friendly people to your site using offline resources, probably best used in the following order:

✔ If you sell a product in offline stores, you can include on the label or packaging a brief description and URL for your online store, such as "For more great products like this one, visit our online store at `http://www.yoursite.com/`."

✔ Take out ads in the traditional venues of your line of business. For example, if your site sells a selection of antique dolls, place an "adversitement" in publications that antique doll collectors generally read. Do so even if your online store is your only store.

✔ Another place that some innovative Web sites are advertising offline is in college newspapers — they're cheap, and they reach a new, excited audience.

✔ Get ads in the industry trade magazines, such as *WebWeek, Internet World, ZDInternet,* and so on. People who read these publications probably shop online. These ads can be a bit pricey, however.

Full-page color spreads look great, but you don't necessarily have to spring for that right away. A smaller ad can do a lot. For example, in the back sections of most trade magazines appear smaller advertisements, some of which are for Web sites and various online stores.

If you already have brochures and other literature about your products and services, one of the most cost-effective forms of advertising your site is adding your URL to your existing print materials.

Hiring an Advertising Agency for Your Site

If you don't have the talent within your company to create and sell banner ads (or any other ads) for your site, you may want to look into hiring an advertising agency to develop an ad campaign for you. This approach has some advantages, including the following:

✔ Advertising agencies who are familiar with the Web have up-to-the-minute information about where to get the best deals for placing your site's banner ads online, as well as print ads offline.

✔ With the rapid effectiveness and equally rapid staleness of banner ads, an advertising agency can keep new ads always cooking for you while you focus on the other needs of your business.

✔ An agency can help coordinate a comprehensive ad campaign in which your online and offline advertising are highly complementary.

Online advertising is changing the way a lot of ad agencies do business, forcing them to respond much more rapidly to their clients' needs. Ads must sometimes be developed literally overnight. Because of the need for speed in selling online, hire an agency that understands online advertising and understands your business.

Here are basic questions you want to ask any prospective agency:

✔ Do your fees fit my budget?

✔ What ads or sites have you already done? (Get URLs and look at them.)

✔ How should my business present itself online?

You may consider hiring an agency to do not just your ads, but to design your entire site for you. If you hire a designer, sit down together and go through the "blueprinting" process described in Chapter 2 and come up with satisfactory solutions for each part of your online store.

An agency can help you get more objectivity, too. After you have an opportunity to see your business through the eyes of others, you may gain insights that help you meet the goals of your online store better.

When designing your ads, or helping your agency design your ads, you can target them better to your intended customers with the help of some up-to-date general information. Check out research that's already been done about online behaviors, attitudes, products, pricing, latest trends, and so forth at www.cyberatlas.com. (Hey, maybe you can even see whether your agency is charging you too much!)

Profiling Customers Using Cookies

Cookies are bits of software that a server stores within a user's browser; the software acts like a scout, finding out all manner of things about the customer and how they use your site.

Cookies let you provide a more customized experience for each customer. Because you can retrieve and store information about your customer in a cookie, you can (for example) select specific Web banner ads for products that may appeal to that specific customer. You can direct them to specials or promotional offers on your site that they may like, based on past visits. In short, cookies can help you sell more.

Some customers don't like the idea of sites having information about them and sites storing anything on their hard drives. Some sites let users know that they use cookies, and they offer to drop them at the customer's choice. Netscape Navigator and Microsoft Internet Explorer both let customers block acceptance of cookies, or they can flash a warning when the customer starts to download a cookie. You, as store owner, want your customers to have the opportunity to reject your cookies because you want your customers to feel that nothing is going on behind their backs.

Affinity-Based Online Advertising

Sometimes an entire site can be an advertisement for a business, but then it isn't an online store, exactly. The sole purpose of these *affinity sites* is to simply create a good feeling about an existing business. For example, many U.S. airlines have "online stores" — but because some of them can't yet sell tickets or take reservations online, they are really affinity sites. (See the Internet Directory portion of this book for more information on airline sites.)

Affinity sites can help build recognition and loyalty for your brand. If you don't have the capability to put up a functioning online store, consider creating an affinity site as a "halfway point" for getting going with selling online. You can put up an affinity site and add electronic transaction capabilities later to turn your site into a store.

Narrowcasting

Narrowcasting refers to the ability to customize on demand, thereby creating a personalized experience, tailored specifically for each client. Narrowcasting is the opposite of *broadcasting*, a term with which people have already become more familiar, which means the ability to send exactly the same information to hundreds of thousands of individuals at once. (It's also different than multicasting, which is the other name for push technology, a more interactive technology I talk about in Chapter 11.)

Chapter 13

Selecting a Database for Your Store

. . . .

In This Chapter

▶ Understanding your database needs and options

▶ Budgeting your database

▶ Keeping up with your database

▶ Protecting customer privacy

. . . .

Databases let you track all kinds of information about your products and your customers. For example, databases can store customer shopping carts, track payments receipts and invoices, and store customer information, inventory information, and order-processing information. Find the right database for your business's needs in this chapter.

Defining Your Database Needs

A database is a way to store information in small bits. Simple databases store information in slots called *fields,* and more complicated databases store information in structures called *records,* which are made up of a number of fields. A field contains a specific item of information, such as the customer's last name — a related field contains the customer's first name, another field could contain the customer's e-mail address, and so on.

For your online store, your database should perform the following basic functions for maintaining and using your data:

✔ Finding, sorting, and displaying the data (such as displaying it on your screen or printing out a report)

✔ Adding new entries (such as for a new customer or product)

✔ Deleting old entries (such as for a discontinued item)

✔ Changing existing entries (such as when a customer gets a new address)

When you ask a database to find some information (such as digging up a customer's address for you), that's called *querying* the database. Each request for information is a *query.* If you have to use a special formula or syntax to tell the database what information you want, that's called *query language.* A query language is usually considered part of the *front end* of, or interface to, the database — you use the front end to extract the information you need.

In your online store, a front end to your database may take the form of a Web page with a CGI script behind it that creates the "formal" database queries based on input from customers.

The data records and the parts of the database that do the actual searching and display of the records are often referred to collectively as the *back end* of the database. A database is designed to retrieve information, based on your queries, from the raw data you store in the back end. The part of the back end that searches is sometimes called a *search engine,* because of the way it metaphorically travels actively across each record looking for the ones it needs.

You find the following two types of databases widely in use:

✔ **Flat file databases:** With a flat file database, you can usually update your database records using a simple word processor.

✔ **Relational databases:** Relational database products usually include an interface for entering and updating your database records; often it uses a graphical user interface (GUI).

If you keep a mailing list, periodically sort through and remove duplicate entries. It may not seem like much, but every stamp and every bit of disk space you save is worth money to your business.

Flat file databases

A flat file database often looks something like a big table with each line representing one record. For example, records may look like these two fictitious records:

Customer, Jan jan@customers.com 123 Any St., Anytown, CA 94000
Browser, Bob bbrowser@mightbuy.net 456 Icy Bl., Eagle Park, AK 99900

Or you could store the same information in small blocks within a single flat file, one field per line, like this:

Customer, Jan
jan@customers.com
123 Any St.
Anytown
CA
94000

A flat file database has several advantages:

- ✔ You can enter the data easily. You don't need any special tools, so it's a great way to start if you've never used a database before.

- ✔ You can write a program easily or adapt an existing program using a programming language like Perl or C to search and retrieve data from your flat file database. (The example Perl script on the CD that comes with this book looks up information in a flat file database.)

- ✔ If you have only a small amount of data or only one kind of data, managing a flat file database is very easy.

- ✔ Flat file databases usually run very quickly because they are so simple.

Basically, a flat file database is great for simple look-up tasks. It may be just the thing for a small site that's accessed by only a few customers at one time or offers only a few products.

One traditional use for a flat file database is for a customer mailing list. Another use of a flat file database appears in the example that comes on the CD with this book — the blurbs about herbs in Herb's Herb Shack appear in a single database file.

However, flat file databases have the following disadvantages:

- ✔ They tend to be very rigid.

- ✔ They slow down quickly when they contain a lot of records.

- ✔ They slow down when several users search the database at the same time.

If you need a more flexible database that can handle lots of users at the same time, can expand to handle lots of data easily, and can help you sort your information in new ways or add new fields, you probably want to go with a relational database.

Relational databases

Relational databases take up a lot of RAM and disk space, and if many visitors use your database, you may find that a relational database takes up a lot of processor cycles, too. However, for the resources you put into setting up and maintaining your relational database, you get a lot in return:

- ✔ Customizable presentations of your data, including specialized forms and reports.

- ✔ A highly expandable storage system that includes the ability to add entirely new categories of information if you decide to do so; most important, relational databases give you the ability to cross-reference different categories of data. Thus, you can use your database to compare lots of different types of information easily.

- ✔ Lots of products and platforms to choose from, because many companies offer relational database products.

Relational databases are robust and powerful. If running your store requires managing a lot of related information, which is true for most stores, a relational database may be the choice for you. For example, a set of related information may be the product itself, its latest price, and its availability (in stock or out of stock?). Another set of related information may be the customer name, customer identification number, and any orders pending to be shipped to that customer. You can store these types of information in your database and thereby keep track of the daily details of your business a lot more easily.

In a relational database, you can create multiple tables and make links between them using *shared fields* (sometimes these fields are referred to as *linked fields* or *joins*). Shared fields means, for example, that the exact same record (or field) containing a customer's identification number point to, say, the customer mailing list and the invoice database. That way, you can link your customer's ID number to the last item she ordered, then link to a list of special discounts she can receive on future orders, then link to a list of other products she may be interested in, and so forth, up to the limits of your time, patience, and creativity.

Some shared fields are truly shared — when you update one, the other one changes automatically. However, other databases require that you enter any update information in both places. Be sure to find out how the specific database product handles shared or linked fields.

A relational database resembles a Web site in some ways — it has a series of tables (instead of pages) with shared fields (which are a little like links) to other tables. Together the individual pages (tables) and the links (shared fields) create a structure for presenting a lot of related information in a clean, understandable way.

Here's why a relational database is better than a set of Web pages when you store information for retrieval: After the information has been broken down into small component parts and stored in a relational database, it's easy to search through quickly when you look for something specific, and it's easy to recombine the information in new ways. For example, you can arrange records into different formats created for specific purposes, such as invoices or shipping labels.

Figure 13-1 illustrates how you can use a related set of database records together to send an order to the correct address.

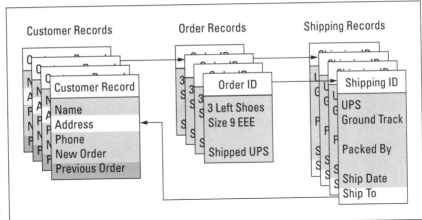

Figure 13-1: Sharing relational database records.

Notice that in Figure 13-1, the customer record is the same as the Order ID and the Shipping ID. In real life, this structure limits you to one order per customer record, because you have to keep coming up with unique numbers for each order. Instead, include a Customer ID on each of the three sets of records. That way, the different tables can share information — linked through the Customer ID field.

The skinny on middleware

Many commercial electronic storefront software products (which are covered in Chapter 6) rely on your database of products or services to create display pages for your store. Basically, the software looks in the database to get product information, puts the information into an HTML template, and posts it on your site. The software that performs these functions is sometimes called *middleware*, because it operates in the middle between the customer, who wants to see your products, and the database, which contains records describing your products.

Middleware consists of specialized driver software that lets CGI scripts query the database (based on user input) and specialized HTML tools to help you create pages that can import data directly from your database.

For example, NetObjects Fusion is a popular middleware product that works with several commonly used databases to create and manage Web sites effectively. (You can get more information about NetObjects Fusion at www.netobjects.com.)

Making the Database Decision

Each of the following factors should contribute to deciding how to implement your store's database or what product to choose:

- ✔ Your database must be compatible with the following items:
  - Your hardware platform
  - Your operating system
  - Your Web server
  - Your electronic storefront software

- ✔ Some database products and storefront software can import data directly from other products (if the formats are somewhat compatible). So you need to ask yourself how you currently store your data and look for a database product that can easily take your existing data. (A positive note: Almost every database program has an export/import ability at least at the lowest common denominator of comma-delimited fields, so there's always a way, wherever there's a will, to transfer your data to a new database.)

✔ Consider what kind of access you want people to have to your database. For example, you need to ask yourself the following questions:

- Will my Web pages have links to the database?
- What fields will serve as searchable fields?
- What kinds of queries will my database need to accept?
- Do I have any data I need to store but won't want others to see?

✔ Think about how information enters your database. For example, do you want customers to fill out forms that store their information directly into the database?

✔ Take any other software that works with your database into account. For example, do you need to coordinate your software with your online cash register to keep a log of customer transactions?

✔ Consider how the database may need to grow and change over the next year. Over the next five years?

The more details you can piece together about your database, the better database selection you can make. If you can sit down and actually sketch out a set of sample records and imagining how they work together, it helps you assess your needs more clearly.

Specifically, doing the following can help you crystallize your thinking about which database to choose:

✔ Make a list of fields you need to include in each complete record. You may need the name, address, phone number, height, shoe size, and so on, for example.

✔ Estimate the length of each field. For example, 40 characters is about right for a name field.

✔ Decide what type of data each field will hold. Differentiate between numbers or text, because mathematical operations may be needed on some numeric fields.

Some fields that appear numeric, such as zip codes or phone numbers, are generally marked as text fields because you don't use them for calculations. Text fields have greater flexibility in formatting on the screen and on paper.

After you get the preceding information together, you can make an accurate product decision and set up your database. You may want to talk to a database developer who can create a customized solution for you, or you may want to buy an off-the-shelf product.

If you plan anything more complicated than the most rudimentary database, you probably need to hire a database administrator (DBA), at least on a temporary basis, to help install and configure your database.

Have the following items in place when setting up your database or hiring someone to do it for you:

✔ Make sure your database works with the rest of your online store. That may mean creating CGI scripts, Web-based ordering forms, and other "bridges" that communicate between the database and your customers. (Also, see the sidebar "The skinny on middleware" earlier in this chapter for more ideas on this topic.)

✔ Configure your data records in a way that makes the information usable today and still makes sense for tomorrow, when your business expands.

Maintaining Your Database

After you get your database up and running, make your database a good friend. Spend time with it regularly, and it won't let you down. That means allocating a regular amount of time and money for maintaining your database — keeping it updated, generating reports, backing it up, and general maintenance.

Besides the costs of initial purchase, installation, and configuration, allow for ongoing maintenance costs in tasks like the following:

✔ Performing daily data entry tasks, such as entering new price information

✔ Creating regular backups and storing them, preferably off-site

✔ Making periodic checks on performance, and some tuning

✔ Making occasional software and hardware upgrades

✔ Dealing with tough problems (that may require a consultant to solve)

✔ Planning expansions as your business grows

Sometimes you need help with your database. When do you need to hire a consultant? Consider putting out the money for a professional in the following situations:

✔ When you need to add fields to your database (to store new types of information)

✔ When you need to retrieve new types of reports or make new queries

✔ When you need to do a software upgrade

✔ When you need to do a hardware upgrade

These procedures are full of tiny bumps and glitches that a seasoned professional is best-equipped to handle. Be sure to call someone with experience administering your specific database product, if possible.

Selecting Database Products

Selecting the best database software for your store depends on the size and complexity of your store, and on how much you plan to do with the database. For example, if you already have order processing and other functions set up in another part of your business, you may want to use your database just for storing information about your products and customers.

Relational databases for a small site

The mSQL relational database product is relatively simple to set up and integrate with your Web server, especially if you run the Apache Web server software. The mSQL database product runs on UNIX platforms, and it requires as little as 8MB of disk space. (For more information about Web servers and Apache, see Chapter 4.)

The ACID test

If you use a database for critical information such as customer bank account balances, you need a powerful and robust database that passes the *ACID test*. In this case, ACID stands for Atomicity, Consistency, Isolation, and Durability. These are the traditional qualities of a database suitable for transactions, such as at your ATM window.

✔ Atomicity means "all or nothing." The transaction either finishes completely, or it is as if it never began.

✔ Consistency means that the database is always in synch with itself, and informally speaking, in synch with the outside world. If your site sells CD players and your inventory database says you have 12.5

players remaining, something is wrong. (Sort of like having 2.4 children.)

✔ Isolation means that transactions can't speak to each other until they finish. That way, no one shares data that was in the process of being updated and is therefore inaccurate.

✔ Durability means that what's done is done. When a transaction finishes, it can't be erased from the database.

If you need this sort of a database, you probably know it already. Most digital cash products meet the ACID test, but interestingly enough, a few do not. For more information about digital cash, see Chapter 15.

---

mSQL comes with the following features:

- ✔ **w3-msql:** A module for converting database records to Web pages, which makes creating a site easy
- ✔ **Lite:** An easy-to-use interface programming language, which makes creating forms for your site easy
- ✔ **mSQLexport:** A tool for making your database files easy to export into other databases in comma-delimited format (fields separated by commas)

After you load the files, mSQL has to be compiled on your UNIX system, but it figures out for itself what kind of UNIX system you use and installs itself accordingly.

Of course, you still need a Perl or C programmer to help you get mSQL set up and working with the other parts of your store — using w3-msql and Lite — but you may not need to hire a full-boat database administrator to get you set up, which could save you a little money.

The mSQL 2.0 database software is available for about $250, or you can get it for free if you're a registered nonprofit organization or educational institution. You can download the software at www.hughes.com.au, which is the Web site of Hughes Technologies, a company in Australia.

mSQL has a couple limitations that you should know about:

- ✔ It can't handle fields longer than about 4K (4,000 characters)
- ✔ It doesn't support the full set of SQL specifications

That means you probably can't use large text files such as documents as field values, and you may not be able to enter some of the more sophisticated SQL queries.

For the Mac platform, FileMaker Pro 4.0, a commercial database product by Claris (www.claris.com), wins hands down for ease of connecting a database to your online store.

You only need one product database, even if you have multiple server machines supporting your store, as in a Web farm. Don't try to update two or more copies of a database. If more than one machine needs access to your database, set up local network connections to facilitate that access — don't duplicate your database on the two machines. That situation will quickly turn into a maintenance nightmare.

Your database and the Year 2000

With the Year 2000 coming up, you need to pay attention to how your database handles date information. (For more information on the Year 2000 and the special challenges it presents to databases, pick up a copy of *Year 2000 Solutions For Dummies,* by K.C. Bourne, published by IDG Books Worldwide, Inc.)

Storing years as four-digit numbers is the best long-term solution. However, other techniques can be effective, such as three-digit years (two digits with a century indicator 0=19, 1=20,

and so on), a consistent two-digit year, or a consistent way of subtracting years from the date (every 28 years the days of the week are the same) and proceeding as before. This provides a good temporary solution if all you have is some compiled code and no access to source code.

Remember to back up your database completely before attempting any date conversions such as these.

Microsoft offers several database products for Windows platforms, which are suitable for use by smaller Windows-based sites. Usually, these databases are an integral part of a server software or operating system that you buy from Microsoft.

Relational databases for medium to large sites

If you need a big, powerful database, look for a major vendor with products such as Oracle, Microsoft SQL Server, Sybase SQL Server, and Informix. To set one of these databases up and make it work, you need to know much more than this book can tell you, and so I just give you the basics about each one.

Oracle (for Windows and UNIX)

Oracle makes the recognized top-of-the-line database product in the industry. Oracle databases are used in mission-critical applications such as ATM machines and credit card processing houses. (Mission critical means that if the database fails, you're likely to go out of business shortly.)

An Oracle database definitely can do anything you need it to do, and it comes with Oracle's own database-compatible Web server software, called WebServer.

Oracle databases are available for UNIX and Windows NT platforms. They cost about $8,000, not including any additional costs for installing and configuring the database to work with the other parts of your online store, or with your middleware.

For more information about Oracle databases, visit www.oracle.com.

Oracle8 takes up a lot more hard drive space than Oracle7, so plan your migration carefully if you upgrade to Oracle8 from 7.1.4 or higher. Oracle8 changes nearly all the structures in your database, from file headers to rollback segment structures. It also offers you the option of using object-oriented technology.

Sybase SQL Server

Sybase SQL Server Professional for Windows NT is probably the best Sybase SQL database product for an online store, and it costs about $1,000. As with any other powerful relational database, you have additional costs for hiring a database administrator to install and configure your Sybase database to work with the rest of your store or with your middleware.

For more information or to download an evaluation copy, visit www.sybase.com.

Microsoft SQL Server

Like most Microsoft things, Microsoft SQL Server began life as a spin-off product. It originally began as a product similar to the industry-standard Sybase SQL Server; however, Microsoft SQL Server now has been specifically adapted to work with Windows NT, and it also works especially well with other Microsoft products and technologies, such as Active Server Pages, FrontPage, and Microsoft Office.

Microsoft SQL Server is relatively easy to install and use, which makes it a nice choice for medium-sized sites with medium-sized budgets. It costs about $3,000 for an Internet Connector License, plus whatever costs you incur for hiring a database administrator to install and configure your Microsoft SQL Server database to work with the rest of your store or with your middleware.

You can get more information about Microsoft SQL Server at www.microsoft.com/sql.

Informix

Informix offers several database products that are suitable for a range of online database sizes and uses. Informix databases run on UNIX systems.

For more information about Informix products, visit www.informix.com.

Informix-SE

The Informix-SE product is great for small- to medium-sized databases. It's relatively simple to install, and relatively low-maintenance (compared to some other relational database products), so it may be a good choice if you don't have the budget available to hire a database support staff. You probably need some help getting set up, however.

If your needs change as your store grows, your Informix-SE database can migrate easily to the Informix-Online Dynamic Server product.

Informix-Online Dynamic Server

Informix-Online Dynamic Server can handle larger databases than the SE product. Also, it can be configured to run on multiprocessor machines, or on a Web farm (a cluster of machines using a local network). You need to budget some support staff time to manage this database.

Informix-Universal Server

This Informix database product stores and serves large multimedia databases, including large graphics, sound, and video files.

Informix also offers some other options for your online store. For example, Informix's Universal Web Connect software lets you integrate your Web server with an Informix database.

If you use the Informix Universal Server, a product called Web DataBlade works with any existing Web server and your Informix database to generate pages on the fly. If you run a Netscape or Microsoft Web server, Web DataBlade speeds up your CGI scripts. When used in conjunction with its associated tools for creating and maintaining Web pages, the Informix Universal Server-plus-Web DataBlade combination lets you administer your entire online site as a database. For example, it maintains links between Web pages for you.

Needless to say, the Informix Universal Server requires some budget for maintenance and support staff, in addition to installation and configuration costs.

 Although the database itself may be fast, some interesting problems can arise with getting connections to a database over the Internet that are fast enough for functions such as authenticating member password information in real time — especially if your site is very busy and provides customers with search capabilities. Some sites create customized solutions to speed up the process of opening a database connection for authentication purposes. For example, you can overcome slow database connections by creating a daemon whose only function is to keep several connections open and ready for use.

Which databases do people really use?

Oracle, Sybase, and Informix databases are popular among online sites with databases ranging from 1GB to 5GB in size. A smaller number of sites use these same kinds of databases to contain between 20 and 100GB of information.

Databases and Customer Privacy

The trust that your customers place in you is the most important asset you have for getting and keeping their business online, and how you treat their personal information contributes to maintaining your side of the trust bargain.

Online privacy is as much about information as it is about relationships and maintaining trust.

After you get all this information about your customers neatly stored away in your database, use the information wisely. Your customers appreciate not having sensitive information about them released into the wide-open free-for-all of the Internet. For example, if you put your customers' home phone numbers into your database, don't make the numbers available on your site.

Some customers may be reluctant to provide you with information about themselves due to concerns that you may use the information in ways they wouldn't want. You can do two things to encourage them to tell you about themselves:

✔ Offer to keep customer information confidential — this is probably the best approach you can take. If you decide to go this route, you can include text on your site saying something like "We don't share the information our customers give us," or "We keep all information you give us strictly confidential."

✔ Offer customers incentives, such as discount pricing on certain products, if they fill out a form or otherwise give personal information at your store. People are a lot more willing to tell you about themselves if they get something in return.

Protecting your customers' privacy includes making sure your site is safe from unauthorized access. Several well-known cases have occurred of hackers breaking into sites on which lots of customer credit card information was stored. Protect their information as if it were your own by doing the following:

 ✔ Encrypt it

 ✔ Put it behind your firewall

 ✔ Limit the number of people who have access to the information

 ✔ Do whatever else it takes to prevent fraud; use your own common sense and think about what kind of protection you'd like to have for personal information about yourself.

Customers appreciate when you use information about them to direct them to specials or to other products they may be interested in. For example, if Sue Smith bought a color printer from you last week, she may appreciate receiving a note that color ink cartridges designed to fit her printer are on sale. This sort of attention makes customers feel special; they feel like you look out for their interests (which you do!). *Real service* such as this is a great business tool, so take a few minutes now and then to figure out how you can use what you know about your customers to help them out and increase your sales at the same time.

Before you comb your database for customer service ideas that make use of private information about your customers, consider these questions:

 ✔ Would you be willing to create a special discount for your frequent customers?

 ✔ Do you have inventory on hand that you need to move out, perhaps by offering a sale price, or a discount to certain customers who have bought them in the past?

 ✔ If your customers tell you where else they shop online, maybe you could place a banner ad on that site and offer the customers that gave you the help a discount coupon?

 ✔ To win first-time online buyers, would you consider offering a steep discount on an initial purchase of your online products or services?

 ✔ If you know your customer's addresses, can you think of something related to where they live that you can supply, such as seasonal needs?

 ✔ Can you supply popular regional items, such as jalapeño peppers in Texas, or maple syrup in Vermont — either to their native regions or to other regions?

Maybe your customer lists will give you some ideas. Ideas such as these will keep your Web-based store dynamic and exciting, which is an important asset for selling online. Your database of customer information is a gold mine for new ideas about how to make your customers happy. (For more ideas about how to make your customers feel special, see Chapter 14.)

Chapter 14

Your Customer Service Department

In This Chapter

▶ Delivering great customer service online

▶ Automating your customer service

▶ Building customer-centered policies that don't break the bank

▶ Keeping in touch with your customers

*Y*our online store's overall goal, like any business, is to create satisfied customers who return again and again. It's a challenge to stand out among all the businesses online and offline, and customer service is one area that promises to be a great differentiator over the next several years. Therefore, the best advantage a business may have to offer going into the next century is its customer service department.

Online Customer Service Basics

You've probably been to a few offline customer service departments — you usually get to a counter and find a single sales person who tries to answer your question or help you. Some service! I'm happy to tell you that your online customer service department can offer three times as much support for your customers, and at a fraction of the price it takes to operate an offline customer service department.

The elements of a successful online customer service department include the following:

✔ One or more phone numbers for customer calls.

✔ A dedicated e-mail address, such as help@yoursite.com (with the right domain name, of course)

- ✔ A chat room and a bulletin board for even better communication with the customers
- ✔ A fax number and postal mail address on your site to offer customers as many ways as possible to communicate with you.

You post your customer service e-mail address and the URLs of your chat room and bulletin board on your site, probably on the home page (the first page), so customers would know how to find these resources. You may want to include the e-mail address for help on every page of your site, perhaps in a footer at the bottom of the page.

Make sure you have adequate staff to answer customer phone calls and e-mail. What good does it do to post this contact information if no one responds?

You can create a centralized "Customer Service Desk," which is essentially just a page of links. Each link at your automated service desk leads your customer to a simple form which she can fill out and submit. Your forms can collect some of the following information:

- ✔ Change of name
- ✔ Change of address
- ✔ Subscription renewal (especially if you accept online payment)
- ✔ Change of password (especially if they know their old one)

Keep forms at your automated service desk simple. Otherwise, you create even more confusion for your customer. Behind the scenes, you need to create CGI scripts that update your database (perhaps in a daily update run around midnight) based on new information gained from these automated customer service entries.

Some electronic storefront software products offer especially good customer service features, such as letting you make real-time updates to your customer's address information (like, while you have them on the phone). If you don't choose to go with one of those products, you can still achieve a lot using automated customer service desks, mailbots, and a few smart policies.

Making Your Customers Feel Great

Bringing smiles to your customers' faces can be a bit of a challenge. The faster you take action regarding a customer comment or complaint, the more likely you are to create a happy customer.

Communicate, communicate, communicate

Invite e-mail and answer it. One thing people expect on the Internet is quick response. One way to invite e-mail is to put a message on your site something like this "We love to hear from you, send e-mail any time to me@mysite.com" (of course you'd put in your own site's e-mail address).

Communication is the best way to overcome any problem or difficulty. If your customer takes the time to tell you about a problem, that means he wants to keep being your customer, no matter how serious his complaint may be.

Using mailbots to respond quickly

If you don't have the staff to respond to customer e-mail promptly, set up a mailbot to provide temporary, automated customer service replies until you can get to it yourself or get someone on it. That way, you know for sure that your customer gets some kind of response from you almost immediately.

Selena Sol's Public Domain Script Archive (www.extropia.com) contains a script for a mailbot that you can easily adapt for your store running on a UNIX Web server, or you can use it as a model for writing a mailbot program on an NT or Mac site. Some hosting services also offer mailbots (also called *autoresponders*) as part of your hosting package. When you use an autoresponder, you compose a message that the mailbot automatically sends out whenever you get an e-mail from a customer.

The message your mailbot sends should be personable and professional. Here's an example of the kind of message your mailbot could send:

> *Dear Valued Customer,*
>
> *Thank you for your recent e-mail message. Our customer service staff will respond to you personally as soon as possible. In the meantime, please accept this automated response to your message, along with our thanks for shopping with us.*
>
> *Sincerely yours,*
>
> *Leslie Lundquist*
> *President and CEO, The Creative Professional, Inc.*

Taking customers right to the top

Make someone who can "do something about it" accessible directly to your customers. Don't make them go through an endless chain of command to get their problem resolved or their question answered.

For example, empower your customer service representatives to take whatever action they feel is appropriate, based on a well-established set of guidelines. (I have been a loyal customer for seven years at a bank that empowers its tellers to make every customer happy and resolve absolutely any issue, up to a certain dollar amount.)

Personal e-mail correspondence from a big-wig at your site makes your customers feel appreciated. For example, you could let your president or CEO personally answer e-mail once every month or so.

Encouraging a community at your site

Find a way to let your customers make themselves part of your site. Allowing your customers to send you e-mail help them feel like part of the total scene. You can encourage a feeling of community at your site by any of the other following means:

- ✔ Set up conferences and bulletin boards where your customers can exchange their ideas and give each other feedback. (See Chapter 11 for tips about setting up bulletin boards and chat rooms, and where to get free programs on the Web to help you do that.)

- ✔ Keep conferences and bulletin board files as an archive and give your customers lots of credit for participating. Use good answers elsewhere on your site, perhaps creating a Frequently Asked Questions (FAQ) list or a list of tips and tricks.

- ✔ Participate in discussions at your site, but don't just set yourself up as the expert. Let your customers answer each other's questions about your products and services, too. Everyone wants to contribute, so make sure your customers feel their contributions are welcome. (Of course, obnoxious contributions are another story — reserve the right to oust anyone who misbehaves, just in case. Most bulletin board and chat room programs have features that let you silence offenders.)

Leave a free-form text field in your customer database called something like "Comments" where unusual or specific information about each customer can be entered. This "misfit" information often is especially helpful when resolving problems.

Chatting and Customer Service

Chat means that you set up a Web page on your site which, when a member types a comment and sends it, it appears on the page for all to see. The resulting page ends up looking a little bit like a movie script, with everyone's comments typed in as you read down the page.

Chat is a great asset in terms of improving customer service and promoting cross-sell opportunities. You should consider adding chat rooms to augment your other customer services with "publisher-to-user" communication, as well as chat rooms where users talk among themselves. (This option costs you very little and creates a lot of goodwill — your staff member doesn't have to be there for that, which reduces your costs.) Several research studies of online commerce have concluded that this type of communication fosters better client relationships, and it assists businesses in these important areas:

- ✔ Marketing products
- ✔ Closing sales
- ✔ Competitive positioning
- ✔ Building communities

You don't need to have a chat room open all the time to make it effective for your site. Just post the hours on your site, so people know when they can stop in. During those hours, someone on your staff can be there to answer questions for the customers (if anyone shows up, and they usually do).

You need to always have someone available who has the authority to make decisions regarding customer policies and procedures. If your online store is open 24 hours per day, that means someone really should be on call, maybe at the other end of a pager, just in case.

Sometimes in a chat room you get a heckler, someone who wants to stir up some trouble or who annoys your customers. Don't let it bother you, and tell your staff members not to take it personally. Just deal with it the best way you can, often by asking that person to keep the comments on a positive level, asking them to leave if they don't respond, and then actually kicking them off the site if they persist. (Your Web server software should provide some instructions for removing people from the site, and your chat room program probably has commands specifically for that purpose, too. Unfortunately, it's a common occurrence that people are rude during chat. But many are nice, too.)

You need to know the etiquette involved in chatting online, such as welcoming newcomers. Participate in a few other chat rooms to see how to run one before opening your own. You can find several chat rooms on the Internet all the time, such as Chat House (www.chathouse.com), CoolChat (www.coolchat.com), and Talk City (www.talkcity.com).

Letting Your Customers Serve Themselves

Yes, you could set up a great customer service department, if only your budget weren't limited, right? Allowing the customer to serve herself to the information she wants lets you create a great customer service department without spending a fortune hiring a staff (it saves a lot of time for the existing staff, too).

You can benefit from putting a lot of information on your site that's traditionally given out by sales staff. Some sites give customers access to lots of information, including their own customer database entries. For example, FedEx lets you track your packages online (www.fedex.com). In addition, many automobile manufacturers put up Web pages where customers can get price quotes directly online, including the following:

- BMW (www.bmw.com)
- Chrysler (www.chrysler.com)
- Ford (www.ford.com)
- Saturn (www.saturncars.com)
- General Motors Chevrolet (www.chevrolet.com)
- Nissan (www.nissan-usa.com)

Conceivably, a manufacturer's entire inventory could eventually be available online. Perhaps then the sales staff could be reduced to a minimum, because customers could find a lot of their own information. For example, General Motors is creating a "configurator" that gives customers online access to essentially the entire voluminous guide that dealers use, as many as 8,000 Web pages. Changes in pricing or options will be immediately posted to the Web. The GM configurator keeps a running total of options the customer selects, and suggests a package if several options are selected that match a standard option package. (Watch out — automated customer service can lead you right into automated sales. By August of 1997, 386 cars had been sold online using a configurator available on a trial basis in the state of Maryland.)

Customer-Pleasing Policies

Remember the days of "The customer is always right?" Hopefully, those days are still around at your online store.

Customer-pleasing policies generate repeat business for your store — you'll never make it if every customer visits only once. You need a few loyal customers to tell all their friends and relatives — that's how you build a terrific business. On the other hand, you can't afford to give away the store. So your policies must have balance.

Mail-order catalogue companies actually provide some good tips for pleasing your online customers. These catalogue companies have already faced the issue of satisfying customers from a distance. Just like a mail-order catalogue company, your store needs to handle the following issues:

- ✔ **Returns and exchanges:** For returns or exchanges of goods, you need to decide whether to pay the customer's return shipping costs or just include an appropriately addressed label with every shipment in case they need to send you a return. (You may want to post your return policies prominently on your site.)

  Print the order number on your return labels, so you can look up the order in your database files quickly upon receipt. Even a return is an opportunity to sell other items, so many companies include a few lines on the return form for the customer to order additional (or replacement) items.

- ✔ **Payment disputes, late payment, or nonpayment:** For disputed credit card payments, the credit card companies' dispute policies may protect you. In most policies, customers are obliged to pay the first $50 of any disputed amount while awaiting resolution. You have to decide on a firm policy for refunds of payments made in cash or by check. (Along with your returns policy, you may want to post your refund policy online, too.)

  For late payments, you need a way to send a polite reminder bill, and for nonpayment you need to decide at what point to write off the debt as bad or refer it to a collection firm. Many companies wait at least 90 to 120 days before taking such action. You can start with a polite e-mail, but you may end up having to follow up with mail through the postal service.

- ✔ **Errors on your part, such as mistaken items and charging the wrong price:** Many stores offer a "we'll make it up to you" policy, such as double the difference between the right price and the erroneous price they charged. It's usually no more than a few pennies, and it makes customers feel good. (This is another good policy to post on your online store.)

> For mistaken mail-order items, if you made the mistake, the least you can do is pay the return shipping costs for the customer. Of course, the best policy is to check and double-check orders to make sure they go out correctly in the first place. Be sure you keep your database records up to date, because that helps minimize mistakes in shipping customer orders.

Keeping in Touch with a Newsletter

In the online environment, your customers can easily forget that you're still out there. A newsletter provides a nice touch that keeps your business alive in the customers' minds.

You can present your newsletter in an e-mail message. That way, you know all your customers can read it without going through a lot of rigamarole. In addition, many e-mail systems now accept and display HTML files as a Web browser would, so you could create your newsletter in HTML and send it to customers by e-mail.

The newsletter can come out monthly, weekly, or whatever schedule is convenient for you. It should offer useful information and perhaps a few "insider" tidbits about what's going on with your site, your business, and your store.

Don't fill your newsletter with blatant sales pitches. Yes, it can offer discounts, coupons, and so on, but work to make your newsletter genuinely useful to and fun for your customers.

Selling Online For Dummies Internet Directory

The 5th Wave   By Rich Tennant

"Now that's what I call a full service selling site - you can sign up for hockey lessons, buy a hockey uniform, and locate the nearest tooth implant clinic all on the same site."

In this part . . .

Turn to this part for a quick guide to Web sites that offer tools, advice, free software, product information, legal news, and a whole host of other resources that can help make your online selling site better, faster, and more successful.

Selling Online For Dummies Internet Directory

• •

In This Directory

▶ Getting HTML tips to improve your site's content

▶ Downloading tools and CGI scripts, free or otherwise

▶ Keeping up with legal information

▶ Locating experts on many topics

▶ Getting ideas from great commercial sites

• •

*T*he Web itself often proves the best source of information to help you with your online business. The *Selling Online For Dummies* Internet Directory presents a comprehensive listing of terrific sites to help you find answers to your questions.

As you peruse this directory, you see icons that point out the following features of sites:

The site contains plenty of graphics that may take a while to download.

$ You must pay for some services at the site.

You find files for downloading at the site.

The site contains sound files.

Exercise your credit card (or other preferred method of payment).

To enjoy some of the features at the site, you must sign in.

The site lets you add your two cents worth on an electronic message board.

Talk to experts, fellow merchants, or potential customers online.

Video clips are a featured element.

Commercial Tools

Even if you can't download your favorite tool for free from these sites, they offer a wealth of information to make your work easier and more efficient.

Adobe Photoshop

www.adobe.com/prodindex/photoshop/main.html

Design and digital image help: Find information about Photoshop, the flagship product for Web designers and any other sort of digital image processing, at this site.

BBEdit

www.barebones.com/

Mac HTML tool: Get pricing information, new product announcements, tips, and hints about BBEdit, the favorite HTML editing tool for the Mac.

Gamelan

www.gamelan.com/

Fun java applets to spice up your site: Gamelan, the Official Directory of Java, offers a big collection of Java applets you can download and use on your site.

GIF Construction Set

www.mindworkshop.com/alchemy/gifcon.html

Create GIFs for your site: Alchemy Mindworks' GIF Construction Set, made for the Windows platform, is a popular tool for creating animated GIFs. It helps you create animations, transparent GIFs, and font effects.

HotSyte JavaScript Connection

www.serve.com/hotsyte/

Create simple applets: JavaScript looks a little like Java, but it's really a scripting language designed to let you extend the capabilities of HTML files. Using JavaScript, you can create simple animations, redirect site visitors if you've moved a Web page, or create unusual Web page designs. The Hotsyte JavaScript Connection offers lots of information about JavaScript and includes links to sample code you can use on you site.

Jamba

www.jamba.com/

Program without being a programmer: Jamba, for Windows uers only, lets you develop simple Java applications with no programming knowledge. You just arrange objects and actions to create animations. At the Jamba site, you can read about Jamba and play with some demo applets.

Java

www.javasoft.com/

Java jamboree: Java made its debut in 1995 as a cross-platform programming language for the Web. It's been a hot topic ever since. Get information about this emergent Web technology at the site.

Kai's Power Tools

www.metatools.com

Get creative with your images: Kai's Power Tools are a must for creating certain awesome effects in your images. Stretch the limits of your imagination at this site.

Luckman WebEdit

www.luckman.com/

Windows HTML tool: WebEdit is the favorite HTML editing tool for the Windows platform. Get product information and tips on how to use WebEdit at the site.

Macromedia Flash

www.macromedia.com/software/flash

Make your site interactive: Flash animation files are extremely small and slightly more interactive than animated GIFs. Flash is much easier than Director to use, too. For a demo, visit Macromedia's site.

Macromedia Shockwave

www.macromedia.com/

Bringing sound and images to your site: Shockwave, a plug-in for your browser, lets you play audio, animation, and movies of CD-ROM quality in your browser window. Files created using Director, Authorware, or Flash can be converted and made playable as Shockwave files. On Macromedia's homepage, you find helpful information and pointers about using Shockwave files on your site.

Marimba's Castanet

www.marimba.com/

Push technology center: Castanet is an award-winning technology for multicasting, often called push technology. You can get information about the ins and outs of using Castanet at Marimba's site.

Microsoft ActiveX

www.microsoft.com/activeplatform/

The (Active)X files: ActiveX lets you create Web pages on your server dynamically, for example, by connecting to your product database and wrapping a template around your product's specifications. Microsoft's ActiveX page offers an overview of ActiveX technology.

Microsoft FrontPage

www.microsoft.com/frontpage/

Easy Web page construction: FrontPage is a Web publishing tool for Windows 95/NT that lets you create Web pages from templates or from scratch. The site includes details about the product's capabilities, as well as some extensions and bug fixes.

Paint Shop Pro

www.jasc.com

Photoshop's country cousin: Paint Shop Pro is a small and cheap program with some capabilities similar to Photoshop's, and some that are nicely complementary. Download the Pro and try it out for 30 days before you pay a dime!

PointCast

www.pointcast.com

Pioneer push technology: PointCast was the first push technology popularly available for the Web. Visit the PointCast site to find out how push technology is changing the Web, and how it may help your business.

RealPlayer

www.real.com/

Put movies and sound on your site: RealPlayer delivers audio and video in smooth-playing streams. You can convert existing video and audio files into RealPlayer files, and you can use the program to deliver live broadcasts, such as concerts and interviews. At the site you can test the RealPlayer for free and download a 30-day trial server package, too.

VRML.org

www.vrml.org/

Find out what VRML is: You definitely need a programmer to help you if you want to develop VRML for your online store. Before you contact a professional to help you get started with VRML, visit this site, which offers a central information source about VRML development.

WebGenie

www.webgenie.com/

Windows Web page development tools: Packed with freeware and shareware utilities for creating Web sites on the Windows platform, Windows users must visit this site before they begin constructing their own pages.

Other Stuff to Check Out

www.aereal.com/instant/
www.ulead.com
www.real.com/devzone/
www.microsoft.com/jscript/

Developing Content

Developing your store's content on you own? Need some help getting started with HTML? These sites give you the help you need. (I still consult several of these sites myself when I have a question.)

Backward Compatibility Viewer

www.delorie.com/Web/wpbcv.html

Browser testing: You must thoroughly test your pages before putting them on your server for the whole online world to see. You can use the viewer found at this site to see how your page appears in different browsers.

Bordertown

www.grafxfactory.com/squinn/
borders.htm

Spice up your site with borders: Bordertown has borders a-plenty, organized by color, and tips for how to use them, including some methods for using invisible GIFs as spacers on your HTML pages. Cool.

CNET's HTML for Beginners Pages

www.cnet.com/Content/Features/
Howto/Basics

HTML basics: CNET offers tips and HTML tutorials for beginners of all levels. This is an excellent site for anyone who wants to improve his or her HTML skills (no matter how long you've been selling online).

How to Do a Searchable Database

www2.ncsu.edu/bae/people/faculty/
walker/hotlist/isindex.html

Databases made easy: Consider how a searchable database could make your site easier to shop, and therefore more attractive to potential customers. Check out this site for an in-depth look at some options for using a searchable database at your site.

Lynda Weinman's site

www.lynda.com/hex.html

Give your site's images a makeover: Lynda Weinman's site is a veritable treasure trove of information about better ways to use graphics and colors on the Web. Here you find the safe palette visibly displayed and discussed in detail, along with tips and hints on getting the most out of your GIFs and JPEGs.

The Slot

www.theslot.com/

Proofreading help: This site offers an editor's-eye view of the good, the bad, and the ugly aspects of English grammar and usage. Many production editors in the real world of the Web use The Slot as a quotable reference for why to do things a certain way (that is, *their* way).

Studio Archetype's Design Process

www.studioarchetype.com/process/
index.html

See how the pros develop their content: Want some tips from experts on how to design a terrific site? Studio Archetype (formerly known as Clement Mok Design) has done some of the most talked-about sites on the Web. You can get a glimpse into their design process at this site.

Sun Microsystems' Guide to Web Style

www.sun.com/styleguide/

Make your Web site shine: How long should each Web page be on your site? What's the most effective way to integrate Java applets in your site? Besides answering these and other exciting questions, Sun's style guide offers rules and tips for creating better Web sites.

Tripod's TechWeb Pod

www.tripod.com/web_tech/

Expert content development help: Visit this great list of links to other sites where you can find all sorts of tutorials, advice, and tools to download. The Pod is "Poderated" by Mr. Don Zereski, VP of Technology at Tripod, Inc., so you know you're getting top-notch advice.

Weblint Page

www.cre.canon.co.uk/~neilb/weblint/

Check your UNIX script: Lint, a classic program for UNIX, catches errors in C programs. Similarly, Weblint catches errors in your HTML files. On this page you find an installable error-checking script.

WebMonkey

www.hotwired.com/webmonkey/
web101

HTML primer: Wonder how to get started with HTML for your store? WebMonkey offers lots of tips, tricks, and tutorials to take the mystery out of creating Web content.

What is Good Hypertext Writing?

kbs.cs.to-berlin.de/~jutta.ht/ writing.html

Address your online audience: This site focuses on writing for the Web, with a solid sense of good grammar and usage. You may find this site a great help for keeping your writing on track when you create content specifically for online readers.

Other Stuff to Check Out

www.quadzilla.com/
info.med.yale.edu/caim/manual/index.html
www.w3.org/pub/WWW/Provider/Style/ All.html
www.typo.com
www.webreference.com/

Design and Advertising Sites

Need some help setting up your store? Looking for a design firm that can show you something great, or an advertising firm to help you attract just the right customers? These sites give you a head start on finding the right partnerships for your business.

CKS Interactive

www.cks.com/

Professional design staff information: Many people consider CKS Interactive, which has designed Web sites for top companies, to be one of the most trusted online design and advertising firms. (If you're not interested in the information about working with CKS

Interactive, visit Holland's Corner at the CKS site and get a taste of Net Breakfast, your daily dose of what you need to see on the Web.)

FlyCast

www.flycast.com/

Make it a banner day at your site: FlyCast can help you enter the (sometimes) highly-profitable world of advertising with banners. FlyCast auctions unsold ad space on various Web sites; a visit to this page could be just the boost you need to take your selling site to the next level.

I/PRO

www.nielsen.com.

Measure your site's traffic: Created by Nielsen of television ratings fame, I/PRO (Internet Profiles) offers an industry standard audit of your online store's traffic. In fact, I/PRO is the leading third-party auditor for tracking traffic on your Web site. You can find lots of helpful information about site traffic at this site.

Poppe Tyson

www.poppe.com/

Professional design staff information: Poppe Tyson is an award-winning advertising and design company that has a knack for creating Web sites. Poppe Tyson differs from other Web-design agencies in that it specializes in advertising for "the considered purchase" — which includes automobiles, personal computers, and movies. Visit this site to find out more about the company's services.

Studio Archetype

www.studioarchetype.com

Professional design staff information: Studio Archetype, formerly known as Clement Mok Design, is the creator of world-class Web sites for major companies and possibly the most respected Web design firm in the business. The company Web site tells you all about the services available through Studio Archetype.

Other Stuff to Check Out

www.cortex.com/
www.linkexchange.com
www.netcount.com/

Electronic Commerce Services

These sites offer technologies and services for the transaction-related parts of selling online. (You can read a lot more about these vendors and services in Chapters 15 and 16 of this book.)

BlueMoney

www.bluemoney.com/

Payment service: BlueMoney, a new entrant to the online payment services arena, offers services somewhat similar to CyberCash (www.cybercash.com), but with a different payment structure. BlueMoney helps new merchants get set up with a merchant bank account, too.

CyberCash

www.cybercash.com/

Payment service: CyberCash, founded by Dan Lynch and Bill Melton, is perhaps the most widely-recognized provider of electronic commerce services online. Their products include payment services for credit cards, digital checks (Pay Now), and digital coin (CyberCoin). Find out more at the site.

CyberSource

www.cybersource.com

Get your products there — safely: CyberSource provides secure delivery of your digital products worldwide. This handy service can also handle tax collection and monitor international import and export laws for you.

DigiCash

www.digicash.com/

Payment service: DigiCash, founded by David Chaum, is the first company to offer anonymous electronic cash and smart card payments. DigiCash, which is implemented by the Mark Twain Bank of St. Louis, is widely recognized in Europe.

First Virtual

www.fv.com/

Payment service: First Virtual, founded by Einar Stefferud (an Internet pioneer) and others, offers an online payment service that doesn't require sending sensitive credit card information over the Internet; First Virtual completes transactions largely by e-mail and existing credit card services.

MilliCent

www.millicent.digital.com/

Payment service: MilliCent, DEC's answer to digital cash, offers a nice system set up with scrip vendors and merchants that accept MilliCent online script for purchases as small as $1/10$ of a cent. Customers can purchase scrip online using a credit card, so they don't have to give out their credit card number repeatedly. MilliCent is currently in a beta testing phase but soon will be released for general use. You can become part of the beta testing phase by visiting the site.

Open Market

www.openmarket.com/

Payment service: Open Market offers the top-of-the-line products (in the $45K to $100K price range) for setting up an electronic commerce site. If you want the best, start here.

RSA Data Security

www.rsa.com/

Online commerce and encryption information: RSA Data Security holds a lot of the patents on public-key cryptography. (The R in RSA stands for Ron Rivest, who has come up with the implementation of public-key cryptography most commonly used for online commerce today.) This site contains lots of excellent resources related to cryptography and electronic commerce, including an FAQ.

Other Stuff to Check Out

www.ziplock.com
www.checkfree.com/
www.hks.net/

Examples

Sometimes, nothing gets the idea across like a good example. This section shows you successful online stores and media businesses that you should visit to get a feel for success. You may even pick up some ideas for your own online selling site.

1-800-Flowers

www.1800flowers.com/

Fresh content and great offline integration: 1-800-Flowers approaches selling online from a retail perspective, and they believe that has made them a successful online business. This site sells flowers online, directing business to local florists. 1-800-Flowers is updated seasonally, for holidays, and so on, offering special bouquets for special occasions.

amazon.com

www.amazon.com/

Easy access to large number of products: amazon.com goes head-to-head with Barnes & Noble for the title of World's Largest Bookstore — but amazon.com does business only on the Internet. Check out the amazing search capabilities available at this site — you can find your title in seconds by plugging in a few keywords into the search engine.

CDnow

www.cdnow.com/

Easy access to large number of products: This site is a great asset for music lovers and is also a real-life success story for the two brothers who started it. Search for a hard-to-find CD by title or artist.

Continental Airlines

www.flycontinental.com/

Good customer service: Continental's site posts flight schedules, fares, and car, hotel, and realtime flight information. Currently Continental Airlines offers bonus miles for booking e-tickets online with the new C.O.O.L. Travel assistant, which requires registration.

Chevrolet

www.chevrolet.com/

Customers serve themselves to product information: Chevrolet's site includes entertaining writeups about the history and romance of many of their enduring models, such as the Corvette and Camaro. You can visit the "Build Your Own Chevy" site and get price quotes online.

CNET

www.cnet.com/

More than just a store: All the Real Audio content available here makes this incredibly ambitious site seem more

like a radio station than a Web site. CNET is a terrific success story, with approximately 1.5 million members. Member registration is free and gives you access to software reviews and a game center, among many, many other features. Get familiar with its friendly and instantly-recognizable yellow-bordered pages today.

Expedia

www.expedia.com/

Fresh content and great customer service: The Microsoft travel site has recently added new features, including real-time flight status information on specific flights. Expedia usually offers a central theme destination with several related articles. You find a hotel directory and a currency converter (which could come in handy for your business in a pinch, yes?), along with weather information and detailed maps.

FedEx

www.fedex.com/

A leader in customer service: Check on a package, or even use the Internet to ship your packages. FedEx integrates its online site with its corporate databases to create the best in customer service online. (The FedEx site went up in November of 1994, with a budget of $100,000. The company believes that they saved at least that much in customer support costs within three months.)

Fodor's

www.fodors.com/

Online store for traditional business: Yes, the trusted name in travel has an online storefront. The personal trip planner section of the site offers an amusing interactive survey that creates a mini travel guide just for you. At this site, you can gather information about cities all over the world. Of course, the company's online store creates a new audience for their offline products.

Ford Motor Company

www.ford.com/showrooms/

Tell the customer everything they need to know: At the Ford site, you can find information about new vehicles, calculate your payments on a particular car, and even apply for credit. (To go straight to the payment calculator, visit www.fordcredit.com/calculator/.)

Lexus

www.lexus.com/

Add-on content creates appeal: The Lexus site includes comparative information about Lexus automobiles versus other luxury automobiles, historical information about older Lexus models, financing information, and a nationwide search for Pre-owned Certified Lexus cars (available through dealerships).

Mercedes Benz

www.mercedes.com/

Bringing the dealership to the customer: Mercedes has descriptions of the cars, a configurator for their newer models, and a form where you can search among over 30,000 cars for a used Mercedes — newer employee-owned cars or older models. (Prices are in Deutschmarks, so I couldn't tell you if the deals were good.)

Northwest Airlines

www.nwa.com/

Special deals for online customers: Northwest's site contains weekend CyberSaver fares, updated by e-mail for those who register. Like many other sites, they offer bonus miles, and special fares advertised online only. They have an online reservations and booking service called WorldWeb.

Southwest Airlines

www.iflyswa.com/

Real-time information: Southwest Airlines features a nice tool for checking flights, fares, and availability. Visiting this site feels a little like talking to a travel agent: You specify your date and time of day for departure, your home, and your destination. It shows you a flight schedule and categories of fares. However, when I called Southwest Airlines on the phone I talked to an agent who found me a cheaper fare. Oh well.

Trans World Airlines

www.twa.com/

Personalized atmosphere and great customer service: TWA offers online booking and notifies registered customers by e-mail of upcoming discounts to destinations to which they fly frequently.

Tripod

www.tripod.com/

 $

Fresh content and more: Tripod gives down-to-earth advice to young people getting out on their own for the first time, and the site asks their opinions in surveys about issues that matter to them. Need to know how to write a resume? Renting an apartment in New York City? Thinking of moving in with your boyfriend or girlfriend? You find fresh presentations of topics like these and more. You can read the articles for free, but to use the chat rooms and join the conferences costs $3 per month. You also get lots of advice about putting together Web sites. (Some very small businesses actually use their Tripod home page as an online storefront if they don't need online transactions.)

United Airlines

www.ual.com/

Excellent customer service and site incentives: United Airlines offers downloadable United Connection software, which lets PC/Windows users make online travel arrangements. Mac users can obtain access to United's online service through CompuServe. Like most of the other airlines, United offers bonus miles for booking online. You can also look up flight information on the site.

US Airways

www.usairways.com/

Excellent customer service: US Airways offers weekend saver fares especially for Internet travelers; those who register receive updates on these specials via e-mail.

Virtual Vineyards

www.virtualvin.com/

Reaching a global market: Virtual Vineyards is probably my favorite online store. Formed as an outlet for small wineries that make excellent wine, selling online grew this business so that they now offer gourmet foods that go with the wines. Virtual Vineyards ships anywhere it's legal to ship.

Other Stuff to Check Out

www.alaskaair.com/
www.americawest.com/
www.americanair.com/
www.bmw.com/
www.chrysler.com/
www.delta-air.com
www.gibson.com/
www.greetst.com/
www.match.com/
www.thetrip.com/
www.saturn.com/car/ipc/index.html

Fighting Spam

This group of sites presents a formidable collection of resources to help you cut down or eliminate the unsolicited junk mail you receive. In this collection, you can find resources to help yourself as an individual and as a business.

Blacklist of Internet Advertisers

math-www.uni-paderborn.de/%axel/BL/blacklist.html

Find out what not to do: It's not nice, but in case you need it, this site offers a blacklist of Internet advertisers. In the blacklist, you find a good explanation of why each party made it on the list. The site contains a nice introductory FAQ about spam, too.

Coalition Against Unsolicited Commercial Email

www.cauce.org/resources.html

Anti-spam news: Here's the online anti-spam organization to watch. They're a grassroots organization advocating the extension of current federal junk fax law to include unsolicited bulk e-mail.

Get That Spammer!

kryten.eng.monash.edu.au/gspam.html

For the avid anti-spammer: You find strategies and tools for tracking down individuals who send spam and a guide for ISPs who deal with spam. For additional information, try the host of links to lots of other anti-spam sites.

How to Filter Out Spam

www.exposure-usa.com/email/spam.html

Wash that spam right out of your Inbox: At this site you find an excellent step-by-step lesson on how to filter spam using your e-mail software. The steps cite Eudora Pro, but they apply to any e-mail software that has filtering capabilities. (One scary factoid I gleaned here: Did you know that some supposedly spam-removal mailing lists could actually be a spam scam to get your name on the spam lists? Beware.)

Spam Media Tracker

www.fofa.concordia.ca/spam/default.html

Spam news: This site claims to be the "Best collection of spam news on the 'net," and I think they may be right. I even found a picture (was it a genuine photo?) of the president of CyberPromotions, which is the world's largest spam company, according to this site.

NAGS Spam Filter

www.nags.org/spamfilter.html

UNIX users get rid of spam: Download a free Perl filter for UNIX systems with Perl installed at this site. This filter works with UNIX programs such as Elm and Pine, and also with POP mail software such as Eudora, Exchange, and Netscape Navigator.

Spam Tools for the Mac

www.fofa.concordia.ca/spam/tools.html

Mac users can forget about spam: Most anyone with a Mac can use the IPName tool, a piece of freeware that lets you translate IP addresses into domain names. Use this handy tool for chasing spammers, but also for monitoring who's visiting your Web site.

Urgent Call to Action

www.tigerden.com/junkmail/

Spam news: This site has a great list of links for information about existing and emerging anti-spam laws, and links to places to complain about spam. Did you know that falsifying e-mail is a felony in the United States?

ZDNet Software Library-AntiSpam Tools

www.software.zdnet.com/roundups/
  spam/mp0897.html

Tools for fighting spam: This site contains the editor's picks with links to several tools to download.

Other Stuff to Check Out

www.scambusters.org/stopspam
www.cs.hmc.edu/~ivl/nags/index.html
com.primenet.com/spamking/
www.csn.net/~felbel/jnkmail.html
www.macintouch.com/spam.shtml
everythingemail.net/unsolicited.html

Free Tools

Real Webmasters visit these site for free goodies, including scripts for things like bulletin boards, chat rooms, mailbots, and so on. Even if your budget doesn't necessitate that you shop for free tools, I bet you can still find something at any one of these sites to make you glad you plugged in the URL.

Apple's QuickTime Site

qtvr.quicktime.apple.com/

Bring interactivity to your site: You find downloadable versions of QTVR plug-ins, useful tutorials, and much more.

Calendar Generator

www.intellinet.com/CoolTools/
  CalendarMaker

Keep customers posted on company events: Need a calendar for your online store? You can visit this site to lay out a calendar for the month and year of your choice using an HTML table.

ColorServe Pro

www.biola.edu/cgi-bin/colorpro/
  colorpro.cgi?

Change the color of your background: Visit this site when you need a quick way to translate a color into its hexa-decimal code, which comes in handy when you want to change background colors on your Web pages (using the BODY HTML tag).

ColorSync

www.colorsync.apple.com/

Match colors: ColorSync is Apple's excellent technology that helps you match onscreen colors to their printed equivalents. ColorSync is a Photoshop plug-in for the Macintosh platform.

CPAN

www.perl.org, www.perl.com

A gem of a site for Perl users: CPAN is the best resource I know of for Perl software and helpful information. This site contains versions of Perl downloadable for almost every platform you can imagine. It's the definitive collection of Perl implementations used by real Webmasters.

CU-SeeMe

www.cu-seeme.com/

Real-time videoconferencing over the Web: You can download a free trial version at the CU-SeeMe Web site and turn your store into a realtime videoconferencing facility — with just a video camera and a microphone. The company maintaining this Web page, White Pine, offers a commercial version called Enhanced CU-SeeMe.

Freedom VR

www.msc.cornell.edu/~houle/freedom/

Ease into virtual reality: An excellent student-written freeware utility that lets you take photographs, then scan or download them into a directory, and easily use them to create a Virtual Reality world, without the hours of processing time needed for QTVR.

GIFWizard

www.gifwizard.com/

Compressing your images: This simple software helps reduce the size of your GIF images, so that they download a lot faster for your customers' browsers.

Matt's Script Archive

www.scriptarchive.com/

Free stuff of all kinds: A resource put together by Matt Wright and used by many Webmasters I know when they need just the "wright" script. The only caveat is that you must keep the copyrights and headers attached to the scripts. The site includes a script for verifying credit card numbers.

Precise Pixel Ruler

www.infinet.com/~microfox/

Just a little animation for your site: Use this pixel ruler for creating things like animated GIFS, when you just want to animate a small portion of an image (the pixels have to line up exactly with the rest of the image or it looks funny).

Selena Sol's Public Domain Script Archive

www.extropia.com/

A storehouse of free stuff: This is probably the Web's most complete collection of free CGI scripts. The scripts mostly work with UNIX systems, but you also find some ports for other platforms. Selena Sol's includes a script for a fully-functional Web store (you can see a demo at the site), scripts for message boards, chat, and many other utilities.

XTML

members.aol.com/ksayward/XTML

Cool table tool: XTML is a free tool written by Ken Sayward that converts Microsoft Excel spreadsheets into HTML tables. Not only that, after you use XTML to create your basic table, you can modify its appearance using HTML tags for cell padding, cell spacing, and so on.

Other Stuff to Check Out

www.perl.com/CPAN-local//ports/
language.perl.com/info/software.html
www.activestate.com/software/default.htm
www.perl.com/CPAN-local//ports/mac/
ftp://sunsite.cnlab-switch.ch/software/
platform/macos/perl/
www.microsoft.com/imagecomposer/
gifanimator/gifanim.htm

Fun Sites

I recommend a visit to these sites when you need a moment to relax, a new idea, or a good giggle to take your mind off business pressures.

Cliche Finder

www.westegg.com/cliche

Flatter than a pancake: Looking for just the right touch to get your point across to a group of old geezers? Here's a great site for you — it's right up your alley.

Cool Site of the Day

cool.infi.net

Fun and good ideas for your site: Started by Glenn Davis in 1994, Cool Site of the Day gives access to cutting-edge Web sites and other "cool" editorial content. Visit to get new and exciting ideas for presenting your products and services online.

Yall.com

www.yall.com

To tickle your funnybone: Full of silly southernisms like the list of ways to drive a Yankee crazy, this site may be just the thing to tickle your funny bone in a spare moment. It offers free digital postcards, including a few of Elvis. If you're a Southerner, it's funny because you get it. If you're not a Southerner, it's funny because it shows you how strange the South really can be.

General Interest Sites

These sites may interest you as a business owner, and possibly on a personal level as well. I picked sites with a wealth of information about personal rights and evolving business practices in the age of online information.

CommerceNet

www.commerce.net/

Growing the Internet: CommerceNet is a consortium of companies, including many big names, dedicated to furthering the growth of the Internet in general, and Internet commerce in particular. Among other tasks, CommerceNet sets up committees that investigate potential areas of difficulty and look for solutions, such as in the area of collecting sales tax online. CommerceNet organizers believe that the majority of companies and organizations in the United States may conduct business online within five years, and they want to clear the way for this explosion in online commerce.

CPSR

www.cpsr.org/

Tying technology to humanity: Computer Professionals for Social Responsibility is a national organization that helps define the nature of the responsibility toward technology. CPSR tries to represent the public's point of view in policy debates, typically those involving the government and large corporations.

The Electronic Commerce Guide

e-comm.internet.com/

General guide to online commerce: The Electronic Commerce Guide contains links to hundreds of resources, including a library, online services, and searching capabilities. The site also has links to Web Week, a leading journal about Web technology and business strategy.

The Electronic Frontier Foundation (EFF)

www.eff.org/

Protecting your rights: The Electronic Frontier Foundation ensures that the principles embodied in the U.S. Constitution are protected as new communications technologies emerge. It is concerned with protecting the rights of individuals in Cyberspace, including privacy rights. The EFF works to shape not just Internet-related policies, but also the policies governing the entire communications infrastructure of the United States.

InterNIC

www.internic.net/

Domain name registration: The InterNIC registers domain names. It maintains a Whois database that can tell you what domain names are in use. The InterNIC has been setting up domain names since the early days, when Internet was the ARPANET, run by the Department of Defense.

The Internet Society

www.isoc.org/

Developing the Internet: The Internet Society is a professional membership organization devoted to encouraging the growth and development of the Internet. Its members come from all over the world, and its membership list reads like "Who's Who of the Internet." Dr. Vinton Cerf, the person who originally conceptualized the Internet and scribbled a design on the back of an envelope in the San Francisco airport, was the founding president of the Internet Society.

Small Business Association

www.sbaonline.sba.gov/

General small business help: The Small Business Association is one of the best and best-known resources for small businesses. Now you can look for business information online with the SBA, including many helpful publications for small business owners.

Other Stuff to Check Out

www.cyberatlas.com/

Getting Listed on Search Engines

Want to get the word out about your site? These sites offer services that can help you get your site a mention on several Internet search engines, which is one of the best ways to start advertising your site. Some of these services charge a nominal fee, some are available for free.

The PostMaster

www.netcreations.com/postmaster

$

Hitting 400 directories: For $75, The Postmaster submits your site to about 400 directories. You can also look at a free trial version that adds you to 25 sites.

Submit-It

www.submit-it.com/

Free site submission: Submit-It offers to submit your site to 20 search engines for free. Additional services include software you can use to submit your own URLs or submission packages ranging from $60 to $400.

The Web Robots Page

info.webcrawler.com/mak/projects/
   robots/robots.html

Read about Web robots: The page contains a FAQ, a guide to the robot protocol, and a mailing list archive. Many files on this site are old, but the standard hasn't changed so they still apply.

Other Stuff to Check Out

www.the-vault.com/easy-submit

Hardware

If you want to do all the development footwork for your online store without leaving your chair, you need to visit some sites where you can purchase hardware and peripherals online. These sites may also offer you some ideas for how to set up your store, too.

Computer Shopper

www.zdnet.com/cshopper/

Hardware for sale: Looking for a place where you can do some serious online shopping for your store's Web server machine and other equipment? Computer Shopper is a great beginning. You get tons of information here — start by clicking the How to Use this Site button.

Internet Shopping Network

www.isn.com

Buy online: Look into the computer superstore for any computer item you may need, or place bids on items from the Home Shopping Network.

NetBuyer

www.netbuyer.com/

Information and reviews: Find review columns and special weekly deals from vendors. Not only that, you can network with other shoppers to get the real scoop about different products. NetBuyer is part of the Computer Shopper online site.

Legal and Business News

Legal resources abound online, especially regarding sensitive issues such as privacy and encryption law.

Bureau of Export Administration

www.bxa.doc.gov/.

Export licenses: If you need export licenses for software, especially encryption software, this is the online site for the government office that can issue the appropriate licenses. For other government branches, look under Government on Yahoo!

The Copyright Web Site

www.benedict.com/

Observing copyright law: This site provides a good guide to copyright issues, especially those involving the Internet.

Cyberspace Law

www.findlaw.com/01topics/
10cyberspace

Legal news: Part of the Findlaw site (www.findlaw.com/), you get information about legal battles and laws that affect Cyberspace. For example, the site offers details on domain name dispute cases.

Domain Names and Trademarks

www.law.georgetown.edu/lc/internic/
domain.html

Domain name news: Visit this site for tons of information about domain name disputes, provided by the Law School at George Washington University.

The Electronic Frontier Foundation

www.eff.org/

Online legal activism: The Electronic Frontier Foundation often writes "friends of the court" memos regarding court cases that affect online rights.

They also offer excellent legal analyses of pending legislation, such as the one they wrote about the CDA when it was before Congress in 1995 that declared it "unconstitutional on its face." And the Supreme Court later agreed.

Electronic Privacy Information Center (EPIC)

www.epic.org/

Legal news: If you want to follow the progress of legislation about privacy, encryption, and freedom of speech on the Internet, EPIC offers one of the best resources.

Findlaw

www.findlaw.com/

Legal news: The Findlaw site offers a searchable index of legal resources. It also contains articles about current topics and court cases that are queried often for reasons of precedent.

Global Contact, Inc.

www.globalcontact.com/

International business contacts: You find a business directory for international import/export trade at this site. Use this site to locate trade leads, sellers, or buyers by descriptions of their products or services.

International Trade Law

itl.irv.uit.no/trade_law/documents/
 freetrade/wta-94/nav/toc.html

A global perspective: You can search the World Trade Agreement and some related documents, plus you find a list of members of the World Trade Organization and their dates of entry.

The Internet Legal Resources Guide

www.ilrg.com

Good general reference source: The Internet Legal Resources Guide provides databases of legal information, articles, and links.

NAFTA site

www.iep.doc.gov/border/nafta.htm

Government documents and border-related information: Includes demographics, geographical information, import/export statistics, and economic profiles.

Nolo Press

www.nolo.com/chunkPCT/
 PCT.index.html

Help yourself to the law: Nolo Press is one of the most widely recognized names in self-help law. The site offers an exceptionally good resource center online that can be very helpful to small businesses. This site features patent, copyright, and trademark information, and links to other online resources about legal issues.

Piper Index

www.piperinfo.com/state/states.html.

State law: Nolo Press recommends this site as possibly the best legal resource online regarding state law. The Piper Index contains a court directory that links to providers of legal information about states, which in some cases includes actual court opinions.

THOMAS

thomas.loc.gov/

Legislation news: If you just absolutely have to check for yourself on the status of any pending legislation before the U.S. Congress, go to THOMAS, the Congressional Web site, administered by the Library of Congress, where you can search by bill number, title, and keyword. THOMAS also carries the proceedings of the House floor. (THOMAS is named in honor of Thomas Jefferson, by the way.)

US Commerce Department

www.doc.gov/

Contact government bureaus: The U.S. Department of Commerce oversees the export of encryption software and other software and hardware products. At this site, you find a list of the individual government bureaus within the Commerce Department.

The United States Copyright Office

lcweb.loc.gov/copyright/

Protect your copyright: This site offers copyright registration applications and other materials online at no charge. Registering a copyright is one of the best ways to protect your copyright, even though copyright actually protects books as soon as they are created. A registered copyright is ironclad against "innocent infringement."

Other Stuff to Check Out

plaza.interport.net/inta/index.html.
www.ssjr.com/interact.htm
www.yahoo.com/Government/Law/Federal/
and www.yahoo.com/Government/ Law/
International_Law/

www.law.indiana.edu/law/v-lib/states.html
home.earthlink.net/~ivanlove/
www.courttv.com/
itl.irv.uit.no/trade_law/nav/
electronic.commerce.html
www.nolo.com/chunkLR/surflocally.html
www.nolo.com/chunkPCT/PCT.index.html

Business and Technology News

These sites offer specialized clippings services and articles about topics ranging from high-tech developments to corporate training and development.

Boardwatch Magazine

www.boardwatch.com

General news: Boardwatch offers its readers a balanced view of the Internet. The magazine includes coverage about the Web, the Internet in general, commercial online services such as AOL, and even small, local BBS providers. Not only that, it's free in return for registration that requires a little demographic information from you. Bonus for online stores-to-be: Boardwatch contains a guide to Internet Service Providers (ISPs).

Good Morning Silicon Valley

www.sjmercury.com/gmsv/

Latest news from the Valley: Want the information straight from the source, or as close as you can get? Visit the *San Jose Mercury News*' Good Morning Silicon Valley site. Things change so fast in Silicon Valley, the site updates four times per day.

News.com

www.news.com/

General technology news: News.com is a premier site offering news about the high-tech world. Toward the bottom of the main page you find links to relevant stories on other major sites such as *Forbes, The New York Times,* and *San Jose Mercury News'* Mercury Center site, written from the heart of Silicon Valley.

Other Stuff to Check Out

www.newspage.com

New Developments

These sites help you keep track of changes and developments in search engines, browser software, and Web server software. They keep you current as new products enter the market and as existing products develop.

BrowserWatch

www.browserwatch.com/

While you keep an eye on what's happening with search engines, why not also keep an eye on what's happening in the world of Web browsers. It's handy to know when you have something new to test your HTML pages with, right?

Search Engine Watch

searchenginewatch.com/

Visit this site to keep up with any changes coming along for the major search engines. You also get helpful information about using search engines effectively.

ServerWatch

serverwatch.iworld.com/

This site keeps up with what's new in the world of Web server software. It offers point-by-point comparisons among several products.

WebCompare

webcompare.iworld.com

WebCompare offers feature comparisons among popular Web server software products.

PR and Marketing

Need some Web marketing savvy to help you bring in customers? Try these sites as a starting point for gathering marketing tips and techniques online, as well as information about what other sites are doing. (Also pick up a copy of *Marketing Online For Dummies,* by Bud Smith and Frank Catalano, published by IDG Books Worldwide, Inc.)

@Brint

www.brint.com/

This site offers a premiere collection of information about issues relevant to contemporary businesses, particularly technology-related issues and management issues. Hosted by an instructor at the University of Pittsburgh Business School, Yogesh Malhotra, this site is excellent for business research. It offers links to mailing lists, discussion groups related to business and technology, and a directory of conferences. Also available are articles, papers, and some case studies.

Adweek Online

www.adweek.com/

Adweek is the principal journal of the advertising industry. This online version contains lots of news and information about electronic advertising.

Alan Weinkrantz Home Page

www.weinkrantz.com

This page is great for PR and marketing managers, especially the section called "Deep thoughts and profundities."

Georgia Tech's WWW User Surveys

www.cc.gatech.edu/gvu/user_surveys/

This site offers some basic and not-so-basic information about who's using the Web and what they're doing. Lots of research, reports, and statistics. Great for doing your demographic research.

Holland's Corner

www.cks.com/

John Holland's site, Holland's Corner, is a great place to get new ideas and new perspectives. Mr. Holland is a designer at CKS Interactive who has a lot of insight about what makes things work on the Web. The best known part of Holland's Corner, Net Breakfast, is a great way to start the day. He offers a list of sites to visit on a daily, weekly, or monthly basis, set up as a calendar with links for each day of the week.

Liszt

www.liszt.com

If you want to know what people are talking about in the fields related to your product or your service, visit Liszt and search for a mailing list on your topic. It's a great way to hear what people are saying, and to get yourself known by contributing to some relevant lists.

Who's Marketing Online

www.wmo.com/

This site covers marketing techniques and reviews other sites with a marketing eye. You can start absorbing the techniques of online marketing here, and you can keep up with the latest news.

Other Stuff to Check Out

www.all-biz.com/

Search Engines

Look for information and also to get your site listed so that your customers know where to find you. These sites let you search for sites using keywords, and most of them also provide reviews of the sites they list. (You should know that not every site is listed on all search engines, so it's good to visit several engines when you're looking for something.)

AltaVista

www.altavista.digital.com/

AltaVista is maintained by Digital Equipment Corporation (DEC). It is a high-quality search engine that you'll want to visit often.

Excite

www.excite.com/

Excite provides reviews of selected "principal" sites in a topic area, and links to other sites that come without reviews. Directory information on Excite comes to you as a topic-by-topic mix of editorial columns and links. By the way, if you'd like to have a (free) search engine for your own site, take a look at Excite for Web Servers at www.excite.com/navigate.

HotBot

www.hotbot.com/

HotBot is Wired's search site. A relative newcomer to the Web, it's colorful and well thought out. It's the easiest site to use when you're trying to find backlinks to your site.

Infoseek

www.infoseek.com/

Infoseek has been around a while. Its design distinguishes itself with a nice navigation system based on sidebars. Its content stands out to me for the excellent international section, which offers Web directories in the native language of each country presented. Among other topics, Infoseek has a special subject heading for shopping, which you might want to take time to visit in particular.

Lycos

www.lycos.com/

Lycos has been active for several years, which is eons in Web time. It's a color-ful hodgepodge of all kinds of informa-tion. One useful feature is a "Top 5 Percent" rating system that makes a try at separating higher-quality sites from those of more mediocre quality. Try it out!

WebCrawler

www.webcrawler.com/

WebCrawler is another search engine that's been around for centuries in Web time. It began as a student project in 1994, and grew rapidly into fame. Now it's been redesigned and updated, with sites divided into topics. Every site is handpicked and reviewed, which makes WebCrawler well worth visiting.

Yahoo!

www.yahoo.com/

Yahoo! is demonstrably the most-visited site on the Web. It's not only a search site, but a valuable resource of sites organized by topic. At the top, there are 14 major topic areas, and much more depth underneath. I find that it's a place I can start a search on almost any topic and come up with something.

Server Software

At these sites you can get lots of information about servers you're considering, and often the sites let you download free or evaluation copies of Web server software for your online store.

Apache

www.apache.org/

Apache is probably the most widely used Web server software. It runs on the UNIX platform, and best of all — it's free.

HTTPd

hoohoo.ncsa.uiuc.edu/docs/setup/
SingleClick.html

Visit this site to download one or more preconfigured versions of HTTPd, a freeware Web server for the UNIX platform. HTTPd is the grandma of Apache server, and many sites still use it. HTTPd is especially easy to install, as you can see when you visit this site.

Microsoft

www.microsoft.com/

Microsoft is, of course, the home of Microsoft Internet Information Server, which is an add-on module for Windows NT 4.0 that makes it into a Web server.

Netscape

www.netscape.com

Netscape offers the most popular Web browser and the Netscape Commerce Server software for online stores. They also offer a plug-ins page where you can download the latest plug-ins for your Netscape browser.

StarNine

www.starnine.com

This is the site where you can get information about WebSTAR, the most popular Web server software for the Mac OS.

Site Maintenance

Need help keeping everything running smoothly? Here are some sites you can turn to for tips and online discussion.

HyperNews Forums Web Mastery Resource Lists

union.ncsa.uiuc.edu/HyperNews/get/
www/html/guides.html

The site features a discussion forum for system administrators and Webmasters (which you are if you're running an online store by yourself, right?). You can post your most troubling questions and share your best ideas with others. You can find information about everything you need to know to run your Web site: HTML, graphics, you name it. Questions are answered in a friendly and knowledgeable way by forum participants.

Netscape DevEdge Online

developer.netscape.com/

Here's a great resource site for system administrators, Webmasters, and programmers who are using Netscape servers or other Netscape software products.

Site Builder Network

www.microsoft.com/sitebuilder/

Microsoft's informative site gives lots of tips on building and maintaining your Web site or online store.

WebMaster Online

www.webmaster.com/

Yes, there is a magazine for everything. And an online version, too, it seems these days. This site is the online version of WebMaster magazine. It offers the latest news and information, and archives of back issues, for almost anything related to running a Web site or online store.

Windows NT Resource Center

www.bhs.com/

Get all kinds of information about running and administering Windows NT servers.

Vendors Online

If the online computer stores don't give you enough information, you can probably visit the vendors you're interested in directly and get more information, maybe even purchase the products you're looking for. You find so many excellent vendors of computers and peripherals, this section can't hope to give a complete list; however, it gives you a look at a few of the ones I found interesting and informative. Try out some others on your own.

Apple Computer

www.apple.com/

The Apple site offers an online store, plus lots of helpful information about Mac server bundles.

Compaq Computer

www.compaq.com/

Highly useful for comparing different server hardware systems.

Gateway 2000

www.gateway.com/

Gateway 2000 lets you configure, price, and order online.

Raptor Systems

www.raptor.com/

Want information about compatibility of Raptor firewall products (some of the most widely-used firewall products) and your operating system or Web server? You can find that info here, along with lots of other useful information about firewalls.

VeriSign

www.verisign.com/

The VeriSign site has great general information and a FAQ about digital certificates. It also offers precise information about applying for and installing digital certificates for Macintosh and Windows platforms.

Other Stuff to Check Out

www.dell.com/

Part V
Accepting Payment Online

The 5th Wave   By Rich Tennant

"Face it Vinnie — you're gonna have a hard time getting people to subscribe online with a credit card to a newsletter called 'Felons Interactive!'"

In this part . . .

Your customers won't plunk down money at your site unless you make it easy for them to do so. In this part, you discover how to encourage selling at your site by giving your customers problem-free — and secure — ways for them to spend their money.

Chapter 15

Money Talks, Sometimes in Ciphers

Concerns about security and privacy sometimes keep people from buying online (and some merchants from offering their wares online, too). For merchants like you, security can be a technical challenge (if you plan to do it yourself) or a challenge to find the available resources to implement it for you.

Never fear — online security and privacy get easier every day (like most things on the Web). This chapter discusses the security and privacy issues associated with the Web and online commerce.

Data Security Technology

Data security technology prevents fraud: either on the part of the customer, or on the part of the unscrupulous merchant (certainly not you, of course, but there are a few out there). When you hear the words encryption, public keys, private keys, digital signatures, and digital certificates the subject is data security technology.

In this section, I tell you what "public key" and all those other weird-sounding words mean, and I show you how the technologies involved can help your online store. Armed with the basics about data security technology, you can reassure your customers that their money and credit card numbers are safe at your online store.

Encryption basics

Encryption is the process of encoding information so that it can't be read casually or by prying eyes. Encryption is the cornerstone of electronic commerce and the heart of data security: It keeps private information private. Encryption also allows people to verify their identity online, where physical cues aren't available.

Encryption creates the very possibility of digital money, because digital money is just a bunch of encrypted numbers (important numbers, though, like your bank balance or the number of pennies in a $100 bill).

Good encryption systems need to have a few basic capabilities; those systems in common use online (such as SSL and SET, described later in the chapter) definitely have these capabilities:

- **Privacy:** Privacy, in this case, means shielding information effectively.

- **Identification:** Identification is the ability to prove the identity of the author of a message or order. On the Internet (or any other open communication channel such as the telephone), a message could be faked. A person's online identity can be established by a password, or in business transactions, by a *digital certificate* (see "Digital certificates" in this chapter for more information).

- **Authentication:** Authentication is the process of determining whether the content of a message has been altered in any way during transmission. Authentication implies that the sender has the credentials needed to send a certain message (if he or she did not, you would instantly know the message had been forged because it couldn't have been sent by the person it says sent it).

- **Verification:** Verification combines identification and authentication. After verification, you know the source and the content of a message is valid and therefore trustworthy.

- **Nonrepudiation:** Nonrepudiation means that a sender can't deny sending a message after it's sent. In particular, it means that senders can't deny signing messages after their digital signatures are attached.

The common components of online commerce — digital signatures and digital certificates — require all these features to work effectively. (For more information about encryption, you can visit the RSA Web site at www.rsa.com.)

Public keys talk in Cyberspace

Well not literally, they don't actually talk, but they certainly help create the trust needed for doing business online. Establishing identity online proves difficult, yet to prevent credit card fraud and other kinds of fraud, the identities of the customers and the merchants involved must somehow be firmly established before online transactions can take place.

Public keys provide a way of establishing identity, just as they are (when used inversely) a way of providing encrypted messages that can be read only by the owner of that public key.

Public key encryption is making online commerce possible. It's more useful on the Internet than other forms of encryption because it doesn't require that any secret encryption keys be sent over the public communication channels, where they could potentially be intercepted. Potentially stronger forms of encryption (including older forms such as DES) do require that secret keys be transmitted somehow, which can leave them vulnerable to attack.

Digital signatures

A *digital signature* guarantees that anyone who reads a digitally signed message can be certain who sent the message. Digital signatures work because they rely on two encryption keys, a public key and a private key, which work only when used together and can't be derived from one another. (If you know someone's public key, don't plan on guessing his or her private key based on that, even if you know quite a bit of math.)

A message encrypted with a private key and decoded with the corresponding public key can be certified as to its owner — thus, the message is said to be *digitally signed.* The very fact that the message could be decoded guarantees that it was encoded with the signer's private key. Conversely, a message encrypted using a public key can be decrypted only by the bearer of the corresponding private key, thus creating a secure communication channel. This two-key encryption process is commonly called *public-key encryption.* Figure 15-1 illustrates the two-way nature of public-key encryption.

Figure 15-1:
Public key
encryption.

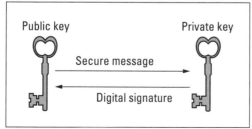

Public key   Private key

Secure message

Digital signature

The birth of a cipher (wrapped in an enigma and smothered in secret sauce)

The most accepted "brand" of public-key cryptography comes from a company called RSA. (RSA stands for Rivest, Shamir, and Adelman, the inventors of the first public-key system that works effectively for encryption as well as for digital signatures.) Whitfield Diffie, Martin Hellman, and (independently) Ralph Merkle originally proposed the concept of public-key cryptography in 1976.

RSA is the most practical implementation available and the de facto standard. For more information about RSA, visit www.rsa.com.

The CyberCash Wallet (www.cybercash.com) creates a digital key pair for you, which then encrypts and decrypts your financial information when sending it over the Internet using the CyberCash system.

How much can you rely on a digital signature? Can a digital signature be forged? The founder of DigiCash, Mr. David Chaum, says, "The best-known methods for producing forged signatures would require many years, even using computers billions of times faster than those now available."

A digital signature doesn't actually guarantee the *identity* of the sender, but rather that the sender is whomever he or she *claims* to be. The digital signature authenticates the message, much like typing in a password authenticates a system login. Signatures and passwords are similar because a digital signature requires a secret key and a login requires a secret password.

DigiCash and blind digital signatures

Blind digital signatures, invented by David Chaum of DigiCash (see Chapter 16 for more about this company), are a slight variant of digital signature technology that actually makes digital cash possible — a blind digital signature adds the element of anonymity while preserving the ability to authenticate the transaction. Before blind digital signatures, the best a person could do was to use a digital check, in which the signer had to be identified. With blind digital signatures, the payer can authorize banks to pay a certain amount without knowing the identity of the payee.

Digital certificates

For online commerce, you need one further piece of trust-creating information — the *digital certificate*. A digital certificate validates the identity of the sender based on the identities of other known entities, such as banks or corporations. A digital certificate can verify any sort of transaction online.

Digital certificates are identity records digitally signed by *certificate authorities* (CAs), which can prove that Jane, for example, is who she says she is when she's online. (In the U.K., certificate authorities often are called *trusted third parties*.)

A basic digital certificate usually contains the following information:

- The owner's public key
- The owner's name
- The expiration date of the owner's public key
- The name of the issuing certificate authority
- The serial number of the digital certificate
- The digital signature of the issuing certificate authority

People usually use digital certificates within very specific contexts. For example, John may have a digital certificate that verifies he is a member of a frequent flyer plan, and another certificate verifying that he has a credit card with a certain number. The merchants themselves would issue these specific digital certificates to their customers.

Market research firms such as Forrester Research predict that digital certificates will come into common use over the next few years, and that people will begin to have as many digital certificates identifying them online as they now have ID cards and credit cards in their wallets.

The Certificate Authority Song

To help you remember the basics of digital certificates, here's a little ditty for you (sung to the chorus of *Simple Gifts*):

When new certificates are made,
We all sign them in so you won't be afraid.
And when they've been encrypted with a key just right,
You can buy on the Internet and sleep well at night.

Understanding the controversy about digital certificates

The U.S. and British governments are reviewing similar pieces of legislation that require certificate authorities to register the corresponding private keys for any public keys within their directories. Opponents of the legislation claim that registering private keys presents the following problems:

✔ It leaves both the public and private keys more vulnerable to compromise because such a storehouse of keys makes a tempting target for hackers.

✔ It offers individuals more plausible opportunities to repudiate their digitally signed documents, such as contracts. If someone can claim their key was stolen and fraudulently used to sign a digital document, it may be possible to get out of otherwise binding contractual obligations.

Getting a digital certificate

Several companies offer digital certificates for business on the Web. For example, at VeriSign (www.verisign.com), to get a digital certificate, you need to prove your identity (or more accurately your business's identity). You may be required to have your application for a digital certificate notarized, and you may need to supply a certified copy of your business license, fictitious name statement, articles of incorporation, tax identification number, and so forth — just as when you open a merchant bank account (see Chapter 16 to find out about merchant bank accounts).

Companies typically offer different "grades" of certificates. For example, digital certificates are available from VeriSign in four grades, designed for different types of transactions; you pay an associated fee for each grade of certificate. Certificates are available for individuals or software publishers, and for Web browsers or secure Web servers. (Visit the company Web site for more information.)

RSA (www.rsa.com), a company that licenses public-key encryption technology, also offers a system for issuing digital certificates.

Corporations may begin offering digital certificates soon, because the SET standard for electronic transactions relies on the use of digital certificates for each party to the transaction. (Turn to "SET" in this chapter for more information.)

Doing business as . . .

Your made-up business name must be filed with the county clerk and published in a local journal, as a fictitious name statement.

I did business as a consultant using the business structure called a sole proprietorship — Leslie Lundquist doing business as (DBA) The Creative Professional. Now, I do business as The Creative Professional, Inc. My business grew and I changed its form; I am the owner of a (very small) corporation. Thus, I now must provide copies of my articles of incorporation to prove that I am a representing my corporation — not myself — for legal purposes in certain circumstances, such as opening a merchant bank account or getting a digital certificate.

As a business, your digital certificate tells your customers that you're who you say you are. Your digital certificate offers them some assurance that you're not just a fly-by-night operation, helping create an environment of trust. Also, if you offer digital products such as online publications, your digital certificate automatically accompanies each download of a publication from your site — it helps prove that you aren't reselling material that you don't hold the copyright to, so your customers can rest assured that they get their information from the proper source.

Data Security Designed for the Web

You and your customers must know that your data travels safely over the Internet using a security technology such as the ones discussed in this section. In fact, if your store and your customer's browser use the security methods discussed in this section, your customers' financial information is safer than it is when a salesclerk runs off to the back room with the customers' credit card in a physical store.

To make customers most comfortable buying on your site, offer secure transmission at their option for all customer data. Also, reassure your customers that you won't sell or otherwise redistribute their personal information without their permission. (You won't, will you??)

SSL

Secure Sockets Layer (SSL) provides secure, encrypted connections be-tween computers. SSL is not a way to do transactions; instead, SSL provides a secure environment in which to operate your shopping cart scripts and your virtual cash register.

SSL works in some sense "beneath" the level of the application that's running; its functionality is set up within the server software itself.

SSL establishes a secure data channel that can provide secure transmission for any kind of data, not just electronic cash. For that reason, SSL can make your customers more comfortable — they know that SSL shields even their personal information as it travels the Internet.

You can use these visual cues in your online store to let your customers know that your site is secure from prying eyes. Any of the following signs tell your customers that you use SSL:

- ✔ The URL of your site begins with `https:` instead of `http:`.
- ✔ When you enter a site or a Web page that's secured by SSL, you usually see a dialog box to notify you.
- ✔ In browsers that support SSL (most newer browsers do, including Netscape Navigator 4.0 and MSIE 4.0), you see a small key or padlock symbol in the lower left corner that's broken into two parts when the channel isn't secure, and appears whole on a secure channel.

Internet trivia: Where did all these crazy names come from?

Quite a few years ago, during the time when the Internet was developing the TCP/IP proto-cols seven layers of protocols described the total workings of an Internet host and network connection using TCP/IP. The names of these layers crop up again and again in the names of Internet products and services. From bottom to top, the layers are: physical, link, network, transport, session, presentation, and application.

Sockets layer (as in SSL) derives from an even older UNIX naming convention. A data chan-nel between two UNIX machines was called a *socket. Secure sockets layer* refers to the fact that SSL treats transport and session layers together as a hybrid connection layer and cre-ates a secure channel at the transport level, for the length of a session, for point-to-point security.

In descriptions of firewall services, you also find references to the application layer, at which many firewalls work, or references to session-based tracking, which means that you track a user through an entire "session" of visiting your site.

To use SSL-based security on your Web site, just follow these steps:

1. **Make sure your Web server software supports SSL.**

2. **Get a digital certificate.**

3. **Turn on SSL in your server after you receive your digital certificate.**

   Your server documentation tells you how to turn on SSL, provided that it has SSL capabilities.

4. **Make sure that your customers know to visit your site using Web browsers that support SSL.**

   All the major Web browsers support SSL, including the following:

   - Netscape Navigator
   - Microsoft Internet Explorer
   - AOL browsers

Many online stores use two servers — one secure and the other unsecure — to speed up online transactions by giving them dedicated resources. (That's one more good reason to set up a Web farm, which I talk about in Chapter 4.) If you have this kind of Web site, you need to move your transaction Web pages to the secure server.

SSL itself doesn't provide transaction services, only a secure channel over which to perform transactions.

SET

SET (which stands for Secure Electronic Transactions) is based on public-key cryptography. SET is a standard for secure electronic credit card transactions, developed and utilized by Visa, MasterCard, Microsoft, and many other companies.

In a SET transaction, each party — the merchant, the credit cardholder, the credit card company, and each bank — is identified with a digital certificate and authenticated with one or more digital signatures. The cardholder is not necessarily identified to the merchant, because knowing that the credit card is valid provides a sufficient level of identification (the credit card company, also a party to the transaction, certainly knows the identity of the cardholder).

When using SET, each party to the transaction has at least two public/private key pairs. One pair encrypts the messages that are transmitted over the network. The other pair is reserved exclusively for the digital signatures. In each key pair, the private keys are used for encrypting or signing, and the public keys are used for decrypting or verifying, respectively.

The SET standard extends digital signature technology similarly to how DigiCash extended digital signatures to include blind signatures (as described in the "DigiCash and blind digital signatures" sidebar earlier in this chapter). SET includes an innovative key element called *dual signatures,* which enables banks or clearinghouses to verify that payment should be sent from a customer's account to a particular merchant for a particular amount, but without disclosing the items purchased or other terms of the transaction.

How is this possible? When the customer signs the order with the merchant, an identical copy of the customer's digital signature is attached to the request for processing that the clearinghouse receives — thus, the name *dual signatures.* The signatures must be identical, because if even one bit of data is different, you can declare the request a forgery.

Heavy use of digital certificates may make transactions take a lot longer to complete. As a result, SET may slow the development of electronic commerce because people won't want to adopt a cumbersome system. SET is currently in a testing and refinement phase. Although several major corporations are going ahead with SET implementations, many smaller companies that provide transaction services are holding off on adoption of SET until the waters clear. Expect things to get moving by mid-1998, when the SET standard is expected to stabilize.

SET is still undergoing testing and refinement, and it is highly complex to integrate with your site. To use SET-based security on your site, use a provider of transaction services that offers SET security, such as CyberCash or BlueMoney. (For more information about transaction service providers, please see Chapter 16.)

Many people may not be accustomed to buying online, and accepting payment online may be a new idea for you, too. You can always choose not to accept payment online. You can offer a telephone or fax number instead. However, online transactions are becoming safer, more popular with online stores, and more accepted by customers every day. It's a good idea to consider accepting payment online, at least in the long-term plans for your online store.

Chapter 16

Accepting Digital Dollars

In This Chapter

▶ Setting up your merchant bank account

▶ Grasping the essentials of credit card transactions

▶ Understanding various forms of online payment

▶ Using hosting services and other transaction services to help you

G ood business sense dictates that you accept as many forms of payment as possible at your online store, even plain old checks through the postal service. This chapter explains some of the better options that you have for accepting payment. Always remember to collect the money!

Your Merchant Bank Account

The first thing you need when setting up your online store, besides the hardware and software for the store itself, is a merchant bank account. Your *merchant bank* is the back room behind your store's back room. Your merchant bank account is where the money actually gets deposited from all the credit card payments, checks, and cash that your customers use to pay for your products.

You need a bank that can serve the needs of online merchants like yourself. Most major banks (such as Wells Fargo, Bank of America, First Interstate Bank, Citibank, and so on) offer merchant accounts as well as consumer accounts. If you don't know where to start looking for a merchant bank, you could start with whatever bank you already use.

As another option, BlueMoney (www.bluemoney.com) offers to help you obtain a merchant account if you purchase their products.

If your business is too new or too small (if you don't make enough money yet) to qualify for merchant banking, you should pay particular attention to companies like First Virtual, which can handle your merchant banking needs as part of the hosting service they provide for online stores. (See "Internet Cash and Credit Service Providers" in this chapter for the details.)

On your way out the door to set up a merchant bank account, don't forget to take the following items with you:

✔ If you're a sole proprietor (you know who you are), you need to show a copy of your business license to the bank.

✔ If you're a corporation, the bank needs to see copies of your articles of incorporation and your federal tax identification number (which the IRS gives you when you incorporate). A new-accounts representative should guide you through the necessary paperwork right there at the bank.

Getting your account set up for accepting credit card payments usually takes about a week (but you can use that time to write your CGI scripts, right?). You should expect to pay a fee to the bank for that basic service, somewhere around $25 per month. Most banks usually charge a small per-transaction fee, as well.

Digital Dollars and Other Forms of Money

Only a small percentage of purchases made offline each year are made using credit cards. Of an approximately $360 billion consumer spending market (that's almost a billion dollars of consumer purchases per day), only about $10 billion worth of purchases are made using credit cards. About $50 billion in purchases are made by check, and $300 billion using cash.

If the world of selling online begins to echo the world of selling offline, you'd be well-advised to accept all the forms of payment mentioned in this section. As customers become more comfortable with the idea of online buying, they're likely to move more into cash-based purchase methods, described later in this section.

For the convenience of accepting credit card payments from customers, you (the merchant) pay a percentage of each transaction as a fee. Similarly, *digital cash processing companies* (such as CyberCash and BlueMoney) charge a small percentage for processing digital cash, check, and coin payments online. However, the convenience of the services that such companies provide make their services at least as worthwhile as a credit card transaction fee. (See "Internet Cash and Credit Service Providers" in this chapter for more information.)

Credit cards online and electronic wallets

The easiest way to accept online payments is definitely by credit card. If you're an international merchant, the credit card companies can even perform the currency exchange for you.

When a customer enters a credit card number and expiration date into their Web browser, SSL or another security program encrypts the data and sends it securely across the Internet to your store's server (see Chapter 15 for more information about SSL). However, you don't know whether the customer has enough credit on the card for the purchase, or whether the actual customer is offering the card. You need to have the customer present a bit of secret information, such as a mother's maiden name, a social security number, a PIN number, or another identifier such as a valid (digital) signature along with the card. This type of information verifies the identity of the cardholder.

After you verify the cardholder's identity, you can relay the card information to your merchant bank or an online credit card processing company. The merchant bank or credit card processing company obtains approval from the customer's bank and returns the authorization to you. Typically, the processor charges you a small fee for each transaction, something like 2 percent.

You can make credit card transactions online easier for your customers (after the first time) by helping them set up an *electronic wallet*. When setting up an electronic wallet, the customer enters credit card data, thus the need to use a card each time she wants to place an order on the Web. See "Internet Cash and Credit Service Providers" in this chapter for more information on electronic wallets.

However, consumers have in the past avoided using wallet software because:

- ✓ Wallets often take between 10 and 30 minutes to download.
- ✓ Wallets are hard to install and set up.

If a wallet takes 15 minute to set up, that's eons in "Web time," so most customers won't do it unless there's a compelling reason. If you do accept credit card payments online, give your customers the option to pay with or without the wallet.

CyberCash, a popular electronic wallet, licensed their underlying security technology to Microsoft, which created the Microsoft wallet. The Microsoft Wallet is the "lightest" and easiest downloading wallet available.

Online credit card transactions

When your customer decides to buy something with a credit card, the following process takes place:

1. **A Web page at your store prompts the customer for credit card information using a form or other interface. (You may need other information, such as the shipping address.)**

   The form you use to request this information should be secured using SSL or some other security technology, such as SET. (I discuss security technology in Chapter 15.)

2. **Your customer enters the information into your form and sends it to your store.**

   If you use a secured form, you receive the information at your store through a protected connection. A SET-compliant application, such as Netscape Navigator, encloses the customer's information in a *slip,* which is the virtual equivalent of a handwritten credit card slip. The slip is then sent to you.

3. **You send the customer's information to your credit card processing institution to obtain authorization.**

4. **After the bank authorizes the transaction, you can ship the goods and charge the authorized amount of money to the customer's credit card.**

Because you shouldn't charge the card until you ship the goods, you experience a time lag between when you can get an authorization and when it's ethical to post the charge to the card. A customers usually consider a reasonable delay okay — customers understand that you can't ship every order the same day you get the order.

5. **To settle the transaction, the credit card processing institution generally piles up charges and credits into a batch and settles them as a group. The processor initiates the transfers of money from your customer's account(s) into your merchant bank account.**

   As online transactions become more common, you and your bank will have the ability to settle transactions immediately, which offers a very efficient and effective way to manage cash flow. Right now, settlement usually occurs daily (at most), but sometimes occurs only on a weekly or monthly basis.

   If the customer returns the good or cancels an order, you generate a credit for the customer's card. Every bank or clearinghouse uses a different procedure for generating credits — you need to contact the banks involved to find out exactly how to issue the credit.

Network Wallet by BlueMoney (www.bluemoney.com) offers another wallet option. To use this wallet, instead of downloading software to the local hard disk, your customer uses a secure channel to fill in information on BlueMoney's Network Wallet Web server. You can use the BlueMoney wallet right away in any online store. (But you have to go to the Blue Money site in advance and fill in your wallet information.)

To set up your online store to accept customer payments using online wallets such as the CyberCash wallet, the Microsoft wallet, and the Blue Money wallet, you work directly with these companies. They help you get everything you need installed and operational on your end of the transaction. Then, you post information on your site that tells your customers which kind of wallets you accept — sort of like going to a restaurant and seeing the Visa and Mastercard placards by the cash register.

Digital cash

Despite the fact that digital cash exists solely in Cyberspace, digital cash spends just like physical cash: You can use it anywhere and it's anonymous.

To use digital cash, a customer basically moves (actual) funds into an escrow account at a bank. Purchases online are subtracted from the "digital funds" escrow account. (Smart cards, described later in this chapter, are related to digital cash, but the funds on a smart card are usable offline as well as online.)

The bank turns the escrowed funds into digital money (which the customer can spend online) in an ingenious way. A person specifies a number that serves as a "seed," which the computer uses to randomly generate a series of unique "serial numbers" that represent digital coins, dollars, or another denomination of money. These serial numbers are then encrypted (essentially "wrapped" in digital envelopes) when the actual funds are withdrawn from the bank and assigned to those funds. The bank never sees the serial numbers at withdrawal time.

Later, as the customer spends the digital dollars, the bank keeps a list of "spent" serial numbers, somewhat like a list of checks that have been paid. The bank can't link a specific "spent" serial number with a specific withdrawal because the serial numbers were encrypted when the withdrawal was made. While digital cash preserves the customer's privacy, no digital money can be spent twice.

One implication of electronic payment

A merchant I know accepts payments from his customers online, but he won't use electronic payment to his suppliers. Because electronic settlement is theoretically immediate, electronic payment to suppliers would take away anything he gained from the *float* (the time between the *commitment* of the funds through a check or other payment instrument) and *settlement* (the time the funds actually change bank accounts). Clever, yes. Upstanding? Maybe.

Digital cash offers the following benefits to you and your customers:

- ✔ If a blackmailer or other criminal accepts digital cash, the serial numbers can be used to identify them.

- ✔ All amounts received digitally must be handled by a banking institution, so less "black market" activity takes place.

- ✔ If you lose digital cash, you only need to remember only the "seed" number to regenerate a series of serial numbers and recover the "cash." (Sort of like traveler's checks, eh?)

Several companies offer digital cash payment services for merchants. See "Internet Cash and Credit Service Providers" for more information.

Digital checks

Digital checks offer an excellent way to pay online, featuring the immediacy of cash while maintaining an audit trail of expenses.

Digital checks resemble digital cash, except that digital checks aren't anonymous. Electronic checks are signed and endorsed online using digital signatures, and authenticated using digital certificates. The digital certificates attest to the identities of the payer, the payer's bank, and the payer's bank account. The check and associated digital certificates authorize the transfer of funds from the payer's bank into your merchant account, much like a fund transfer using an ATM card.

A payer must register with their bank or a third party to obtain the proper certificates before using digital checks.

Digital coin (for smaller purchases)

If your online store sells small items such as photographs, data records, news clips, cartoons, recipes, greeting cards, and so forth, you may want to look into accepting customer payments in digital coin.

Digital coin lets your customers make small purchases (normally considered too small for a credit card) using digital cash. Purchases for as little as $1/10$ of a cent can be made practical using digital coin.

CyberCoin

CyberCash (www.cybercash.com) is perhaps the most popular vendor currently offering digital coin services, which they call CyberCoin. For example, ESPNNet SportsZone offers daily passes ($1 per day) to the premium services available on its site using the CyberCash CyberCoin service.

To make the processing of such small payments feasible and cost effective as a credit service (instead of a debit service like MilliCent), CyberCash bundles the purchases together and batch-processes them like a credit card transaction, keeping a nominal percentage as a transaction processing fee.

MilliCent

Another digital coin service from Digital Equipment Corporation (DEC) is called MilliCent. With MilliCent, customers buy *scrip* from an electronic scrip broker, which they can then use at any online store equipped to accept MilliCent scrip. A customer can use her credit card to purchase scrip in specific amounts ($10, for example), keep the scrip in storage on her hard disk drive, and use the scrip to purchase items for as little as $1/10$ cent or as much as $5.00 at a time.

Because MilliCent is a prepayment system, it helps online stores avoid the difficulties and costs of transaction settlement. Customers give out their credit card numbers less frequently online, which they appreciate. Customers make MilliCent payments through a downloadable wallet.

You can get information about signing up to be a MilliCent vendor, customer, or scrip broker at www.millicent.digital.com.

Smart cards

Smart cards have a lot of appeal for merchants, because they act just like cash. Settlement is instantaneous, without the need for credit transaction processing (which saves you, the merchant, some dollars).

Smart cards are portable digital money. You can load them up with digital cash at your local ATM (or at home using the Personal ATM product recently released from VeriFone) and take smart cards to the store with you. Then as you make each purchase, the card is debited by the merchant's computer.

In some ways, this process may sound just like paying for your groceries with an ATM card, but it's really more like a phone card that's not just for phones — the money is in the card, not in your bank account.

Computers and televisions equipped with smart card slots (usually smart cards fit into PCMCIA slots) are becoming more common, and hopefully accepting payments over the Internet using smart cards will soon be commonplace.

Smart cards contain microprocessor chips that can create and store digital signature keys and digital certificates (to go along with the digital cash they store). The only thing that seems to be holding up the widespread use of smart cards is the legislative and legal quagmire over regulating the certificate authorities.

Internet Cash and Credit Service Providers

This section acquaints you with several companies that offer transaction processing services for your store. These services can be useful to you if you choose to operate and maintain your own Web server (that is, you choose not to hire a hosting service for your store), but you don't want to invest the resources (basically, money and programmer expertise) in creating the programs that let you process credit card and digital cash transactions yourself.

Most of these services require you to install the appropriate software on your Web server and make sure your customers have access to the related client-side software to go with their Web browsers. To ensure easy access, put the customer software on your site for downloading.

CyberCash

CyberCash (www.cybercash.com) is an example of a business I tend to call a transaction processing house. CyberCash, and businesses like it, offers to take care of processing all your credit card, debit card, digital cash, and digital check transactions for you, over the Internet, for a small fee. They take the information, and you end up with the money in your merchant account.

You still need a merchant account at a bank to work with CyberCash — otherwise, where would CyberCash put all your money? (See "Your Merchant Bank Account" in this chapter for the details on merchant bank accounts.)

To use the CyberCash service, you install some software on your server, and then you ask your customers to use a CyberCash wallet when making their payments on your site. (CyberCash offers a downloadable consumer wallet for your customers and a virtual cash register for your store.) When your customer enters information into the wallet, he or she specifies a credit card number or a bank account to which purchases can be billed. The customer's purchases are consolidated and billed on a monthly basis by CyberCash. (CyberCash stores the transaction records in such a way that purchases are anonymous, thus protecting your customer's privacy.)

To make it easy for your customers to use the CyberCash Wallet, you can set up a link to the CyberCash Web site on your site.

The CyberCash system runs on all major Web servers, including Windows NT, several major versions of UNIX (Solaris, HP-UX, and IRIX), and Macintosh computers.

Virtually every electronic storefront package and hosting service supports CyberCash for their transaction processing. (See the discussion of electronic storefront software in Chapter 6 for details.)

If you run a CyberCash Register on your server and your customer uses a CyberCash Wallet, you don't need any other security system on your site for financial transactions, because the two set up a secure channel between them. However, you would need another form of security, such as SSL, if you intend to protect other types of sensitive data. (See Chapter 15 for more information on SSL.)

DigiCash

If you plan to accept smart card payments at your site, consider DigiCash (see "Smart cards" in this chapter for more information). DigiCash is well-accepted in Europe, because of the popularity of smart cards there, and it is growing in acceptance throughout the United States as smart cards gain acceptance here. The DigiCash system is based on cash, not credit cards, so it relies on physical banks rather than credit card processing companies.

DigiCash transactions save you money because you don't pay credit card transaction fees.

The DigiCash server-side transaction software works with all major Web servers. Customer software is available for Windows and Macintosh platforms.

DigiCash itself isn't a transaction processing house — DigiCash just provides transaction software. DigiCash does not partake in your transactions, because they are cash transactions. That means you and your customers gain more security and more privacy, automatically.

The DigiCash software creates a secure connection between its client side and server side software, so you won't need any other security system at your site to protect online purchase transactions, only to protect other sensitive information.

Your customers must install the DigiCash client software on their home computers before they can make a purchase at your online store using DigiCash.

You can download the DigiCash software for your server from the DigiCash Web site (www.digicash.com). To use DigiCash at your store, you need a merchant account at a bank that accepts DigiCash. You can find a complete list of banks that accept DigiCash on the DigiCash site.

BlueMoney

BlueMoney (www.bluemoney.com) deposits proceeds from your credit card sales directly to your merchant account. You activate their Gateway service for a one-time fee and then you pay an extremely minimal per-transaction cost if transactions exceed a certain number.

BlueMoney offers to help you set up a merchant account if you don't already have one. It also features the Network Wallet, a consumer wallet, which can be set up in a browser window and used immediately for online shopping (the customer does not need to download any software).

BlueMoney also offers an electronic storefront product that ties in easily with their transaction services and Network Wallet. Basically, it offers a fully-functional storefront designed to add transaction capabilities to an existing site. Their storefront runs on most Web servers, including Apache, Stronghold, and Netscape. The storefront includes a shopping cart, layout templates for setting up displays and inventory control, and a built-in price database that's updatable remotely using password authorization. You can download an evaluation copy of the BlueMoney storefront at the company site (www.bluemoney.com).

If you use only the storefront without the gateway service, you get it in manual transaction mode, which means that you process your own credit card transactions offline.

Besides credit card transactions, the BlueMoney storefront can handle fax, phone, mail, ecash, and COD orders. (You should run an SSL-capable server for capturing this sensitive customer information on your site.)

Because BlueMoney uses First Data Corporation (a credit card clearing-house) to process your credit card transactions, you have to sign up with First Data. (A merchant signs up with a clearinghouse through their merchant bank or through a transaction services provider such as CyberCash or Blue Money.) That could be a cost item (perhaps $300 or more) if you switch credit card processors to use BlueMoney's services.

BlueMoney's gateway service can save you the cost of buying and annually renewing a digital certificate. (Digital certificates are described in Chapter 15.) This benefit increases in value as the SET standard proliferates for online credit card transaction processing.

ICVerify

For Windows platforms, ICVerify (www.icverify.com) enables your store to accept credit card and debit card transactions using a secure, Web-based form on your server. Your script passes along relevant customer information, such as the account number or credit card number and the amount of the transaction, to ICVerify. The ICVerify server obtains authorization for the transaction and returns the information.

The ICVerify solution could save you money if you have programming resources on staff and already run a secure Web server.

ICVerify is a commonly-used solution for online transaction processing; you can find lots of scripts for easy customization. However, you definitely do not want to try this option without a secure Web server. (See Chapter 5 for discussion of Web server software that offers security features.)

Other Online Transaction Services

What if you don't have the staff resources available to install, configure, and maintain electronic transaction software? In that case, you may want to consider one of the options detailed in this section, which can save you time and money.

First Virtual

First Virtual got going about a year sooner than most other electronic commerce service providers because of the simple technology involved — it relies on e-mail only, along with the traditional credit card and banking services networks.

You can think of First Virtual as an online mall, but one that requires a membership to shop there. The shoppers at First Virtual must register and receive a PIN number. When they make a purchase, you (as the merchant) report the transaction to First Virtual in terms of the item purchased, the cost, and the customer's PIN number, not in terms of the customer's credit card number. Then First Virtual confirms each customer's purchase by sending e-mail to the customer's e-mail address of record — "Did you buy this?" If First Virtual gets a yes, the financial side of the transaction (authorization, posting, and settlement) is completed offline in the normal way for credit cards, not through the Internet. That way, only the banking networks handle the most sensitive information.

First Virtual has over 2,000 merchants and over 10,000 registered customers. In addition to hosting online stores that sell physical goods, First Virtual has a special online mall for information products, which is called the InfoHaus (www.infohaus.fu.com). It's designed specifically for online stores that sell digital products, and it lets such businesses get going quickly and inexpensively.

To become an InfoHaus seller, you just upload your information products using a simple process, along with a description of each product and a price. For any buyer who requests the products and provides a shoppers' PIN, InfoHaus automatically delivers the goods. You receive payment from First Virtual after about 90 days, when First Virtual is reasonably sure that the customer won't return the goods. Your payments go directly (using the ACH system) into the bank account you register with First Virtual when you sign up, and you receive notification by e-mail when a payment has been deposited.

The waiting period for payment poses the only drawback to the First Virtual service. If you're a small business, it may be difficult to wait 90 days before receiving payment for your goods. However, the InfoHaus service is reasonably priced, which helps offset the difficulty of the waiting period. There's a nominal set-up fee plus a small per-transaction fee. Products sold through the InfoHaus, incur an additional 8 percent InfoHaus service fee.

You find helpful CGI code on the First Virtual Web site for InfoHaus sellers who need help putting together forms for taking customer orders. However, the code requires at least minimal customization before it works for your products.

CyberSource

CyberSource (www.cybersource.com) offers transaction processing services, in addition to services for secure electronic distribution of software and other digital products over the Internet. CyberSource handles the complexities of export controls and sales tax collection for you, too. (For more information about export controls and taxes online, see Chapter 19.)

For an annual product registration fee, you can register your product with CyberSource, and they prepare it for digital delivery. They deliver an encrypted bag of bits (BOB) and a separate Electronic License Certificate (ELC) which contains a key to unlock the bag of bits once the license is signed.

If your product is digital, and if you use a solution like CyberSource for your online transaction processing and electronic fulfillment, you only have to think about customer information databases and site traffic in your own store's back room. You have more time to spend on updating your site's product displays and getting a great advertising plan going.

Wave Systems

Another, newer site that's in the business of distributing your content securely over the Internet and helping you collect payment is Wave Systems (www.wave.com). Wave's WinPublish service encrypts your content, which you can then serve on your Web site. When your customer selects an item for purchase, the file goes back to Wave, where it is unlocked and down-loaded to the customer. Your store's account with Wave is credited for the amount of the sale. All your customer needs to do to make a purchase is get an account set up with Wave.

Paying bills online with CheckFree

You can already pay your personal and corporate bills using CheckFree software and a modem (www.checkfree.com). CheckFree Corporation (founded in 1981) currently offers online invoicing and payment services to over 100 million customer and business accounts, including 21 of the nation's largest billers. You may want to investigate the options available to your business for letting your customers pay their bills to you online; it can save you time and money.

Some research firms predict that 30 to 40 percent of households will use the Internet to pay consumer bills by 2010 (which sounds like the distant future but isn't really so far off). Why not collect your payments online, at your Web site?

No transactions, but lots of site traffic: The Internet Mall

The Internet Mall is one of the oldest malls on the Web. It doesn't handle transactions for you, but it is so venerable that it seems worth mentioning. Actually, it's very easy to join and very reasonably priced. It's almost like a classified ads page or clearinghouse for online businesses.

For $24 per year, you get a basic listing on The Internet Mall, which includes a summary description of your product or service and a link to your URL. For a yearly fee you get a premier listing. To join, you step through a form, and in the next two to three days, your listing appears on the mall pages.

You can pay for your listing by credit card or by check sent in the U.S. Mail. You have to fill out the form online before mailing a check,

though, to get a submission tracking number so they can tell who sent the check. The address is furnished online when you fill out the form.

The Internet Mall is basically a large engine that customers search based on keywords in your description. So if your description at the mall includes the words "large widgets," any client search on the keyword widgets would find you. The mall is also arranged in categories, very simply and conveniently, so that customers can find you that way if they just browse for a certain type of product or service. I found a category called Authors and Books that I may yet go back and join.

Accepting Payments Internationally

For the moment, your international online business benefits most by the fact that the major credit card companies can convert almost any currency to almost any other currency in the world for you.

Traditionally, businesses that import and export internationally use one of the following methods of payment:

- ✔ Cash in advance
- ✔ Letters of credit from a bank
- ✔ Draft payments

None of these payment methods are currently available to online stores, however, though I expect to see them coming from international banks that offer online payment services in the near future.

Several online stores already do a significant overseas business by credit card. For example, Virtual Vineyards (`www.virtualvin.com`) receives many orders for California wines from Japan, where such wines are very expensive. The Internet Shopping Network (`www.isn.com`) also makes a notable percentage of its sales to customers outside the United States.

International shopping may become more common when currencies can be converted online in real time, without the use of credit cards. Expect transaction service providers, such as CyberCash, to begin working with international banks so these service providers can extend currency conversion services to the Internet when the market is ready for it.

The travlang Web site (`www.travlang.com`) has an excellent currency converter — you can convert Chinese renmimbi to Russian rubles if you want. Alternatively, the GNN site has a currency conversion program (`gnn.com/cgi.bin/gnn/currency`) gives you instant conversions between major world currencies. If you target sales in a specific country, consider creating pages on your site in the native language of that country; then post your prices in the local currency.

Hooray for the underdogs — like us!

Major U.S. corporations such as IBM traditionally have divided up the world into geographical territories and focused on developing specific relationships with distributors of their products in those territories. Online stores can circumvent those geographical distribution agreements and offer more attractive prices than the distributors who do have rights.

Geographical sales territories may disappear, leaving local distributors to focus on installation, support, and service in an environment of global international distribution.

Remember, the minute you open your online doors, you compete with major international corporations. It can seem a little bit scary, but it's a great advantage to your business to have potentially international reach while maintaining the lesser overhead costs of a small corporation — you aren't bound by their territorial agreements. The big guys are worried about that fact, actually.

Part VI
Looking at Legal Necessities

The 5th Wave   By Rich Tennant

CRICHTENNANT

POLICE

POLICE

"They were selling contraband online. We broke through the door just as they were trying to flush the hard drive down the toilet."

In this part . . .

To keep the channels of commerce flowing freely, you need to remain unencumbered of any legal complications, including copyright infringement (a big problem on the Internet), improper tax collecting, and not observing the laws appropriate for your selling territory. In this part, I tell you how to steer clear of the legal issues that may present a speed bump in your plans to sell your wares online.

Chapter 17

It's the Law

Selling online enables your business to reach a customer base that extends far beyond the limits of your normal governmental jurisdiction. As a business owner, you must know and obey the laws that apply to you at home and in the areas where you ship your products. Otherwise, you may end up in a lawsuit or in jail. This chapter provides an overview of some legal issues that affect your business.

Finding Out the Law

From the day your online store opens, you are immersed in a worldwide marketplace. You must know the laws that apply to every place you do business, because the same laws apply to business in the online world that apply to business in the physical world.

For example, did you know that it's illegal to ship wine or any other alcoholic beverages to a dry county in the United States? And plenty of dry counties still exist in the South, particularly in the Texas panhandle, where 34 contiguous counties are dry (an area about the size of Vermont and New Hampshire put together). And that's just in Texas. Other states also have dry counties.

Perhaps the most important question you may ask is, "How can I find out what the relevant law is?" Sometimes you need to do a bit of research, online and otherwise, to find sources that tell you the law that affects your business.

More and more municipalities and other governmental bodies have Web sites, making it easier to find out what you need to know to conduct your business legally in a worldwide marketplace. For starters, you can look in the Internet Directory portion of this book for online sites that offer legal information.

Knowing Export Restrictions

You can't legally import several products, including some types of hardware and software, from the United States. In addition, the United States only allows restricted trade (or no trade at all) with some nations.

If your U.S. business sells online and you're not familiar with United States export law, take time to review the Export Administration Act of 1979 (available at www.bxa.doc.gov/). This document contains lists of products that require licenses for export and countries with which the United States has trade restrictions.

If you plan to market your products specifically in other countries, you may also wish to study the import laws of those countries. (You can find Web sites to help you with this in the Internet Directory that comes with this book.)

You can incur a fine of over $100,000 from the United States Treasury Department and the State Department for each instance of exporting to a Denied Person, Specially Designated National, or Restricted Country (the lists of people and countries that fit into these categories change almost weekly).

Fulfillment service providers, such as CyberSource (www.cybersource.com), update restricted trade information for the U.S. on a near-daily basis. If you start receiving a lot of orders from overseas, you may want to consult a professional service provider like CyberSource or an attorney.

If your store needs a license to export a technical product, such as hardware or software, the U.S. Department of Commerce can tell you what type of license you need, general or individual, and the Bureau of Export Administration (BXA) issues the license for you. You can get the details at www.bxa.doc.gov/.

Exporting Encryption

Currently, you run into a lot of red tape regarding exporting commercial products with encryption keys longer than 40 bits from the United States. Pending legislation may increase the readily-exportable key length to 56 bits, but the construction of the legislation requires that keys must then be escrowed, which makes the software objectionable to most parties concerned.

If your product contains strong cryptographic algorithms and you wish to sell it on the Internet, you should consult an attorney. Some sites check the zip code of anyone wishing to purchase or download such products, but it's unclear what your liability is in case someone falsified that information. Better get professional help.

Collecting Sales Taxes

As a store owner, you must collect all sales taxes due on any products you sell and convey those tax revenues to the proper taxing authority in each jurisdiction in which you sell products. Otherwise, you can be ordered to cease and desist and fined for back sales taxes.

Collecting sales taxes could become a nightmarish endeavor online because of all the possible jurisdictions within which taxes must be collected. If perhaps you don't feel up to the challenge of collecting sales taxes nationwide or worldwide, hosting services can provide sales tax collection as a service to you. (See Chapter 3 for the details.)

Several of the electronic storefront products discussed in Chapter 6 include tax calculation features. Also, within the United States, the Direct Marketing Association can give you help with collecting your sales taxes. Although they focus on the mail-order catalogue industry, the DMA can help you find software programs that calculate the taxes to be collected, based on the shipping address of your customer (by zip code). (These programs often contain other essential information, such as restrictions in shipping certain products to certain zip codes.)

What's Right with My Copyright?

Copyright law, the law that protects original works of authorship, is one part of a general category of laws governing intellectual property, which is more or less anything original that someone thinks up.

Entire volumes have been written on intellectual property laws. As the owner of an online store, you must focus on copyright law as the law pertains to intellectual property. You must be aware of intellectual property laws so that you don't inadvertently infringe on a creator's rights by using their creation on your selling site.

What's protected

According to the copyright laws of the United States, copyright protects all original work the moment the work is created — the work belongs to the author. (The copyright law encourages authors and artists to spend their efforts creating valuable works, allowing them to charge others for copies.) Copyright protects certain materials online, including the following:

✔ Postings to Usenet, mailing lists, and bulletin boards, including individual messages and entire threads

✔ E-mail messages

✔ Software, including applications, patches, add-ons, and utilities

✔ All kinds of data files, specifically:

- Text, hypertext, HTML files, and formatted documents

- Multimedia works (such as interactive books)

- Databases

- Visual image files, such as clip-art files, textures, and other images

- Sounds and music files, including MIDI files

- Animation loops

The Internet actually doesn't add much to existing copyright laws and precedents. The laws are clear. What the Internet adds is more ways to get around the laws. Because it's so easy to copy and redistribute materials online, people often "borrow" something by copying from someone else's site without asking them.

Don't borrow; it's against the law. In addition, you don't want people using images you paid good money to create for your store, so don't do that to someone else. Instead, get creative and make something of your own. Doing so enhances and differentiates your online presence more, anyway. Make yourself proud.

Typing things in from a book to use on your site doesn't make them original work, either. I was quite surprised today when, in researching this book, I found a short section from my own first book, *Digital Money* (co-authored with Mr. Dan Lynch), right there on a company's Web site.

Someone owns everything on the Internet unless the site clearly states that the work is in the public domain. Ask permission in every case if you simply must use a portion of someone else's work. By asking, you may obtain permission, or you may be offered a license to use a specific work or portion of a work in return for a fee. Because the Internet has no borders, be sure that any licenses you obtain for using copyrighted works at your online store include worldwide rights.

Protecting your own work

Copyright laws in the United States follow guidelines laid out by the Berne Copyright Convention, which favor the owners of the work. The Berne rules state that anything created after April 1, 1989 is automatically protected as the work is created.

However, laws in other countries sometimes require a little more fore-thought. For example, some countries still require the word "copyright," the date, and the name of the copyrighting entity to appear with the work. Some countries require the phrase "All rights reserved." Place these words in any files you create for your site, such as displays of your products — it can't hurt. For best protection, copyright notices should appear at least once on every page of your site.

The U.S. Copyright office (`lcWeb.loc.gov/copyright/`) offers registration for your copyrights, too, for even more protection.

You may think that your company owns the copyrights for any work created by freelancers. In fact, the law states that works created after January 1978 by freelancers, contractors, designers, and so forth can't be considered works for hire unless both parties sign a contract stating so. For example, unless you signed a contract that states otherwise, your freelance artist still holds copyright to the artwork she created for your business's annual report last year.

Born to be free — or not

Some people fight vigorously to protect their intellectual property, while others believe ideas are free, so should intellectual property be. Perhaps the difference matters little to you as a business owner, because you always want to check with the owner of an intellectual property before you use it.

Using technology to protect your work

Because copying digital bits is so easy, you want to take some strong steps to protect your business against unauthorized use of your materials online.

Two innovative solutions have been developed to address the difficulties of protecting copyrights in the Internet environment: digital watermarks and cryptographic wrappers.

Digital watermarks

The practice of watermarking, in the offline world, dates back to the Middle Ages. Italian papermakers used watermarks to prevent others from claiming their craftsmanship. Watermarks still appear on fine stationery and on important documents, such as bank checks, to prevent forgery.

Digital watermarks work like watermarks on stationery, but you apply them using digital methods.

You can apply digital watermarks to the following items:

✔ Images

✔ Sound

✔ Other products, such as software

Table 19-1 recommends some tools to get you started with watermarking certain types of products.

Table 19-1	Great Watermarking Tools		
To Watermark . . .	**Try This**	**Producer**	**URL**
Images	IBM Digital Library	IBM	www.software.com/is/dig-lib/home.htm
Sound	Liquid Audio	Liquid Audio	www.liquidaudio.com
Other products	ThingMaker	Parable	www.parable.com
	DigiBox	InterTrust	www.intertrust.com

Digital watermarks can be made visible or invisible, depending on the needs and intentions of the maker. For example, the Vatican uses visible digital watermarking technology from IBM to protect images displayed online from its extensive and valuable collection. That way, scholars can study the images in great detail, but the Vatican need not fear that cheap posters based on its collection may show up on the streets.

Previous digital watermarking technologies provided visible watermarks that were reasonably easy to remove using a digital image processing program such as Adobe Photoshop. IBM's watermarking tool, Home Page, is more sophisticated; the tool creates watermarks that can't easily be removed.

Put it in a plain brown digital wrapper, please

Wrapper technology, such as IBM's Cryptolope (`www.cryptolope.ibm.com`), is more sophisticated than watermarking. If your site distributes photographs, articles, software, or any other products that are "made of bits," a wrapper encrypts the item and protects it as you send it on its way to your customers.

A good content wrapper can do things like send information back to you whenever your product is used, and it can notify your Web server when someone tries to open the wrapper (perhaps illicitly). Your server can store "rules" that let you grant or deny access based on the content inside the wrapper and any licensing agreements that pertain to it. Some wrappers also handle digital payment for the items inside the wrapper.

Digital wrappers are a little more expensive to produce and use than digital watermarking, so you use them for exchanging or delivering things online that are relatively valuable, such as software products.

Several electronic delivery service (EDS) providers, such as CyberSource (`www.cybersource.com`) offer delivery of digital products using wrapper technology.

Public domain works and fair use rules

Some authors choose to put their work in public domain rather than protect it with copyright law. Works clearly in the public domain may be freely quoted, used, and adapted. For example, the scripts available on Selena Sol's Public Domain Script Archive (`www.extropia.com/`) are in public domain, and you can use these scripts freely on your own site.

Small excerpts from copyrighted works may be used for specific purposes: reporting events, reviewing the work, creating educational materials, and creating parodies.

A particular use is probably fair use if it does not deprive the rightful copyright holder of income from the work. Needless to say, uses of copyrighted material that help *you* make money probably would not be considered fair use.

The rules of fair use are very conservative. If you have a specific question about fair use for materials in your online store, such as using excerpts from musical pieces designed to help you sell the recordings, seek the advice of an expert attorney in this area.

Protecting Privacy

Customers appreciate your efforts to keep their personal information private, whether by using encryption tools such as SSL, or by refusing to sell your customer information to other parties.

Unlike physical goods, once information has been communicated, it can't be returned or taken back. And it's easy to pass along, because you don't lose information when you share it with someone else. Therefore, if you communicate information about customers without their knowledge or permission, you have the potential to do them permanent injury in the area of privacy.

Customers outside the United States are even more accustomed to privacy rights than U.S. customers. For example, in Germany, it's against the law to send someone unsolicited sales material. (So much for spam in Germany, I guess.) Instead, a business must find ways to direct its advertising so that it attracts the potential customers to request the materials. And in German advertising a law prohibits saying anything that isn't *verifiably* true. A shocking thought for multilevel marketers, I think.

In Europe, it's also against the law to export personal financial data from one country to another. In contrast, the personal information industry thrives in the United States today, estimated at $3 billion per year in 1990.

Your business has a right to expect privacy online, too. The law protects the rights of businesses, especially concerning trade secrets. Here are other ways in which privacy is protected, both online and offline:

- ✔ The privacy of company information is protected by business confidentiality and trade-secret laws.

- ✔ The privacy of materials in preparation for publication is protected by the Privacy Protection Act, which actually came about as a means of protecting the First Amendment rights of journalists.

✔ The privacy of membership in groups is protected by the constitutional right of freedom of assembly. This means mailing lists, bulletin boards, and online services have a right not to disclose their members' names, especially in any situation where disclosure may lead to an effort to damage or destroy the organization. (This law hasn't been tested in court yet.)

✔ The privacy of e-mail messages is protected by the Electronic Communications Privacy Act, which originally was intended to help the cellular phone market. This law was actually put to the test in the case of *Steve Jackson Games vs. United States,* when Secret Service agents mistakenly seized a company's entire electronic bulletin board contents, which included a lot of private messages between employees. (Be aware, it could happen to your business, too.)

✔ The privacy of personal information in databases is protected by various laws about personal data privacy, such as banking and medical records, but no single law states an overall nature of personal information privacy rights.

✔ The privacy of personal affairs from public view is protected by common law privacy rights.

For information about privacy laws and pending legislation that could affect your business, you can visit `www.epic.org/privacy/bill_track.html`.

Monster Stories of Multilevel Marketing

Multilevel marketing (MLM) is illegal, online or anywhere else, but it remains a big problem in online sales. (You know what a multilevel marketing business is, right? It's a "business" whose only product is recruiting other investors.) Imagine I offer you a business proposition — you pay me $250, and I give you a "business kit." The kit includes instructions for you to make money by recruiting 10 new salespeople and charging them $250 each. So there's no way to make money in this business without recruiting other people. Why is this illegal? Because it's mathematically impossible for some people to make money off of this. Because of this exponential explosion problem, some U.S. laws treat situations of this kind as lotteries.

An executive at a large media site explained MLM to me something like this. There's actually nothing wrong with paying people for recruiting other salespeople. It's when the only way a business makes money is through recruiting new salespeople that it's illegal.

In evaluating an MLM opportunity, make sure you are selling products rather than just recruiting salespeople. And, preferably, that you're selling good products, like Amway or Mary Kay. Standard disclaimers apply — I'm not a lawyer, nor do I play one on television.

Many sites that let subscribers put up free home pages find themselves filled with pages advertising thinly-veiled MLM schemes. As fast as the sites can uncover and take down the pages, new ones arise. Large sites often work directly with the FBI to track down and prosecute the owners of these sites. The FBI gets involved on these cases because the operations cross state boundaries.

Be very careful to stay out of any shady investment deals online. If the offer sounds too good to be true, it probably is. And needless to say, don't start any yourself or you're likely to end up in jail. The FBI is getting very good at tracking down the perpetrators of these sorts of "deals" online.

The Scarlet Letter: Pornography Online

Legislation has been introduced in Congress that may legally require online vendors of adult material to restrict access to their sites by children under age 17.

If you sell adult products online, consider working with blocking companies like SurfWatch (www.surfwatch.com) to get your site added to their lists of sites that can't be visited by minors.

Internet hosting services generally do not want to take the risks associated with hosting pornographic materials; therefore, presenting adult pictures, stories, or any sort of pornography can be a major problem on some hosting services or ISPs. Check out the rules of your ISP for specifics.

Chapter 18

Wading through the Gray Areas

. . . .

In This Chapter

▶ Disputes over domain names

▶ Unwanted linking

▶ Web sites and Internet jurisdiction

. . . .

*T*he topics discussed in this chapter represent *clearly* gray areas: for example — how to guarantee the ownership of a particular domain name, how to prevent unwanted linking to your site, the legal status of digital signatures, and jurisdiction in legal cases involving online stores. Because these are gray areas, it's difficult for this chapter to offer any specific guidance other than "be aware."

Before suitable precedents can be established in these gray areas of the law, court cases will be filed and decided upon. The ramifications of these court decisions must be worked out over time, and eventually they will begin to shape the world of online commerce in important ways.

Several states are proceeding with legislation in some areas (such as the validity of digital signatures for binding contracts), and some federal legislation has been proposed, but eventually laws and practices tend to be challenged in court.

In this chapter, you find out how to avoid some possible pitfalls caused by unknowingly venturing into these uncharted areas of the law.

Domain Name Disputes

You may have heard about cases in the media where two parties want the same domain name. But what you may not know is that the InterNIC (www.internic.net) has a domain name dispute resolution policy in place.

What is a trademark?

A *trademark* is a right of ownership placed on a specific word, phrase, or symbol that identifies a particular product in the marketplace. (A trademark is different than a *copyright,* which is ownership of a specific created work.)

A federal trademark can be registered with the U.S. Patent and Trademark Office (www.uspto.com) in Washington D.C., and you can also get a state trademark through your state government. Ideally, you register a trademark even before you begin to use it (to get maximum protection), but later is better than never.

Similar to a trademark is the idea of *trade dress.* Trade dress is a look and feel associated with a certain product brand. Trade dress also is protected by law. Unique design elements that distinctly identify your online store, such as color scheme, layout, and graphics, are protected legally as part of your business's trade dress.

By the way, the symbol ™ protects a trademark before it is registered or while the registration is being processed. After a trademark is registered, the ® symbol is used. You can use the ™ symbol even before you apply for a registered trademark.

If you feel that someone is using your rightful domain name unfairly, having a U.S. or foreign trademark on the term identical to the second level of the domain name (that is, the name without the www or the com parts) helps you the most.

If you hold a trademark that someone uses as their domain name and you want to complain to InterNIC, follow these steps:

1. **Send the owner of the domain name (which InterNIC calls the *Registrant*) a letter stating that the Registrant's use of the domain name violates your legal rights as holder of a trademark.**

2. **Present evidence of your current trademark registration to InterNIC, along with a copy of your letter to the Registrant.**

   InterNIC looks up the date that the Registrant activated the domain name. If the activation date is prior to your trademark date (or if the Registrant holds another U.S. or foreign trademark for the same name), InterNIC allows the Registrant to continue using the domain name.

The same name can be trademarked for different industries (as long as the double use doesn't cause confusion, in the opinion of the trademark office), such as between Delta Airlines and Delta faucets.

If the activation date for the Registrant is after your trademark date, InterNIC sends the Registrant a request to provide evidence of its own trademark identical to the second-level domain name.

If the Registrant doesn't provide the evidence requested by InterNIC within 30 days, InterNIC assists the Registrant in finding a new domain name. If the Registrant refuses to do either, InterNIC puts the domain name *on hold*. Neither you, the Registrant, nor any other party can use the domain name.

InterNIC waits until the parties provide a resolution or a judge issues a court order stating which party has the right to use the domain name.

If you can't work it out with the party who is using your trademark in their domain name, you must file a lawsuit before you can proceed any further with registering your domain name.

If you hold a trademark that someone uses in their domain name, you can file any of the following types of lawsuits:

✔ If you think the public may confuse your company and the Registrant's company (because you offer similar products or services), you can file a trademark infringement lawsuit in federal court.

✔ If no similar product or service is involved, you may want to file a federal anti-dilution lawsuit. This type of lawsuit has been used successfully by businesses trying to get control of a domain name. The Trademark Dilution Act implies that you must only show that the other use is weakening your trademark; however, you must have a well-known brand in order to make this type of suit work.

✔ If both parties are located in the same state, you can file a *state trademark lawsuit.* Many states have the same trademark infringement and anti-dilution provisions as the federal laws, and filing a state lawsuit can be a lot cheaper.

Usually, just the inconvenience of having to wait while your domain name and your Web site are put on hold provides enough impetus for the two parties to reach an agreement. The party holding the trademark in question definitely holds the upper hand in such a situation.

The word *Internet* is a federally registered trademark, so don't plan to use it in your business name. In fact, the U.S. Patent and Trademark Office won't even allow you to use the word *Internet* in your product descriptions, because a trademark has already been issued for that word. You have to describe your Internet product using "Global network of computers" or a similar phrase. Gee.

Duking it out over domain names

What happens when two parties want the same domain name? Several cases (which have been covered in the media) have been resolved successfully:

✔ **McDonald's:** Sometimes, Cybersquatters come along and register several (even hundreds) of well-known domain names, just in hopes of obtaining money when the domain name's more-likely owner gets ready to register it. For example, as part of a story, a writer registered the domain name mcdonalds.com before the well-known McDonald's got to it. McDonald's didn't want to be part of the writer's story and didn't like having its name used. The dispute came to a relatively peaceful resolution in which the writer gave up the domain name and McDonald's made a charitable contribution.

✔ **Candyland:** Children have enjoyed the Candyland board game (made by Hasbro, Inc.) since 1951. Imagine how Hasbro felt when they discovered that the domain name candyland.com had been registered by a site that featured pornographic materials. Hasbro sued the Web site owner under federal trademark law and obtained an injunction preventing the continued use of the domain name for that purpose.

✔ **MTV:** An MTV employee registered the domain name mtv.com. A trademark suit was filed in the matter, but it was later settled out of court.

✔ **Intermatic:** Intermatic, Inc. was the victim of a Cybersquatter who had registered over 200 domain names (199 besides Intermatic, that is). Intermatic filed suit to prevent the squatter from using the name, and won on the basis that its trademark extended back 50 years and the squatter's registration would dilute Intermatic's trademark.

✔ **Kaplan:** Princeton Review registered the domain name kaplan.com, just to keep its competitor, Kaplan Education Centers, from using it. Eventually the dispute was settled and Princeton Review gave up the domain name.

✔ **PETA:** A group called People for Ethical Treatment of Animals was extremely dismayed to hear that their acronym, PETA, had already been claimed by the group called People Eating Tasty Animals (using the domain name peta.org). Last I checked, this domain name was still on hold at InterNIC.

The Netiquette of Linking

Little or no legal precedent has been established yet to govern the common practice of *linking* to other sites. Many people believe that the very act of putting your store online means that you invite other people and other stores to link to yours. If a questionable group links to your store, what's a person to do?

At this point, you can't legally do much to prevent other sites from including links to your Web site. If they do, the best course of action is to send e-mail to that group requesting that they remove their link to your site. For example, if the group who linked to you is the Unwanted Giant Lizards of Yesteryear (say, `www.unwanted.com`), you can send an e-mail to `Webmaster@unwanted.com` and request that they remove their links. You can monitor the traffic that's actually coming from any questionable sites, too. (See Chapter 12 for more information on monitoring who visits your site.)

More than a legal question, linking is a matter of *Netiquette.* Always ask permission of any site you'd like to link to.

Electronic Jurisdiction

Jurisdiction in the electronic realm is an entirely different ballgame than in the physical realm. Most importantly, you should know the following about electronic jurisdiction:

- ✔ You can set up your online business in a particular state or province in order to take advantage of favorable business laws in that jurisdiction.
- ✔ You need to be aware of and obey the laws where your business customers reside (to avoid messy legal problems for yourself).

For example, many U.S. corporations are set up in the state of Delaware, because its laws favor corporations (particularly the tax laws). As the scope of business transactions on the Internet increases, you may find a province, state, or country that has just the right laws and taxation policies to make your business sing. Go for it, the world is only getting smaller.

One example of favorable jurisdiction that has come to light early is the situation with gambling online. Yes, casinos are springing up everywhere online, and not everyone is happy about that. In a case brought by the state of Missouri against the Coeur d'Alene Indian tribe of Idaho, Missouri sued to stop the tribe from sponsoring an online lottery, saying that the game promoted unregulated gambling in Missouri. In response, the tribe states that it answers to tribal law and to the state of Idaho, not to Missouri. The tribe has succeeded in moving the case to Federal court, where it has filed a motion for dismissal. Indeed, what is the proper jurisdiction for online gaming? Although citizens of Missouri are gambling at their computers, the Web server machines are located on tribal land in Idaho.

More cases of this type are likely to arise, and you want your business sitting firmly on the side of the law to avoid time-wasting and potentially expensive legal battles.

Ultimately, the answers to these questions of jurisdiction will determine not only the issues of legal jurisdiction when lawsuits result from Internet business — the answers to these question will also determine the jurisdiction of governments for the purpose of taxation. These decisions will affect all businesses online, including yours. A lot still needs to be sorted out in the gray area of selling online to a market that stretches far beyond your normal geographic reach.

However, some progress is being made on the related but simpler issues of business conducted over the Internet using e-mail, telephone, online chat, and so forth. A California plaintiff recently filed suit in California against a New York company, over some business that had been conducted primarily by electronic mail. In a strong opinion issued from the California Court of Appeals, Second Appellate District, Judge Arthur Gilbert wrote that current technology "has increased the number of transactions that are consummated without either party leaving the office." In addressing the crucial issue of what is required to establish a state's jurisdiction in a case, Judge Gilbert said, "There is no reason why the requisite minimum contacts cannot be electronic." Judge Gilbert's decision basically brings e-mail to the same level of acceptance in business dealings that telephone, fax, or paper transactions already hold. This is a major step forward in determining some crucial aspects of online jurisdiction.

Your online store may meet the standards for *requisite minimum contact* in another state, and you may indeed be held accountable for certain laws in whatever region your customers live. On the other hand, a good case can be made that passively presenting information online, or engaging in a transaction that doesn't involve the participation of the site operator, doesn't constitute the requisite minimum contact. Observe this gray area rather closely over the next few years. But don't let it stop you from selling online; whatever decisions the courts ultimately reach will need to take into account the needs of the existing online business community.

Part VII
The Part of Tens

The 5th Wave   By Rich Tennant

"I've been in hardware all of my life, and all of a sudden it's software that'll make me rich."

In this part . . .

Welcome to the part of the book that gives you quick and easy tips on some key online selling issues, including rules to observe at your site (rules that can make or break the success of your store), ways to increase the number of customers that visit your site, and pitfalls that you want to avoid.

Chapter 19

The Ten Commandments of Online Selling

. . . .

In This Chapter

▶ Knowing the rules

▶ Playing by them

. . . .

*L*ike everything else, selling online has its absolute musts and must-nots. This chapter offers one perspective, in a not "wholly" serious manner, although the guidance these commandments provide should definitely keep you honest enough to apply for wings.

Thou Shalt Not Commit Spam

The issue here is Netiquette. *Spam* (which means bulk e-mailing thousands of e-mail messages as a way to advertise) is low-down and dirty. It wastes everyone's time and disk space. Limit your advertising to acceptable methods and venues, and you build a better business.

For lots of information about good ways to advertise online, please see Chapter 12.

Thou Shalt Not Sell Thy Mailing List without Permission

Privacy concerns many Internet users. Don't give out information without explicit permission from your customers. Protect their interests, and your customers will love you for it.

If you want to query your customers about the availability of their mailing info, include a "yes-or-no" checkbox along with the question "May we share this information with others?" when you ask your customers to fill out a form containing personal information at your site.

Thou Shalt Not Steal Thy Neighbor's Images

Copyright laws definitely apply on the Web. Ignorance is no excuse for breaking the law (especially now that you're up to speed with this book to help you).

For example, no matter how great that picture of the beach would look on your site that sells suntan oil, you can't use it unless you get express written permission from the owner of the image. This commandment applies to text, too.

For more detailed discussion about copyright laws, please see Chapter 17.

Thou Shalt Not Treat Thy Neighbor's Resources as Thine Own

Many Internet Service Providers limit the amount of downloading a customer can do each month (by the way, if you pay to have customers download your product information, you may want to change ISPs).

If you link your page to someone else's page (whom I assume is someone you don't know) and say "everyone see this great product," and if the extra downloading costs them money, you're basically stealing. Instead, obtain permission to use the image, and then copy the image to your own site for viewing.

Thou Shalt Not Create Images Too Big for Downloading

You know how mad it makes you when you have to wait longer for your fries at the fast food joint. Just imagine how your customers feel when you keep them waiting for 10 minutes while they download a picture of your product? It's impolite to your customers and bad for business. No one should be held captive to download times, even for five minutes.

Keep images to about 40K, really. Other files, such as software files, may acceptably require longer to download. You can prepare the customer for a wait with phrases like "Our latest product upgrade is big, it will take the file about 20 minutes to download."

Thou Shalt Not Establish Multilevel Marketing Schemes Online

Multilevel marketing means that the only product a business sells is getting more people into the business. Eventually, somebody is a big loser, while the initial investors recoup their investment many times over.

Beware, these types of businesses are illegal. The FBI investigates these setups online.

Thou Shalt Not Post Adult Materials on Sites That Children May See

If you have an adult-oriented product, get your site a rating so that parents can protect their children. Companies like SurfWatch (www.surfwatch.com) or standards like the Platform for Internet Content Selection (PICS) are good places to start for doing your part as a business person to protect children on the Internet. 'Nuff said.

Thou Shalt Update Thy Site Regularly

People look to the Web for current and timely information. Update small things weekly or more often. For example, you can add a weekly special or change your greeting, or you can add a link to your latest press release.

Plan to create a whole new look quarterly to semiannually, which means doing things like changing the page layout, redesigning the navigation tools, changing the placement of ad banners, and generally restructuring your site if needed.

Part II gives some helpful advice about making changes to your site, but if these tasks are beyond your abilities, don't be afraid to hire a professional. (I include the URLs of several design firms in the Internet Directory section.)

Thou Shalt Use High Production Values

High production value means a lot of things. It means rich backgrounds, music, textures, images, and all that. It means text that's easily readable and clear. It also means that the site operates smoothly from the customer's viewpoint.

Nothing turns customers off faster than a site filled with typos and bad links.

Part III gives you a good starting point for creating content with high production values. In particular, Chapter 10 tells you some ways to check your site for common mistakes before going live.

Thou Shalt Organize Thy Site Simply

Nothing is more intimidating than getting lost in Cyberspace. If it's not immediately clear to a newcomer where each page leads — for example, where the prices are, if they're on a separate page from the product descriptions — your site needs better organization. (As the site grows more complex — for example, if your product list grows — you may need a site map to help your customers get around.)

Get people who are unfamiliar with your site to test it and see how well-organized it really is. Think of it from the new customer's point of view.

Chapter 20

Ten Ways to Get More Traffic to Your Site

· ·

In This Chapter

▶ Getting customers to your online store in droves

▶ Building your online business

· ·

*B*y 2002, approximately 175 million people may be on the Web. Wouldn't it be great to have even a tiny fraction of all these people visiting your online store?

Meanwhile, Jupiter Communications, another well-known research firm, estimates that businesses currently spend $86 million per year on direct online marketing and advertising, and that they may spend close to $1.3 billion by 2002, while sales revenues grow from about $940 million now to about $7.7 billion in the same time frame.

Obviously, you can make lots of money through selling online, a veritable gold rush of the 1990s. If you want to tap into this online business gold rush, you need for those paying customers to find you.

They say that the three most important factors in creating a successful retail business are "location, location, location . . ." And of course you need to make your location known online, too. How do you go about that? Read on.

This chapter contains some tips gained from the experience of the most successful online stores. Try any or all of the tips mentioned in this chapter and watch your Web site traffic increase — which should pay off beautifully as the electronic marketplace grows.

Get Listed on All the Major Search Engines

Submitting your Web site information to the big search engine sites is the number one way to get more traffic at your own site. Unlike buying an ad on a search engine, getting listed with a search engine doesn't cost you anything.

To get listed, send your URL to the site. The site may send you a form to fill out, or they may just add you to the search engine without any further information from you. The search engine you apply to gives you the details of their approval process when you apply.

Services such as Submit-It! (www.submit-it.com) can help you get your site listed — often for a fee, although a few are free. Several sites that can help you get your site listed on search engines are given in the Internet Directory section of this book.

Some search engines allow you add your Web site to the search engine directly, which I include in the following list. To submit your URL to sites individually, use these URLs:

- **AltaVista** (www.altavista.digital.com/cgi-bin/query?pg=tmpl&v=addurl.html): After you fill out the form, it may take two to four weeks before your site appears on AltaVista.

- **Excite** (www.excite.com/add_url.html): It takes about three weeks for your site to appear on Excite after you fill out the form.

- **HotBot** (www.hotbot.com.addurl.html): HotBot is sponsored by Wired magazine, and it's definitely a hot site to get listed on.

- **Infoseek** (www.infoseek.com/AddUrl?pg=DCaddurl.html): Infoseek keeps an excellent array of sites, which it groups by category.

- **Yahoo!** (add.yahoo.com/fast/add): Yahoo! has a team of Web surfers who actually visit sites submitted for the search engine, so sometimes you experience a slight backlog.

For the most current information about major Web search engines and news about any changes they make, visit Search Engine Watch at searchenginewatch.com/.

Use Metatags in Your HTML Files

Be sure to use the metatag `NAME=keywords` in your HTML files; then include keywords that place your page in the topic areas you'd like (see Chapter 9 for an example of this technique). Be sure not to overstuff your metatags by repeating exactly the same word lots of times; use synonyms, such as (for an auto repair shop whose owners have a flair for stock car racing) "mechanic, grease monkey, cars, hot rods, automobiles, hot cars, racing." The search engines won't accept your page if you use the same word over and over and over again.

Use lowercase letters in your metatags; it's important to getting the search engines to find you. Just trust me on this one.

Optimize Your Site's Title

Be sure the `TITLE` tag in your HTML files contains a short descriptive phrase about your site. "Welcome to my site" wouldn't be an optimal title for getting your site to show up on Yahoo! under "Hot Cars," for example, but "Detroit steel" may do the trick.

Similar to the metatags, the `TITLE` tag helps the search engines find your site and index it in the most appropriate category. That's why a pithy title is an important element of your store.

Buy an Ad on Yahoo! or Another Top Site

To get the most for your advertising dollar, buy on a site that has lots of traffic. Luckily, quite a few sites, especially search engines and top media sites, now have over a million visitors per month. These sites can serve as key elements in increasing traffic and sales at your Web site, too.

In general, the more traffic the site has, the more likely you'll pay for your ad.

Where to start? Yahoo! has the most visitors of any Web site, almost 15 million unique visitors during the month of August 1997, and over 17 million in October 1997 (as projected by Relevant Knowledge). But at least 19 other sites get well over a million visitors per month. Consider these (and notice how the overall numbers are going up):

Top 20: August 1997		Top 25: October 1997	
Yahoo!	14,822,000	Yahoo!	17,208,000
Microsoft	12,012,202	Netscape	13,945,000
Netscape	10,824,802	Microsoft	13,945,000
AOL	8,251,103	Excite/Webcrawler	11,793,000
Infoseek	7,946,467	AOL.com	9,968,000
Excite	7,597,988	Infoseek	7,622,000
GeoCities	7,127,869	GeoCities	7,080,000
MSN	6,170,267	MSN	6,487,000
Lycos	4,883,459	Lycos	6,071,000
AltaVista	4,657,826	CNET	4,940,000
CNET	3,976,232	AltaVista	4,926,000
ZDNet	3,521,996	ZDNet	4,251,000
WebCrawler	3,233,339	Hotmail	3,201,000
RealAudio	2,260,248	CNN	3,163,000
Four11	2,202,307	WhoWhere/Angelfire	3,134,000
Pathfinder	2,129,904	Four11	2,848,000
Hotmail	1,936,296	Pathfinder	2,577,000
ESPN	1,931,467	RealNetworks	2,547,000
Tripod	1,754,563	Wired	2,483,000
CompuServe	1,720,862	MSNBC	2,472,000
		Tripod	2,174,000
		ESPN	2,075,000
		USA Today	2,001,000
		Weather Channel	1,902,000
		Amazon	1,894,000

For more statistics of this type, you can visit CyberAtlas at
www.cyberatlas.com.

If you want to place an ad on a site but can't find a link to get more information, try sending e-mail to '"webmaster" at that site's domain name (for
example, webmaster@yahoo.com) or any e-mail address the site lists for
obtaining general information.

Form a Strategic Partnership

Work out a deal with a complementary site to offer your product or service using a button click. That's what Greet Street (www.greetst.com), a vendor of online greeting cards, did, when they made a deal with Hotmail (www.hotmail.com), a popular e-mail service provider. You see a button on Hotmail that takes you directly to a selection of Greet Street greeting cards. I get lots of Greet Street cards from Hotmail e-mail addresses now, so I know that Greet Street's plan is working. (Incidentally, on a logistical note, to make server performance better for this sort of interaction, Greet Street has co-located a server machine right beside Hotmail's server machines. See Chapter 3 for more information on co-location.)

Some deals of this type involve payment to the partner as a sort of "ad space" deal. However, you may work out a deal whereby one partner gets a small percentage of the proceeds of each sale the other partner makes at their site. (A similar type of royalty partnering arrangement has begun to start a trend — for example, larger sites such as amazon.com now offer "associate" partnerships, in which an associate who sends a buying customer to amazon's site gets a small percentage of the proceeds of that sale.)

Give Something Away

Have you tried a contest or a promotion that can draw in traffic with the chance of winning something neat? If you have a travel site, for example, you could offer a free trip someplace. Then just promote your store in your usual ways and see how much your traffic increases.

Advertise in the Traditional Print Media

Many people still aren't online — to bring in new prospective customers from among those who aren't avid Internet users, try placing an ad in a newspaper or magazine related to your product or service.

For example, a professional chef I know recently put up an online site selling information related to food costing and equivalents (www.chefdesk.com), but he didn't get as much traffic as he wanted until he put ads in the magazines related to his profession.

Offer Revenue Sharing to Sites that Send You Traffic

Revenue sharing is a hot trend right now among Web businesses. When a site sends you business, you can share a percentage of your profits with the site.

At least one popular hosted storefront, ViaWeb Store (www.viaweb.com), now supports the revenue-sharing model. Big sites like amazon.com (www.amazon.com) and CDnow (www.cdnow.com) also use it.

Get Active on Discussion Groups, Bulletin Boards, Chat Rooms, and Usenet

Your personal knowledge and reputation can do a lot to bring customers to your site when you share answers to questions on discussion groups. It's a traditional and well-accepted practice online to share information freely, because of the academic heritage of the Internet.

Don't be too blatant about advertising your products when you share your knowledge; let the product information develop naturally from the discussion.

Look for More Information at Yahoo!

At Yahoo! (www.yahoo.com/Computers_and_Internet/Internet/ World_Wide_Web/Announcement_Services), you can find information about promotional services, tools for search engine submission, and other ways to get the word out about your site.

Chapter 21

Ten Mistakes to Avoid When Selling Online

In This Chapter

▶ Watching out for the chuckholes

▶ Playing by the rules

*M*any people getting started with selling online make the same mistakes. You can avoid them now that you know about them.

Getting Stuck in Offline Mode

Simply putting up a catalogue and an 800 number is not online commerce.

Well, you may want to keep the 800 number at least as an alternative until SET or other security becomes more widely used online, but unless you ask your customers for feedback about their experience at your site, you can't call it online commerce.

However, just presenting an online catalog deprives your customers of interactivity. Instead, use CGI to create a message board where your customers can enter their comments, and offer an e-mail address where they can reach your customer support center.

Sending Spam

Spam sounds like a good idea to those who aren't net-savvy. (You should have heard me trying to explain it to my dad.) After all, spam offers an unbelievably cheap way to reach millions with your direct e-mail advertisements. Wrong. What you don't know is how thoroughly you will be ignored, chastised, and ostracized if you spam.

Actually, you should think of spam as stealing. The Internet Service Providers and the individuals who receive the advertisements are paying for your spam, because ISPs have to store it on their servers, and individuals use up their time and perhaps their paid-by-the-minute connections to read it or just delete it.

Forgetting Navigation Buttons or Bars

Put navigation buttons on every page of your site. Navigation on every page gives your customers that element of control they need to feel comfortable in your online store. And if they're not comfortable, they won't be sticking around to buy.

Valuing Beauty over Use

Making a site that's graphically beautiful but totally unintuitive to use — that's what I call the "Lost in Hyperspace" problem.

Graphic designers love to do what they do best — design artwork and page layouts. An inexperienced customer may not know that the picture on your site is really a clickable image map.

All of the stuff that is accessible to most of your clients may seem quite pedestrian to your designers. That's okay — reign the designers in a bit and keep your site elegantly simple.

Not Answering E-Mail Quickly Enough

Customers definitely judge you on your response time to their e-mail. If you can't get to your e-mail right away, you should set up a mailbot, which is a computer program that responds automatically and at least acknowledges the receipt of a message, perhaps saying that a human response will be coming soon.

Skimping on Your ISP

It seems like a good idea at the time — save some money, get a smaller connection, you can always upgrade later. Some smaller providers can't really afford enough equipment to make sure their customers have access. (Netcom went through a terrible time in its early days, and so did AOL more recently.)

Actually, it's such a major pain to move your site that you won't ever want to do it. It requires a full backup, to the last iota (two backups would be better), and then possibly several hours of downtime while you lose money because customers can't reach your online store. Just put the money up for an ISP who can handle your business, and leave it at that.

Forgetting Regular Backups

Don't even think about not backing up all the files on your site at least three times a week. Better yet, do your backups and have a RAID array with several hot spares. When you're in business online, you need reliability to spare.

Posting Un-Proofed Content

When you rush, you think, oh, I'll look at it once it's up there and fix it if I need to. But you know what? You never seem to have time to fix those little things unless they're a disastrous misspelling of someone's name or some other real blooper. Take time to do it right the first time. Be proud of your professional-quality Web pages.

Undertesting Your Site

There's just no substitute for getting your hands dirty. Click around on your own site. You end up with lots of interesting observations to show for it. Don't assume for a minute that different browsers behave the same way, or even that the same browser behaves the same way on different platforms.

Ignoring Privacy Issues

Privacy is the cornerstone of trust. Without trust, your business won't be around long. This could be the last mistake you ever make in selling online.

Appendix

About the CD-ROM

● ●

*T*he CD-ROM that comes with this book is packed with great software to help you get your online store up and running. Read this appendix for the details on getting the most out of the CD.

System Requirements

If your computer doesn't match up to most of the following requirements, you may have problems in using the contents of the CD:

- A PC with a 486 or faster processor, or a Mac OS computer with a 68030 or faster processor
- Microsoft Windows 95 or later, or Mac OS system software 7.5 or later
- At least 8MB of total RAM installed on your computer. For best performance, Windows 95-equipped PCs and Mac OS computers with PowerPC processors should have at least 16MB of RAM installed
- At least 50MB of hard drive space available to install all the software from this CD. (You need less space if you don't install every program.)
- A CD-ROM drive — double-speed (2x) or faster
- A sound card for PCs (Mac OS computers have built-in sound support.)
- A monitor capable of displaying at least 256 colors or grayscale
- A modem with a speed of at least 14,400 bps

If you need more information on the basics, check out *PCs For Dummies,* 4th Edition, by Dan Gookin; *Macs For Dummies,* 4th Edition, by David Pogue, or *Windows 95 For Dummies,* by Andy Rathbone (all published by IDG Books Worldwide, Inc.).

How to Use the CD with Microsoft Windows 95

To install the items from the CD to your hard drive, follow these steps:

1. **Insert the CD into your computer's CD-ROM drive.**

2. **Click the Start button and click Run.**

3. **In the dialog box that appears, type** D:\SETUP.EXE.

   Most of you probably have your CD-ROM drive listed as drive D under My Computer. Type in the proper drive letter if your CD-ROM drive uses a different letter.

4. **Click OK.**

   A license agreement window appears.

5. **Read the license agreement, nod your head, and then click on the Accept button. After you click on Accept, you'll never be bothered by the License Agreement window again.**

   From here, the CD interface appears. The CD interface lets you install the programs on the CD without typing in cryptic commands or using yet another finger-twisting hot key in Windows.

   The software on the interface is divided into categories whose names you see on the screen.

6. **To view the items within a category, just click the category's name.**

   A list of programs in the category appears.

7. **For more information about a program, click on the program's name.**

   Be sure to read the information that's displayed. Sometimes a program requires you to do a few tricks on your computer first, and this screen tells you where to go for that information, if necessary.

8. **To install the program, click the appropriate Install button. If you don't want to install the program, click on the Don't Install button to return to the previous category screen.**

   After you click on an install button, the CD interface drops to the background while the CD begins installation of the program you chose.

When installation is done, the interface usually reappears in front of other opened windows. Sometimes the installation will confuse Windows and leave the interface in the background. To bring the interface forward, just click once anywhere in the interface's window.

9. **To install other items, repeat Steps 6, 7, and 8.**

10. **When you're done installing programs, click on the Quit button to close the interface.**

    You can eject the CD now. Carefully place it back in the plastic jacket of the book for safekeeping.

To run some of the programs, you may need to keep the CD inside your CD-ROM drive. Otherwise, the installed program would have required you to install a very large chunk of the program to your hard drive space, which would have kept you from installing other software.

How to Use the CD with Mac OS

To install the items from the CD to your hard drive, follow these steps:

1. **Insert the CD into your computer's CD-ROM drive.**

   In a moment, an icon representing the CD that you just inserted appears on your Mac desktop. Chances are, the icon looks like a CD-ROM.

2. **Double-click on the Read Me First icon.**

   This text file contains information about the CD's programs and any last-minute instructions you need to know about installing the programs on the CD that we don't cover in this appendix.

3. **Double-click the CD icon to show the CD's contents.**

4. **To install most programs, just drag the program's folder from the CD window and drop it on your hard drive icon.**

5. **To install some programs, open the program's folder on the CD, and double-click the icon with the words "Install" or "Installer."**

   After you install the programs that you want, you can eject the CD. Carefully place it back in the plastic jacket of the book for safekeeping.

What You'll Find

Here's a summary of the software on this CD. If you use Windows, the CD interface helps you install software easily. (If you have no idea what I'm talking about when I say "CD interface," flip back a page or two to find the section, "How to Use the CD with Microsoft Windows 95.")

If you use a Mac OS computer, you can enjoy the ease of the Mac interface to quickly install the programs.

Apache Web Server

You find two versions of Apache Web Server the CD: Version 1.2.4 runs only on UNIX; version 1.3b2 works with NT as well as on UNIX platforms. Many of the major online stores on the Web today use this server software. For updates and more information, visit www.apache.org.

Herb's Herb Shack

You can borrow the HTML templates and CGI script from this sample to help you set up a database search function for your site. Look at these files from the CD, by opening the HERBHERB folder, or, if you would like to modify the files, you can place them on your computer.

To use the CGI code, the file herb.cgi needs to be placed on a Web server in the CGI-bin, in a folder called WEAVE.

FreedomVR

You get a freeware program from Honeylocust Media Systems that lets you take photos, put them into a folder, and nearly instantly create virtual reality on your site. You may find it a lot easier than some other methods out there. For more information, visit www.mcs.cornell.edu/~houle/vr/freedom.

To use this program, you must place the program files on your Web server in the same directory as the HTML page that you want the program to work with. For complete installation instructions, see the Honeylocust Web site, at www.honeylocust.com/vr/doc/install.html.

Links Galore!

Links.htm is an HTML page that you can open up in your Web browser for point-and-click access to all of the Web sites listed in the *Selling Online For Dummies* Internet Directory.

To view the links page, open your Web browser and choose File⇨Open (or Open File, depending on your browser) to open the Links.htm document from the Links folder on your CD-ROM.

Microsoft Internet Explorer 4.0

Internet Explorer 4.0, from Microsoft Corporation, is the latest version of the popular Web browser from Microsoft, including support for CDF-based Web channels. In addition to Active Channels, Explorer 4.0 includes components that allow Windows users to use the Active Desktop as well as Active Screen Savers.

Netscape Navigator 4.0

Netscape Navigator 4.0, from Netscape Communications Corporation, is the latest and greatest Web browser from the folks at Netscape. It features such enhancements as faster start-up time, faster loading plug-ins and Java applets, and drop-down menus for quicker and easier navigation. The latest HTML standards are also supported in this version.

Screen Ruler

Screen Ruler is a great Web development tool from Micro Fox Software. Objects and distances can be easily measured in pixels, which comes in very handy when designing Web pages and other screen layouts.

WebGenie

You find a collection of Web utilities designed for Windows platforms, including the following:

   ✔ **Banner*Show:** A Windows application that generates JavaScript-based rotating banners for your Web site. With Banner*Show, you don't need to be a programmer to make your Web site look fancy.

- **CGI*Star Pro:** A Windows scripting tool that automatically generates Common Gateway Interface (CGI) scripts to e-mail the contents of HTML forms to your mailbox. With CGI*Star Pro, you can get information from people who visit your Web site.

- **Guestbook*Star:** An all-in-one guest book creator complete with JavaScript functionality. You can use Guestbook*Star to find out who's been visiting your Web site.

- **Link*Launch:** Can be used with either JavaScript or CGI development to create drop-down lists on your personal Web site. Using this WebGenie tool can help to organize your Web site.

- **Site*Sleuth:** A Web site traffic reporter tool that enables you to monitor your small business Web site and see how it is being visited.

- **Site*Sponsor:** An inexpensive CGI tool that can be used to increase the number of advertisement banners for your Web site. Site*Sponsor gives smaller Web site operators an incentive for displaying your banner on their site.

- **Smart Shopping*Cart:** Allows you to create your own interactive shopping on the Web without creating your own CGIs or storing log files on your own server. WebGenie runs the CGI for you.

- **WebGenie's Shopping*Cart:** Gives you the ability to manage order records on your own server and import the data easily into a database. You get everything you need to create your own online shopping on the Web.

After you install the WebGenie software, the installation routine asks you if you would like to launch the program. This feature of the installer does not work. To launch the program, exit the installer and click Start⇨Programs⇨WebGenie Software, and select the icon for the program you want. If you are installing Guestbook*Star, the installation routine does not place icons in the WebGenie program group or on the Start menu. To run Guestbook*Star, run C:\Program Files\WebGenie Software\GuestbookStar\gbstar.exe.

For more information on WebGenie products, visit www.webgenie.com.

If You've Got Problems (Of the CD Kind)

I tried my best to include programs that work on most computers with the minimum system requirements. Alas, your computer may differ, and some programs may not work properly for some reason.

The two likeliest problems are that you don't have enough memory (RAM) for the programs you want to use, or you have other programs running that are affecting installation or running of a program. If you get error messages like Not enough memory or Setup cannot continue, try one or more of these methods and then try using the software again:

- ✔ Turn off any antivirus software that you have on your computer. Installers sometimes mimic virus activity and may make your computer incorrectly believe that it is being infected by a virus.

- ✔ Close all running programs. The more programs you're running, the less memory is available to other programs. Installers also typically update files and programs. So if you keep other programs running, installation may not work properly.

- ✔ Have your local computer store add more RAM to your computer. This is, admittedly, a drastic and somewhat expensive step. However, if you have a Windows 95 PC or a Mac OS computer with a PowerPC chip, adding more memory can really help the speed of your computer and allow more programs to run at the same time.

If you still have trouble installing the items from the CD, please call the IDG Books Worldwide Customer Service phone number: 800-762-2974 (outside the U.S.: 317-596-5430).

Index

• E •

(continued)

(continued)

IDG BOOKS WORLDWIDE, INC.
END-USER LICENSE AGREEMENT

READ THIS. You should carefully read these terms and conditions before opening the software packet(s) included with this book ("Book"). This is a license agreement ("Agreement") between you and IDG Books Worldwide, Inc. ("IDGB"). By opening the accompanying software packet(s), you acknowledge that you have read and accept the following terms and conditions. If you do not agree and do not want to be bound by such terms and conditions, promptly return the Book and the unopened software packet(s) to the place you obtained them for a full refund.

1. **License Grant.** IDGB grants to you (either an individual or entity) a nonexclusive license to use one copy of the enclosed software program(s) (collectively, the "Software") solely for your own personal or business purposes on a single computer (whether a standard computer or a workstation component of a multiuser network). The Software is in use on a computer when it is loaded into temporary memory (i.e., RAM) or installed into permanent memory (e.g., hard disk, CD-ROM, or other storage device). IDGB reserves all rights not expressly granted herein.

2. **Ownership.** IDGB is the owner of all right, title, and interest, including copyright, in and to the compilation of the Software recorded on the CD-ROM. Copyright to the individual programs on the CD-ROM is owned by the author or other authorized copyright owner of each program. Ownership of the Software and all proprietary rights relating thereto remain with IDGB and its licensors.

3. **Restrictions on Use and Transfer.**

    (a) You may only (i) make one copy of the Software for backup or archival purposes, or (ii) transfer the Software to a single hard disk, provided that you keep the original for backup or archival purposes. You may not (i) rent or lease the Software, (ii) copy or reproduce the Software through a LAN or other network system or through any computer subscriber system or bulletin-board system, or (iii) modify, adapt, or create derivative works based on the Software.

    (b) You may not reverse engineer, decompile, or disassemble the Software. You may transfer the Software and user documentation on a permanent basis, provided that the transferee agrees to accept the terms and conditions of this Agreement and you retain no copies. If the Software is an update or has been updated, any transfer must include the most recent update and all prior versions.

4. **Restrictions on Use of Individual Programs.** You must follow the individual requirements and restrictions detailed for each individual program in the Appendix of this Book. These limitations are contained in the individual license agreements recorded on the CD-ROM. These restrictions may include a requirement that after using the program for the period of time specified in its text, the user must pay a registration fee or discontinue use. By opening the Software packet(s), you will be agreeing to abide by the licenses and restrictions for these individual programs. None of the material on this disk(s) or listed in this Book may ever be distributed, in original or modified form, for commercial purposes.